MARY QUEEN OF SCOTS

T0382634

MARY QUEEN *of* SCOTS

A STUDY OF THE LENNOX NARRATIVE IN THE UNIVERSITY LIBRARY AT CAMBRIDGE

With SOME REFLECTIONS *on her* ENVIRONMENT *in* FRANCE & *on her* MARRIAGE NEGOTIATIONS

BY

MAJOR-GENERAL R. H. MAHON

C.B., C.S.I.

F.R.HIST. SOCIETY

CAMBRIDGE: AT THE
UNIVERSITY PRESS
MCMXXIV

CAMBRIDGE
UNIVERSITY PRESS

University Printing House, Cambridge CB2 8BS, United Kingdom

Published in the United States of America by Cambridge University Press, New York

Cambridge University Press is part of the University of Cambridge.

It furthers the University's mission by disseminating knowledge in the pursuit of education, learning and research at the highest international levels of excellence.

www.cambridge.org
Information on this title: www.cambridge.org/9781107666009

© Cambridge University Press 1924

First published 1924
First paperback edition 2014

A catalogue record for this publication is available from the British Library

ISBN 978-1-107-66600-9 Paperback

PREFACE

THE CAMBRIDGE MANUSCRIPT of the first Lennox Narrative has exceptional value as a source of independent information of what took place at Kirk o' Field. It is undoubtedly the story of one who was in a position to know the truth though not necessarily to tell it; unfortunately it is incomplete. The other connected narrative—Buchanan's Indictment—is written without personal knowledge, from information supplied by those whose interest it was to create the most unfavourable impression possible.

The object of this volume is rather to draw attention to the clues which can be unwound from a study of the Paper, than to follow them to a conclusion.

The numerous writers who have described the story of the fall of Mary Stuart, have followed a well-beaten track with amazing regularity, different ruts perhaps, but the same roadway leading always to an *impasse*. The chief difficulty of the "defence" is that nine-tenths of the evidence comes from enemy sources, and of the "prosecution" that, however genuine the case, the testimony is obviously garbled.

In these circumstances it appears necessary to apply the *argumentum a priori*; to deduce from the conditions which influenced her adolescence whether the woman was likely to fill so vile a part, and the first two chapters are devoted to this.

Then it is necessary to apply one's common sense to find a solution to the problem of the Casket Letters, at least of the two first, which are so obviously beyond the power of human genius to forge in their entirety; in Chapter IV I offer an interpretation to which the chief objection is that it is so simple that it makes one hesitate to adopt it, in the face of so much previous examination.

Yet I would remind the reader that to demolish or explain away the evidence on which the case against the Queen is based does not clear up the mystery of the death of her husband. In this volume I have not attempted to do so. I claim only, working on the material that the labour of others has provided, to indicate a line of thought which needs further research to justify it. In the archives of the foreign capitals, I feel sure there is much still to be found which will confirm the views here set forth.

R. H. M.

1924.

CONTENTS

The discussion of the years of Mary's misfortunes is so often prefaced by an exaggerated conception of her virtues or her vices, that it seems necessary to arrive at the *juste milieu* before proceeding further. The influence of the Reformation on her character, has, I think, been neglected. I aim herein at showing the effect that contact with this great movement must have had upon her.

MARY STUART

No historical problem has presented a more perplexing tangle of conflicting evidence than, as Andrew Lang calls it, "The Mystery of Mary Stuart." Nor has the solution of any similar problem been more frequently disconcerted by the discovery of fresh testimony, many hundreds of pages of the laborious works of Goodall, Robertson, Whitaker, Laing, Froude, to mention only a few of the host of writers, have been rendered unnecessary or inaccurate by knowledge acquired since their day. Yet, though it behoves the general reader to be cautious in accepting much that is to be found in these and other histories of the Queen of Scots, we could scarcely do without the mass of information they have brought together.

In all these older stories and, as I think, also in those that are more modern, there is failure to present a true picture of the chief actor in the drama—of Mary Stuart herself. It is the object of this chapter to bring together such information, much of it derived from comparatively recent research, as will enable the reader to form a conception of the characteristics of the woman who entered on her disastrous years at the age of 23, in the year 1566. It may be that this is not fully relevant to the consideration of the Lennox Papers, but I conceive that it is essential to get away from the stereotyped traditions which have been handed from one author to another, and in doing so we shall obtain light on some dark places of the Manuscript.

The impression derived from the works of historians of the 18th and 19th centuries whose reputations stand highest is that

Mary, brought up at a frivolous and licentious court, was a young woman of erotic tendency, wedded to luxury and display; and yet, though the combination is almost an antithesis, she had, we are told, vigour, energy, tenacity of purpose, all the faculties necessary to conceive a great purpose. Her uncle the Cardinal of Lorraine was her "preceptor in profligacy," her heart was "steeled by her education" to fierce untamed tigerishness; she was "bold, remorseless and unscrupulous"; she expressed "delight in murder"; she had in short a "wild woman's passionate nature." Through another pair of glasses we find her a "gentle administrator," the "most amiable woman of her age," famed for her accomplishments. Yet a third commentator finds her filling her position as Queen of France with a "soul superior to the admiration she caused," shining equally in the court as in the "necessary formalities of state" with a "native firmness of resolution."

From so much variety and much more if it were worth repeating we have to ascertain the truth. A part of the harsh judgment is pure invention, some of it is gained from contemporary statements of her enemies, made when religious excitement gave rise, as never before or since, to a flood of coarse calumny from which no reputation was exempt. It would be equally unimpeachable if the historian of the future should base his views of the conduct of the Great War on a study of the publications issued by the Propaganda of the combatants; deliberately designed, as they were, to deceive. On the other hand a great deal of the encomium is founded on imagination, and the whole as applied to one who at the time she was held to exhibit these remarkable qualities was still but a child, is too exaggerated to be credible.

The court of France, in the first half of the 16th century, was gay and splendid beyond any other in Europe; so much is true, and that court under Francis I was lax in decorum; but the historian who dwells at length on Brantôme's account of Francis' indiscretions, and by context brings them into relation

with Mary's youth[1], neglects to tell that he had been dead more
than a year before Mary, at the age of $5\frac{1}{2}$, arrived in France. Even
the reflexion of the immoralities of the late King could not have
touched her mind at that age. In truth, Catherine de Médicis,
whether as wife of Francis' successor or as widow, ruled the
court in Mary's time with strict propriety. Any approach to
indecorum was frowned upon, transgression was severely
punished,—"La cour qui du temps du feu roi étoit très licen-
cieuse est aujourd'hui assez regulière," says the Venetian,
Contarini. Even the "fact" of Diane de Poitiers, already, before
Mary's advent an old woman, as age went then, blends into the
picture without scandal when we read of her assiduity in domestic details, supervising the royal nursery, even nursing the Queen
in her confinements! Henri himself had the grace not to flaunt
his *affaires amoureuses*,—"Il les tient si secrètes que personne
ne peut en parler." Catherine herself tells us that, "La chose
du monde de quoi il étoit le plus marri, c'étoit quand il savoit
que je susse de ses nouvelles-là."

Ladies of royal rank were in fact guarded with almost
oriental strictness, more especially until they were given in
marriage, and the guardians of Mary's childhood were little
likely to permit her to come in contact with vice or to imbue her
with any spirit of idleness. Margaret of Angoulême, Queen of
Navarre, was perhaps more an example and a memory than a
guide, for she died not long after Mary came to France, but in
more than one respect it would appear that Mary, in common
with many others, endeavoured to model their lives on hers,
which even the vile scandal-mongers of the time did not succeed
in smirching. In frequent and immediate contact with Mary's
life was her "aunt," as she called her, Margaret of Valois, afterwards Duchess of Savoy, whose piety and learning as well as
her liberal sympathies with reform, must have had an effect on
her young pupil. In the quiet retreat of Meudon, with her
Grandmother, the Dowager Duchess of Guise, she spent much
of her time away from court associations, and at Blois and

[1] *Mary Stuart*, by F. A. Mignet.

St Germain-en-Laye, where, with the children of France, she received her education, the King and his court were only occasional visitors. Her French *Gouvernantes* were chosen with immense care, Lady Fleming, who came with her from Scotland, was dismissed not long after the arrival in France because of the King's undue friendship, and thereafter only French women were appointed, but the incident of Lady Fleming happened when Mary was too young to appreciate the significance of the reason. We may say with confidence that Mary's contact with the French court, properly so called, was very limited, probably it was not more frequent than that of the Princess Victoria with the court of William IV. It would be difficult to say that the moral atmosphere of the latter was superior to that of Henri II! Brantôme, who was perhaps not impartial, wrote, "La cour de Catherine de Médicis étoit un vrai paradis du monde et école de toute honnêteté, et l'ornement de la France."

Nor was there wanting the example of other great ladies of the court, celebrated for their virtue, whose names and lives are at once a guarantee that Mary's character could not but benefit by knowing them, and an impugnment of statements already referred to as to her vicious upbringing. Louise de Montmorency, sister of the Connétable and mother of the Chatillons, Madeleine de Mailly their sister, to whom Catherine wrote that it overpast all reason to destroy unfortunates for conscience sake; Eléonore de Roye, Princesse de Condé; her sister Charlotte de Rochefoucauld; Anne d'Esté, Duchesse de Guise, daughter of Renée de Ferrara, who wept at the cruelties of Amboise[1]; Madame de Crussol, of whom it was said that she was the mainspring of the Huguenots, and the close friend of Catherine; Jacqueline de Longwie de Montpensier, "Who sought but the

[1] Anne d'Esté's friend and companion was Olympie-Fulvie Morata, a woman celebrated for the purity of her morals. She died in exile for her adherence to the new doctrines. It is worth noting too that when Anne arrived in France for her marriage with Francis of Guise, then Duc d'Aumale, she was accompanied by Madame de Parroy, who was later "Gouvernante" to Mary, and was, it may be assumed, a person of liberal views.

peace and the public tranquillity, and of whom it was believed
that she could have prevented (had she lived) all the troubles that
arose after her death," yet she died asking a protestant minister
to administer the Viaticum; and many others, all of them opposed
to persecution, and liberal in their views as to religious freedom.
It has been truly said that the Reformation in France was a
woman's movement; the court ladies were deeply tinged with it,
the singing of psalms and reading the Scripture in the vulgar tongue
became fashionable, Catherine herself had her favourite psalm.

There were men too, leaders of thought in the kingdom, who
worked for reform and reconciliation; Charles de Marillac, who
died, says de Thou, of grief for the evils which afflicted the
Church; Michel de l'Hôpital, the Chancellor, ardent champion
of religious peace, whose "Mass" the Parisians laughed at,
saying he was the greatest Huguenot of them all; broad-minded
Cardinals as de Bourbon, and Armagnac, who were stout
Catholics but advocates of argument rather than the faggot;
bishops in plenty, as Saint-Gelais, Carracioli, Froissac, Gérard,
Morvilliers, Monluc of Valence.

The idea of moderation and of finding a formula which
would reunite the Church, dominated the minds of the leaders
of France in the years when Mary was growing into womanhood;
it formed the *motif* of much of the political correspondence of
the period. The Assembly of the Estates General of France which
closed in January 1561 showed how widely spread was the idea;
the Venetian Ambassador wrote that the common people in
many places were still Catholics, that is of the old faith, but that
the nobility, men as well as women, were for the most part in-
fected by the new doctrines. Catherine herself was at *that time*
sincerely anxious to bring about such alteration of the Roman
ritual as would content the Protestants or at least the Lutherans,
the English Ambassador stated the fact and it is not doubtful.
It is not enough to say that all this was mere *camouflage* intended
to conceal the effect of political pressure, it was too widespread,
too deep, too sincere, too obviously desirable to be accounted
for thus.

It was Francis, Mary's husband, who wrote, though we must assume that Catherine and the Cardinal of Lorraine were behind the pen:

I see the King (of Spain) my good brother, following a course full of delay and difficulty...which is not the method by which one should proceed to obtain the issue so wished for by a number of unfortunate consciences....It is certain that if both sides do not lay aside all passion and unanimously embrace this holy work...the Church of God will never be in repose and peace, nor shall we ever see ourselves free of the troubles and calamities which these divisions bring to all Christendom....I have by the advice of a great number of persons of consequence in my Council, whose opinions I have heard willingly ...(decided to press for the assembly of) a Council General, to which liberty of thought and access shall be guaranteed to all those received by the Church....As for me the conservation of my Kingdom being most dear, I intend, if the Pope, who is the chief and common Father has not some alleviation (to propose), to search for it myself and to assemble so many people of importance, as will suffice to put in tranquillity the consciences of my subjects, and establish a real reformation of the morals which are depraved by the vice of mankind.... (Francis to the Bp of Limoges, 18 July, 1560.)

If Francis was under Mary's (evil) influence, as some of our historians tell us, we must then credit her with a pronouncement so broad-minded as the above. I am afraid, however, that neither Francis in his seventeenth nor Mary in her eighteenth year can receive the merit, though no doubt both were in accord with the idea. *En passant* it may be said that this letter serves to indicate also the intention of its composer to maintain the Church in France as a national unit, and on another occasion Catherine wrote: "Il (Le Pape) n'a nulle autorité sur ceux qui portent le titre de roi ou de reine," the papacy was, in short, concerned with the principles of religion and not with the ordering of kingdoms.

Catherine herself had put the situation to the Pope in a letter dated 4 August, 1561:

The number of those who are separated from the Roman Church is so great that it is not possible to coerce them by severity or force of arms. The party is so powerful by the adhesion of the nobles and magistrates, it is so united and acquires every day such increase of strength, that it is formidable to the kingdom....Many of the most zealous Catholics believe that it is not necessary to cut them off from the Communion of the Church, that they may be accepted without danger and without evil effect, and that a reunion of the Greek and Latin Churches may be achieved.

Several of Mary's subsequent actions in Scotland betray her independence of the papal authority in temporal affairs, and her French education in such things asserted itself.

It would be useless to touch on the religious atmosphere of the land in which Mary spent her youth and imbibed her ideas without a closer consideration of the views held by the Cardinal of Lorraine, whose influence with her was perhaps greater than any other. Rightly or wrongly he was regarded as secretly a reformer and Philip of Spain always suspected his orthodoxy; Vargas, Spanish Ambassador in Rome, did not mince matters; "I am told," he writes to the King, "that the Cardinal of Lorraine is damned and a heretic, or to speak plainly, is one of the protestants[1]." This was in January 1561, and a few months later Chantonnay, Spanish Ambassador in Paris, wrote to his master an account of a conversation between Throgmorton and Mary, Throgmorton was exhorting her to adopt the new religion, he said she would find herself alone in her country if she did not do so, that the Cardinal was affected to it, if he would confess so much. Mary is represented as replying that she would rather be alone in her views than be a protestant: "As to the Cardinal," she said, "she thought she well knew his mind, having heard him preach publicly many times, and she understood him clearly[2]." This, it is true, is a somewhat ambiguous statement, and it may be argued that Mary did not believe in the Cardinal's alleged leaning to reform, but apart from the fact that Chantonnay is not likely to have known accurately what passed between Mary and Throgmorton, there is the evidence of Brantôme: "Je l'ay veu souvent discourir de la confession d'Augsbourg et

[1] Döllinger, *Beiträge zur Politischen, Kirchlichen und Kultur Geschichte etc.*, vol. I, p. 349.
[2] Teulet, *Relations Pol. de la France etc.*, vol. II, p. 163.

l'approuver à demy[1]." Here again it is open to question whether these discourses were not political, as indeed Brantôme suggests, rather than the result of conviction.

There is, however, broader ground for thinking that the Cardinal was not bigoted and was sincerely anxious to heal the schism in the Church by compromise. I have quoted on a previous page the letter sent by Mary's husband, Francis I, to the King of Spain, which undoubtedly was the work of the Cardinal, and we should remember that it was he who was instrumental in appointing the broad-minded Michel l'Hôpital as Chancellor, after the *émeute* of Amboise; he who at the assembly of Fontainebleau expressed the King's desire that in future those who attended the preachings should not be molested if they came unarmed; he again of whom it was said: "La première idée d'un concile national étoit venue du Cardinal"; he who met Theodore de Bèze, Calvin's chief lieutenant, at St Germain: "Avec l'intention bienveillante de chercher les termes de rapprochement plutôt que les termes qui éloignent[2]." And of this colloquy von Pastor says: "Die rede des Kardinals war in der Form äusserst gemässigt, so dass der versöhnlichen partei ihren Eindruck nicht verfehlen konnte[3]." Even Brantôme, who liked to have a sly dig at the Cardinal on occasion, could not conceal his admiration: "Aussy ce grand personnage M. de Bèze, le (the Cardinal) loua fort...l'un et l'autre ne se pouvoient exalter assez." Finally it was he who presented to the Council of Trent the 34 Articles which permitted, *inter alia*, the communion in both kinds, and the study of the Scripture in the vulgar tongue. It was of this that the Spanish Ambassador in Rome said, "In quos fines saeculorum devenimus."

At the interview at Saverne, when the brothers Guise met the Duke of Würtemburg, it was recorded by the Duke that the Cardinal had said, "I have read the confession of Augsburg and the three chief Lutheran theologians. I entirely approve of their

[1] *Œuvres*, vol. v, p. 194.
[2] De la Ferrière, *Lettres de Catherine de Médicis.*
[3] von Pastor, *Geschichte der Päpste*, Pius IV.

doctrines. But I must conceal my opinion for a while in order to gain others whose faith is feeble[1]."

It is true that the extremists of the new religion declared that the Cardinal's broad-mindedness was wrung from him by personal fear of the effect of revolution; of this there is no proof, on the contrary it can hardly be doubted that he was sincere when he wrote: "Pour remédier aux maux qui accablerent la France que demandait-il? La réformation du clergé. Il faut que l'on voie une telle réformation...que le commencement puisse retirer et rappeler les devoyés et éteindre le feu qui croît tous les jours." Even if we attribute to him the motive of mere personal aggrandisement or even personal security, the fact remains that in the cause of France he exerted his great abilities, and we will find that in the matter of Mary Stuart and the Spanish Marriage he sacrificed his niece and to some extent himself, because that marriage would have been detrimental to French interests.

That he acted with severity against the Calvinists is true, but according to the views of the age they were revolutionary in their aims: "La crise religieuse du XVI siècle n'était pas simplement religieuse, elle était essentiellement révolutionaire." (Guizot.) A contemporary writer saw in their teaching a return to republicanism; that the power of the sovereign was derived from the people; that the nobles were no greater than they. In Scotland, Knox preached openly that the subject was entitled to resist the prince, if moved by conscience. At such a time it is not strange that views of this kind should be mercilessly repressed. The Cardinal of Lorraine as a great officer of the State could not be backward in rooting out a heresy against the princely caste, whatever his opinions might have been on the question of religious reform[2].

[1] Paul van Dyke, *Cath. de Médicis*, vol. I, p. 238.

[2] In this connection it is interesting to remember that, according to Archbishop Spottiswood, the Superintendents and Ministers assembled to draw up the Book of Discipline for the guidance of the Scottish kirk did not favour a break away from the ancient faith, "But to purge it from the corruptions and abuses only, that were crept into

It was suspected at the time that the Cardinal of Lorraine aimed at the establishment of a Gallic Church of which he should himself be Patriarch, but if this be so there seems to be no reason for supposing a desire to renounce the papal supremacy, though it may well be that he hoped thereby to advance a step towards "reasonable reformation" by adding to his power of imposing his own views.

The character of the Cardinal of Lorraine has been painted in dark colours by many historians, and, as far as England is concerned, this was due to no little extent to the fact that he was the stubborn opponent of Nicholas Throgmorton, Elizabeth's Ambassador in France, whose many machinations to stir up trouble made him a thorn in the flesh of the French rulers. To the Calvinists in general he was Antichrist, and to John Knox, whose vocabulary was extensive, he was the "cruel and conjured enemy of God and of all godliness." To such outpourings it is not necessary to give much consideration, the religious sectaries of the day exhausted every epithet to describe the errors of their opponents, "be my brother or I will beat in thine head," was the nearest approach to amity that was reached in the 16th century! It is, however, when we come to the judgment of the French writer M. Mignet (1851) that we find ourselves confronted with serious charges, which, coming from such a source, cannot be disregarded. Francis I, he tells us, prided himself on his unblushing licentiousness, "his second in this work of debauchery and corruption was Mary Stuart's uncle, the opulent and libertine Cardinal of Lorraine." Mr Froude adopts this and goes one better, he tells us that the Cardinal was Mary's preceptor in profligacy.

But for such statements there is insufficient foundation; we should clear our minds of such imaginings. Francis I was

the same....But these advices took no place, John Knox who then carried the chiefest sway, liking the course best which stood in extreme opposition against the Church of Rome..." (April-May, 1560). From this one sees the more or less accidental nature of the course of events which in the end caused Mary's destruction.

already 30 years old before Charles of Guise was born, and before
he was old enough to have a share in the King's unseemly proceedings, that monarch was approaching the decay which he
brought upon himself. I presume that M. Mignet's verdict was
founded on Brantôme, the pleasant historian of the lives of the
"Grands Capitaines François." But Brantôme was anxious to
pose as something of a Paladin, and while admiring and greatly
extolling the genius of the Cardinal, he had the same view as
Hotspur, of one who might "have been a soldier but for these
vile guns," and he seldom lost an opportunity of saying so.
Howbeit, even Brantôme did not go further than to say: "Il
éstoit bien autant mondain en ses jeunes et beaux ans, aussi a il
eu très bonnes fortunes, que je dirois bien." He says also in
another place, presumably after the Cardinal, or rather the
Archbishop as he was then, had sown his wild oats: "Il éstoit
fort religieux." But in any case I prefer the more recent judgment of von Pastor (1920): "The youngest of the French Cardinals, he shamed the others by his strict correctness of life. In
his diocese of Rheims he worked earnestly for the education of
a qualified clergy[1]."

That he was a man of vast ambition, greedy of power and
perhaps, like his peers, not too scrupulous how he obtained it,
seems indubitable. It may be that in his early years as Archbishop of Rheims, to which dignity he was inducted at the age
of 14 (!), he was what Brantôme suggests, but even so we should
be chary of too much condemnation, remembering that the age
took slender objection to irregularities of princes, whether of
the Church or not, which to us seem shocking; at least we can
place to his credit evidence of a subsequent reform, and we
should suspend final judgment until a more exhaustive criticism

---

[1] von Pastor, *Geschichte der Päpste*, Pius IV. It seems probable that
M. Mignet, followed by Froude, has mistaken John of Lorraine, who
was also Cardinal of that province, and who *was* the companion of
Francis' follies, for his more reputable nephew Charles. At all events
M. de Bouillé describes Charles as presenting a theme on Theology
to Francis in 1544, which was only a couple of years before the King's
death!

be available[1]. There is no shadow of evidence that he acted otherwise than as an honourable guardian to his niece; not a word in contemporary correspondence of any weight supports such an idea; the letters sent by him to Marie of Guise, during Mary's minority, would alone prevent any other conclusion.

Though the time was one in which extraordinary genius developed, yet there was in the minds of men a baseness which seems to indicate how little the refinement of the Renaissance had purified the masses. The vilest libels were invented, the most senseless scandals; the chastity of Mary in relation with the Cardinal was called in question, of Margaret of Navarre with her brother Francis, of Marie of Guise with the Cardinal Beton, of Elizabeth of England; William of Nassau had murdered his wife, Mary Stuart poisoned Francis I, Philip had poisoned Isabel. The honour of every person prominent in the disputes was, at one time or another, dragged through the mud to satisfy party rancour, and every artifice was used to stir up strife; forgery was almost a fine art, there are numerous cases in the record; Cecil had a servant whose name has come down to us who was skilled in opening sealed packets and mastering their contents before forwarding them again, Throgmorton boasts of success in a similar practice. The Ambassadors of the Powers had their spies in the households of the great and, judging from the nature of the "news" they provided, they were of a low type; even in the secretariat of the grim Philip himself was one who dared to report what was going on[2]. In Scotland almost every man, noble or simple, had his price, and chivalry was a mere form of words; in France, if the standard of the "gentles" was higher, that of the literate class next below was base. We should remember these things when passing judgment on those whose character has been defamed.

---

[1] In his *Histoire des Ducs de Guise*, M. René de Bouillé can hardly be said to have presented an exhaustive study of the famous Cardinal. It is rather a history of the times in which he lived, and there is yet room for a true portrait of the man himself.

[2] John de Castillo who after many years of successful duplicity was discovered and torn to pieces by four horses.

My purpose in thus briefly referring to the moral atmosphere
which surrounded Mary's youth, is, not to express a final opinion
on the merits or demerits of the Cardinal of Lorraine or of the
leaders of party at the time, but to show that it is unjust and
inaccurate to represent Mary Stuart as embarking on a career of
misgovernment and crime in Scotland as the result of vicious
training at a profligate court in France. In fact, she led a more
sheltered life there than would have been the case had she
remained at home, and to suggest, as a modern writer has done,
that she "breathed the atmosphere of scandal, she was familiar-
ised with sights and thoughts of cruelty...persecution was not
hid from her...," is to suggest what is not true. The inference
that she was naturally cruel is too far removed from reality to
merit a moment's credence. Every action of hers up to, let us
say, to avoid controversy, the end of 1565 was the very antithesis
of cruelty; the Bishop of Mondovi, not a favouring witness,
wrote: "The Queen could easily have made her position secure
by punishing a few ringleaders, but being too prone to pity and
clemency she exposed herself to the risk of being a slave and a
prey to those heretics with danger even to her life...." Lenience
even to weakness was so marked a trait in her character that the
idea of cruelty is altogether absurd. I do not desire to beg the
question of her guilt in the crimes which led to her fall, other
than to say that if guilty the change of nature was astonishing.

One other deduction from the foregoing should be made; we
know that before leaving France, Mary said to the Ambassador
Throgmorton: "I mean to constrain none of my subjects"
and shortly after her home-coming in her answer to the
General Assembly she said: "The Queen neither has in times
bypast nor yet means hereafter to press the conscience of
any man, but that they may worship God in such sort as they
are persuaded to be best" (Keith, III). Though her detractors
would have us believe that this attitude was mere duplicity,
adopted to conceal the development of very different intentions,
yet it is so entirely in accord with the general aspect of the toleration which held the minds of so many in France with whom

Mary was in contact as described above that I hold it for perfectly genuine.

We cannot overlook the *fact*, for it is a fact, that the awakening of Mary's powers of mind was accompanied by the spirit which influenced those around her, and this involves the admission that to find a *via media* in the great religious controversy was to her, as it was to them, a guiding principle. Whether we attribute this to mere political exigency, as it probably was in some cases, or to sincere conviction, as it certainly was with many, does not greatly matter; Mary had little to do with politics during her sojourn in France, her toleration was, I think there is no doubt of it, the outcome of sincerity.

It is well to remember that a *via media* did not at the time present such difficulties as afterwards grew out of the controversy, there is nothing unreasonable in the assumption just made. Both sides desired reform and the dispute as to the Eucharist had existed for centuries without splitting the Church asunder. Accord, or at least a compromise with the Lutherans, was conceivable, and if achieved, the sanguine hoped that the Swiss Reformers would fall in or be overwhelmed. At the very time of Mary's closest touch with affairs in France the question of the constitution of a new General Council was in debate. In February 1561 the German princes had come to agreement at Naumberg; France had undertaken to abide by the decisions of a General Council provided that the "Princes of Germany would allow thereof." Elizabeth was in communication with the Duke of Saxony, and had expressed herself with little reserve on the disputed matter, "There is but one faith," she said, "all the rest is a bagatelle." We have seen already the action of the Cardinal of Lorraine when the Council did ultimately assemble. The Spanish Netherlands were suffering for conscience sake, and William of Orange-Nassau was finding himself. The Emperor, under the influence of the Electors, was inclined to take sides with France to insist on reform. The Pope himself, Pius IV, preferred conciliation to violence. Spain alone stood four-square to the storm.

Here then was ground enough to lend hope to Mary that patience and the efforts of Europe would find a solution. We need not accuse her of duplicity in this matter of religion. It is true that on many occasions she declared herself a faithful daughter of the Church; that she would die as she had lived in the Roman faith. But here is no contradiction. Savonarola died in the faith; Luther adhered to the popish supremacy long after he initiated reform; Margaret of Angoulême-Navarre died in the practice of the Roman Church; very many of the great names referred to above, ardent reformers though they were, claimed the right to die as members of it.

It is, I think, beyond question that Mary was honestly anxious to meet Elizabeth, "When we see each other she will know my heart better than she can judge my letters," she said. She had a great secret to impart; true she only refers to it specifically after her fall, and it may have been connected with the murder, yet the terms of her reference to it precluded that it was altogether confined to this: "Would to God that you knew what I know." "You shall declare that we have some matter of great weight... which we cannot commit to the credit of any person nor to writing"; "Her desire is still to reveal into her Majesty's self in her own presence that which she will not else to any living."

Was this only a ruse to gain admittance to Elizabeth's presence at a time when this was denied her? I think not; what she had in her "heart," in the early days before Darnley came on the scene, had some connection with the subsequent appeal. That it concerned religion is I think probable, any form of heterodoxy would seem to Mary a matter of tremendous importance, she would fear eternal damnation if it were published before general acceptance rendered it orthodox. She had not the virile courage of her sister Queen. Her secret, whatever it was, died with her.

Cecil, his greatness notwithstanding, was insular in his views. Like many Englishmen of his time and indeed of times long after his, he could see no good in men or measures out of France; he consistently regarded Mary as aiming at the Romanisation of

England. In this he was probably wrong, but it is hard to blame him that he took no chances; yet it may well be that had he worked sincerely to bring Mary and Elizabeth together in personal conference, issues would have developed to bring the security he desired. The probability is that Mary dreamed of a harvest of great things which more experience would have told her were beyond her capacity to bring about. She had her girlish vanity of her power of persuasion, with Elizabeth a common ground was likely, with the courtly de Bèze she might have anticipated a compromise. The coarse violence of Knox was a disillusionment, and in Scotland she was driven more and more within herself.

Of her mental and physical vigour can so much be truly said as is suggested by her admirers or detractors? *Prima facie* one would hardly expect to find robustness; her father died at 31 from an obscure brain disease a week after her birth, his constitution undermined by the excesses which contemporary writers relate; her two brothers died in infancy; her mother died at 44 from an ascitic dropsy; of her English progenitors, Henry VII died of consumption and none of his stock was healthy, of his grandchildren two died young, and the three who survived, Mary, Elizabeth and Edward, were all tainted. Mary Stuart certainly did not start life with a good record behind her, and in fact we find her sickly at frequent intervals during her childhood, though perhaps such illnesses should not be insisted on as evidence of delicacy. But when she came to adolescence her health became a subject of discussion among the Ambassadors when writing to their sovereigns. The year after her marriage, she being then in her 17th year, it was reported that she could not live long, and the commentary was, "God take her to him as soon as he pleases," this commentary, one of several of like sort, is useful to remember. This woman Queen of Scotland, snatched from the power of England in her infancy and brought up by England's hereditary enemy, was not wanted, and from the beginning England would fain be quit of her.

The Florentine Ambassador thought her consumptive; she was subject to long fainting fits, and this continued to be the case after her arrival in Scotland. She had some chronic complaint of the spleen, probably inherited from her mother, which caused her almost constant pain, especially after fatigue or excitement. She became worse after the birth of her child, she nearly died of it in 1566, and was reported thereafter to be much broken in health and constantly ailing.

Physical vigour must be ruled out, and the picture of Mary leading her levies armed with a "dagg" (pistol) and wearing a "secret" (under coat of mail) appeared so absurd to Randolph who reported it, that he added: "If it be true that I heard." A good horsewoman she probably was, we read of her favourite horses, Bravane and Madame la Réale, in the early days at Blois, but whether the hunting of which we hear a good deal involved anything like the exertion which a straight riding young lady of to-day will undertake, is open to doubt. Yet it is true that on occasion under strong excitement she did perform feats of endurance, as for instance her ride to Dunbar after the murder of Rizzio and her ride to Dundrennan after Langside, but we have glimpses of the physical exhaustion that followed, and we know that the 40 mile ride to Hermitage and back to Jedburgh nearly killed her. Undoubtedly she was naturally delicate and far from equal to the arduous task that fate had allotted to her.

As an instance of "historical" judgment let me quote Mr Froude's conception of Mary's activity at the end of 1563: "Without illness or the imagination of it, she would lounge for days in bed, rising only at night for dancing or music, and there she reclined with some delicate French robe carelessly draped round her....." For this there seems to be no better foundation than is derivable from letters written by Randolph: "I understood that the Queen kept her bed, being somewhat diseased (=overtired) of over much travail she took a night or two before, dancing over long to celebrate the feast of her nativity....But I think rather it was a great cold she took (*as she says herself*) being so long that day at her divine service...." A week later, he says: "The Queen's disease (whereof proceeding I know not) daily increaseth; her pain is in the right (left ?) side...on Saturday she was out of bed but took no pleasure in company nor in talk with any...." As a pendant to this let us glance at a picture of Elizabeth painted by the same artist and related to the same month of December (1563): "In the midst of encompassing perils Elizabeth bore herself bravely. The death rate in London at the end of December was still 200 a week, the country was smarting under the disaster at Havre. The French difficulty was likely to lead to a great war in which Spain would take a part and Mary Stuart married (to be married ?) to a catholic prince, formed the ominous centre round which clouds were forming. Yet Elizabeth, to the world appeared to be given up to amusement." The contemporary statement reads: "The Queen is entirely given over to love, hunting, hawking, and dancing, consuming day and night in trifles, nothing is treated earnestly, he who invents most ways of wasting time is regarded as one worthy of honour." Challoner who wrote this was no doubt jaundiced, but why it should be noble of Elizabeth to amuse herself while her kingdom was in danger and naughty of Mary to dance and catch cold at her birthday party, is a problem only worth considering because it shows that it would be unwise to accept too hastily Mr Froude's, and I am afraid a good many other estimates of Mary's *naturel*.

It is noticeable in many references to the Queen of Scots that she is represented, as it were, "fully fledged" before she was in fact emerged from childhood, and often enough the historian attributed to her responsibility for things of which she knew nothing. "The Queen of Scots is a great doer here and takes all upon her," and again, "The Guises and the Queen of Scots rule all in Paris." To these reports of Throgmorton, Froude adds that though but nineteen years old she was dextrous and energetic beyond her years; of the same period we are told, "If Mary Stuart had influence enough to give direction to her uncles, there was more danger than ever." All this relates to July 1559, and Mary was not nineteen but sixteen and a half! It is too much to ask one to credit that she could have *influence* at such age with men like either Francis or Charles of Guise, and as to ruling all in Paris, or shining in the affairs of state, as another critic says she did, the idea is laughable. Women, at least royal women, were not encouraged to rule in France, and nobody knew this better than Throgmorton, who wrote a little later that the salic law "precludes women from authority though she be a daughter of France"; and the same Throgmorton who in July 1559 describes Mary as ruling all, tells us in December 1560: "During her husband's lifetime there was no great account made of her, for that being under the band of marriage and subjection of her husband...there was no great occasion to know what was in her...." We may say without hesitation that up to her departure from France, Mary had no experience of statecraft. In the contemporary histories of De Thou and Regnier de la Planche, when treating of the political happenings of the reign of Francis II, there is not so much as a single reference to Mary or her influence.

The fact is that Sir Nicholas Throgmorton's despatches were coloured with a great deal of exaggeration, especially where they concerned the Guises whom he detested, and any item tending to excite opinion against the Queen of Scots was, as he well knew, acceptable in England. More than once he deliberately used Mary's name where the matter concerned Catherine, as for instance when he reported, "The young French Queen has sent to the Duchess of Valentinois to take account of the King's jewels," it was not she but Catherine who did so, not unnaturally Catherine was not slow to indicate to her rival that her day was over. It is very likely that when he referred to "ruling all" he should have used Catherine's name and not Mary's. Sir Nicholas, like most of his kind, wrote what he hoped would further his interests, and one can hardly blame him at a time when others of his class did the same thing, but one does feel inclined to blame those later-day "historians" who blindly accept such things without proper consideration.

Another instance which is useful as showing the kind of

undercurrent which was constantly setting against the "Young French Queen" is also due to Sir Nicholas; he reported the escape of the Earl of Arran, who was held in France as a kind of hostage for the good behaviour of his father, the head of the Hamiltons, and he said that, on hearing of Arran's disappearance, Mary expressed the desire that if recaptured he should be treated "as an arrant traitor," which is much the same as asking for his head in a charger. I do not think there is a word of truth in the story which was admittedly hearsay only, Arran's life would have been perfectly safe had he been retaken, noblemen were not so lightly destroyed in those days of class privilege. But the pith of it lies in the end of the letter which was addressed to Cecil: "Sir, methinks if these matters could be speedily insinuate to the Earl of Arran's father and kinsfolk...it would serve well to the advancement of the Queen's (Elizabeth) service." The service in question was to induce the Hamiltons to join in the rebellion against the constituted authority in Scotland! The bearer of this precious epistle was one Sandy Whytlowe, "greatly esteemed by John Knox...." "He is very religious and therefore you must let him see as little sin in England as you may." The sixteen year old Queen had indeed need to be "dextrous beyond her years" to deal with such people as these.

And of this dextrous, resolute, purposeful Mary, how much is there in reality? Nothing! Married to the sickly boy Francis, then Dauphin, when she was a little more than 15—they had been brought up together as children and as children they continued to the end of Francis' short life—neither he nor she had any real contact with the affairs of state. We see them at the gorgeous ceremonies of the wedding, or the coronation, stiff in their splendour of brocades and velvets, bejewelled and unreal like marionettes. One can imagine the scene not very dissimilar to an eastern marriage with its ostentatious display of gems and cloth of gold. The little Queen faints at the altar and is revived with the sacramental wine, at the subsequent court functions she is carried away "swounding." Preliminary to the marriage she is made to sign three secret documents which, failing her own heirs, cancel the right line of the succession in Scotland, in favour of the house of Valois. She is represented as, "Having taken advice of her best and most singular friends, especially of the Most Illustrious Cardinal of Lorraine and of My Lord the Duke of Guise her uncles." Certainly there was not much precocious resolution or far-sighted political acumen about this, rather one must say a singular absence of such qualities and a very childlike submission. Even M. Mignet, who was not gifted with much power to perceive Mary's inwardness, says: "We cannot fairly charge her with this fault, so young was she and submissive to the will of others." Elizabeth when it suited her purpose could recognise Mary's youth as we gather from a conversation between Mary and Throgmorton, "The Queen your mistress doth say that I am young and do lack experience. But I have age enough and experience to behave myself towards friends and kinsfolk, friendly and uprightly" (July 1561).

It is true enough that young people developed then at an earlier age than is the case to-day, but I cannot find any indication that Mary was exceptionally precocious. Education was conducted somewhat on the comprehensive lines recommended by Pantagruel to his son, and we read accounts of the wide learning of many great ladies of the time, but, perhaps because of her delicacy, Mary does not seem to have been very advanced. She understood Latin but could not speak it, whereas her "sister" Elizabeth could carry on a conversation in Latin, Italian or French. Of Mary's Italian I find no mention, but one assumes that the Queen Mother would make Italian a rule in the royal nursery; in later years she was "reading" Spanish. Her English was limited, at least she could not write it, and she excused her "ill English" declaring herself "more willing than apt to learn that language," this was at Tutbury in 1569, and we must conclude that on her first arrival she had very little "English" at all. Even of Scottish one must be doubtful. It is not a great step from the dialect of southern Scotland to the English language, and if she could not speak the latter we may doubt if she was fluent in the other. It is true that Throgmorton relates a conversation with Mary which he expressly states was carried on on her part in Scottish and on his part in English, and we must accept this as fact, though as he was at least a fair French scholar and the meeting was in the presence of French people it is remarkable that a language should be chosen in which both were somewhat halting[1].

We should remember that her baby talk while she remained with her mother was almost certainly French, and while in France there is reason to believe that she was made as *French* as possible for political reasons. There are as far as I know no authentic autograph letters of Mary's in the Scottish dialect; a few lines by way of postscript have been added in some cases, and in these the Scottish is somewhat "broken," for instance, "Wat ever bis sayed bi sur off my gud mynd, and that ye sal persayve, command mi to our bruder." (Postscript to Earl of Argyll, 31.3.1566.) Here is a mixture of English, Scottish and French which does not indicate fluency in the first two! I have gone a little further into this question of language than is necessary for the immediate purpose of this chapter, because it will be useful in connection with matters of later date. One thing is certain, Mary's natural language in which she thought and wrote was French.

Apart from the question of languages in which she probably had no great skill, Mary was undoubtedly well educated and refined by contact with the Art of the Renaissance. Whatever faults may be attributed to Francis I, at least he did much to bring France in touch with the creations of the great artists of Italy, and Catherine de Médicis continued and expanded the movement initiated by him, as indeed the great-grand-daughter of Lorenzo the Magnificent could hardly fail to do. Francesco Primaticcio was engaged in painting his frescoes at Fontaine-

---

[1] When opening her first parliament Mary wrote her speech in French but read it in "English," that is, presumably in Scottish, no doubt a translation made for her by a secretary.

bleau in Mary's time; Philibert de l'Orme was at work on the
Châteaux of St Maur, Anet, Meudon, which Mary wrote of as
"Cette belle maison de Meudon." An almost endless line of
great painters had already passed away, but Titian, Tintoretto
and Veronese were still at Venice and Michelangelo at Rome,
Leonardo had died at Amboise within recent memory. In
France no great painter had arisen, but France had taken and
made its own other forms of expression of genius; Leonard
Limosin was executing his exquisite enamels, it is quite possible
that he made a portrait of Mary, for many of the royal family,
including her husband Francis, were among his studies; Bernard
Palissy was perfecting his bizarre masterpieces, and those wonderful examples of the ceramic art known to us as Oiron, more
correctly, St Porchaire, ware, decorated the palaces of Henri
and the Château of his mistress at Anet, many bearing the inter-
laced crescents which formed his badge and the monogram of
H and D—Henri-Diane; Catherine had added to these the works
of the famous potters of Gubbio and Urbino which we name
comprehensively, Majolica.

But perhaps it was the art of the weaver and embroiderer
which in Mary's time was most characteristically French, and
many of the great ladies employed their leisure with the needle
creating the immense tapestries which we so much admire.
Mary was herself a skilful needlewoman, and of Catherine,
Brantôme tells us that in this art, "Elle éstoit tant parfaite qu'il
éstoit possible." At Amboise the tapestries were famous, at
Fontainebleau we may suppose that Mary saw the creation of
Antoine Caron's *chef d'œuvre*, the "History of Mausolus and
Artemisia," which Catherine had ordered as a memorial of her
grief and widowhood, with its woven motto, "Ardorem extincta
testantur vivere flamma," "Though the beloved is gone, these
testify of the living love." Years after, Mary had woven a motto
on her "cloth of estate" which read, "En ma fin est mon commencement." "It is a riddle I understand not," said Cecil's
correspondent; perhaps it might be read, "I end as I began,
unwanted."

Certainly up to the date of her leaving France this unosten-
tatious Mary had neither shown nor had opportunity of showing
any remarkable qualities, unless the obedience and affection
apparent in all her letters may be classed as such. And after her
arrival in her kingdom one searches in vain for evidence of
resolution and far-seeing diplomacy. She is in the hands of her
"brother," the Lord James, and of Maitland of Lethington,
content, as Throgmorton put it, "to be ruled by good counsel
and wise men," and if these two had been to Scotland and Mary
what Cecil was to England and Elizabeth how different a story
would have been to tell! All a blind, say her enemies, firm in
her intention to re-establish the Roman faith, she played with
the reformers merely to gain time, *elle recule pour mieux sauter*.
But whence is drawn the evidence from her immediately preceding life in France that this was her scheme? Everything
connected with it seems to point in the opposite direction. And
then the destruction of the Gordons to which she lent her name
and her presence, if not her wishes. Was it far-seeing policy on
the part of this unscrupulous, papistical Queen to destroy the
mainstay of the Religion in Scotland? To hunt the man who
had offered to come to her and to reinstate the Roman faith?
I am afraid one can only see in this incident that "submission
to the will of others" which is mentioned above. And her
marriage with Darnley, in which one of our historians sees
evidence of "firmness"? We shall deal with it more fully, but
was it not rather evidence of petulance and inability to play the
cards her position gave her? We shall see!

And of her murder of Darnley or acquiescence in his murder,
if she did so? Could she have done anything more damnably
foolish, I am not thinking of wickedness, but of pure foolishness?
Not only the fact itself but the manner of doing it. She is on the
eve of a settlement with Elizabeth on the subject which filled
her mind—the acknowledgment as to succession—Bedford has
brought her a letter from Elizabeth—representatives are to be
sent immediately to London—Elizabeth has been Godmother
to the child—nothing could be of greater importance than to

retain the good opinions of the English parliament shortly to be called, many members of which were Catholics who looked rather to the Englishman, Darnley, than to the "foreigner," Mary. And the manner! An astute woman supposed to be well instructed in the alleged (but apochryphal) lore of Catherine de Médicis, the art of poisoning, in which the egregious Buchanan gives her skill; quite capable, they say, of arranging an effective "daggering" during one of his many unsavoury escapades, or better still an open trial for treason, to which he was deeply liable, a hundred and one ways of doing it, would she have chosen the clumsy method of gunpowder in circumstances which inevitably brought suspicion from every quarter? But they say, this was a *crime passionel*, and to this type no laws of sense apply. Even here the prosecution stultifies itself, for we are told that she and her lover had exhausted every intimacy many months before; there was no reason for haste, every reason for delay, the inconvenient husband had even declared his intention of leaving the country and the lovers to themselves, but they must needs prevent him from doing so, and having brought him into the limelight they do away with him with as much noise as possible; finally the marrying with the chief villain and the pitiful subterfuges of the "clenging" and the carrying away to Dunbar, which we are told were arranged by the bold, unscrupulous Mary herself to mock God and the world, with hasard of her crown, estate, dowry, life and honour.

Truly her annalists cannot have it both ways; if guilty, a set of adjectives less expressive of strenuous evil-doing must be employed to describe her; if innocent, they must be content to place her on a lower pedestal, for in neither case did she show outstanding qualities. The opinion may be hasarded that if Mary had passed through the same school as Elizabeth, a Mary more fit to cope with wild Scotland might have resulted.

A little "diamond heart" resolution would have won the day at Carberry Hill; a touch of imperious will and a faculty for "achieving a great purpose" would have carried all before it after Lochleven; a determination to endure would have avoided the fatal flight into England; a little insight into Elizabeth's difficulties, even supposing her honour to be spotless, should have warned her not to trust her sister queen too much. Mary possessed none of these.

As it is I can only find a graceful, charming, delicate girl, easily given to tears, "*une petite reinette ecossoise* qui n'a qu'à sourire pour tourner toutes les têtes," brought up to believe herself by divine intervention a ruler, but totally untrained by contact with affairs to take her position; sincerely anxious to play her part and passionately resenting any infringement of her royal dignity. So used to homage and the observance of a court etiquette in which royalty could unbend without any thought of reciprocity that she had no defence against the rude manners of Scotland. Witty and vivacious during the few years she had of success, she may have said that Elizabeth was about to marry her "horsekeeper[1]" or that Catherine was "a merchant's daughter," but if she did she condemned herself as a bad politician. In truth there is nothing to show that her abilities were more than moderate or perhaps I should better say they were not of that high order which some panegyrists with mistaken zeal would attribute to her. She was loyal to those who stood by her and infinitely trusting, unfortunately without that peculiar gift of selecting the trustworthy.

I have no wish to present Mary as a paragon of the domestic virtues, her mode of expression would shock even a young woman of to-day, but her age was the age of Rabelais; men and women lived nearer to nature than we do, the plain wood that we veneer was then in its natural state! With Rabelais himself she may have been acquainted during his Curacy of Meudon; with his satires she was certainly acquainted, and no doubt the decadence of religion was a theme on which she heard a great deal. Yet, as often happens, it was the women who maintained the purest ideas on the precepts of religious teaching, and virtue among women stood then in no less regard than is the case to-day. I might even go further and say that the fierce controversies

---

[1] Robert Dudley, afterwards Earl of Leicester, Master of the Horse.

produced champions more ardent than we know, and those who adhered to a high moral standard did so with an intensity that is not so necessary now.

That Mary's moral standard was high I do not doubt for a moment, I mean particularly the physical quality of virtue. It would be so from no higher consideration than laws of custom which shielded royal ladies more than meaner mortals, but it was so also because she was naturally religious and modest. In other moral qualities possibly there was the same deficiency which was common to all the princes of the time. When Niccolo Machiavelli wrote *The Prince* he was not so much propounding a new theory as summarising a state of things of which he had experience: "As the generality of mankind are wicked and ever ready to break their word, a prince should not pique himself in keeping his more scrupulously, especially as it is always easy to justify a breach of faith on his part." It is certain that princes and their ministers did understand and practise the "art of feigning and dissembling" recommended by the author, and as his work was addressed to Catherine's father it would be too much to suppose that the idea was absent from the education of her children—besides, the book contained a great deal that is beyond reproach even from our ethical viewpoint. While I should be sorry to say that Mary did not possess this particular attribute of 16th century sovereignty, it is quite certain that she made a poor hand at it. Catherine, Elizabeth, Philip, to mention the three principals only, were past masters in the art of deception, and they all regarded Mary as a tiro. Surrounded by traitors and naturally frank and confiding, she no sooner embarked on a policy than it was reported in the courts of Europe.

From her early letters there is not much to be gathered, they lack spontaneity and are evidently for the most part dictated or supervised. Here and there are sentiments which are likely to be natural, as for instance her annoyance that Madame de Parroy should have put about the suggestion that she was stingy in the matter of giving away her cast-off clothes, and that she was unlike her mother. If we are to take the letters literally the pin-pricks inflicted by this lady of her suite weighed so heavily on her mind that her life was endangered.

In another of the early letters, written by the Cardinal to Marie of Guise, we meet those exaggerated encomiums of the young Queen which seem to have misled so many. "She daily grows in dignity, wisdom and virtue...she is as perfect and accomplished in all things as it is possible.... The King delights to pass an hour in her society, she understands so well how to entertain him with wit and wisdom as would a woman of twenty-five." No doubt it was kindly of the uncle thus to write to the lonely mother in Scotland, but we cannot forget that this all-accomplished young lady was at the time only ten years old!

The Flemish Jesuit Nicholas Floris, called de Gouda, wrote of her in 1562 a little sketch which I think sums up her situation then and afterwards, "What I would ask you should a young lady do in such circumstances? She is devout, has been nurtured in princely luxury and numbers scarce twenty years, she is alone and has not a single protector or good councillor.... The men in power are taking advantage of her gentleness....In the opinion of good men it is absolutely necessary she should marry a strong Catholic Prince...She is well nigh destitute of human aid...."

Those who condemn Mary as an adulteress, a murderess and a treacherous liar, must do so on evidence, evolved after the event, by enemies whose good faith is very doubtful, but to endeavour to supplement the record by presenting her as just the kind of woman who would be capable of such things is more than an injustice. If Mary at the point of death in October 1566 had then passed the border, there would not have been even a suggestion of evil in her life.

CHAPTER II

Read in connection with the preceding chapter, I aim now at showing that the Queen of Scots was actuated by higher motives than mere ambition in her project of the Spanish marriage. The explanation offered seems to be a necessary link in historical facts which are otherwise unconnected.

THE MARRIAGE NEGOTIATIONS
OF MARY STUART

A CONSIDERATION of the negotiations which centred round the marriage of the Queen of Scotland, in the light of knowledge which the liberal publication of contemporary archives permits, will be another aid to form a truer estimate of her character. The subject necessarily leads far afield, I hope none of it is irrelevant, but I am conscious that much remains to be done to make it complete. What follows in regard to the Spanish negotiations is set down rather in the hope that further investigation may be made to confirm or destroy the thesis advanced, than to maintain it as proven. There are many hundreds of contemporary documents which have not yet been printed, and it may well be that the editors of those we have, not having this particular matter in view, passed by as unimportant items that would be of great use.

Of her first marriage with the Dauphin Francis, who for a short year and a half raised her to the throne of France, little need be said. They were affianced almost as babies, brought up together and married as children, Mary being 15 years and 4 months old and Francis 13 months younger. There is considerable contemporary evidence that they were sincerely attached, and that Mary tended her sickly boy husband with devotion. It is beyond doubt that his early death was the result of an abscess of the inner ear and no question to the contrary was thought of at the moment. Yet it is useful to recall the statement, falsely attributed to the Bishop of Ross, that Mary had caused her husband's death by poison. The mere idea that she would wil-

fully forfeit her position as Queen of France is too absurd to
mention were it not to emphasise the vile nature of the stories
which Cecil's correspondents did not hesitate to communicate[1].
The Ambassador, Throgmorton, wrote to Elizabeth, "On the
6th of this present he (Francis) departed to God, leaving a
heavy and dolorous wife, as of right she had good cause to be,
who by long watching with him during his sickness, and painful
diligence about him, and especially by the issue, is not in the
best tune of her body, but without danger." Throgmorton is
not always reliable, but here he gives a glimpse of the real Mary.

As a young widow, the Queen became at once the object of
political intrigue. Not that her kingdom, poor and undeveloped,
was itself a prize worth struggling for, but as a strategic base it
was of decisive importance. It was life and death to England
to prevent the dominance of France or Spain in Scotland; and
both France and Spain were jealous each of the other. When
Mary, yet a child, was sent to France and, with the approval of
the Scottish Estates, affianced to the heir of the French crown,
her fate was sealed. It became England's policy to foster the
protestant party against their Queen, and to employ all the
resources available to minimise the French ascendancy. Had
England not been successful it was not a secret that Spain would
have attacked France.

One of the stereotyped traditions that surround the Queen
of Scots is that she was *amante passionée*; that she was "struck
with the dart of love," as Lennox puts it, for Darnley; destroyed
by an overmastering attraction for Bothwell, with minor
episodes, as Chastelard and Rizzio. Nothing could in fact be
less probable. To suppose a princess of her upbringing capable
of arranging her matrimonial affairs on the basis of personal
inclination is to forget all the *convenances* which hedged royal
ladies of the time with impenetrable closeness. Royal alliances
were first and last matters of political negotiation and national
advantage; there was not a princess alive with a greater appreciation of her duty than Mary: "She will never yield to any marri-

[1] Wilson to Burghley, 8 November, 1571.

age, how fit or profitable soever it be for her, unless she see that
her reputation (that is her princely dignity) shall not diminish
by the match." Thus wrote her secretary in December 1564,
and he had opportunity of knowing her mind. Princely dignity
was with her a fetish; nurtured by the notion that as Queen,
crowned of Scotland and presumptive of France, she was as
one set apart by divine will. Not healthy ideas for a young
woman, but tending to keep her from disposing of herself by
that mere human frailty that we call "falling in love." As a
French princess, which she was in effect, it would scarcely occur
to her that she should have a voice in her disposal, though as a
sovereign she might claim some authority in the decision. She
had seen her friend and playmate, Elizabeth of France, promised to the Prince of Spain, yet transferred to his father, the
grim Philip, as a chattel would be, but therein she would see no
occasion to murmur. We find her "offered" by her uncles to
various negotiators without reference to herself.

The first proposal for her was undoubtedly the one that
continued to appeal to her throughout the ensuing four and a
half years after the death of Francis—that is the marriage with
Don Carlos, only son and heir to the King of Spain. There is a
strange similarity in the story of Mary and Carlos; round each
of them has sprung up an extensive literature, the mystery of
Don Carlos is not less the subject of controversy than the
mystery of Mary Stuart. Both were educated without the
advantage of parental guidance, each lost a parent in earliest
infancy. The cataclysm which engulfed Mary took place at
almost the same time as that which destroyed the prince, it is
not unlikely that there was inter-connection between the two
events. Malice and servility inspired contemporary writers to
misrepresent the facts in each case, and whatever basis of truth
may have existed, the tales are tarnished with gutter rumours
of no credibility. Mary had her Buchanan; Carlos, his Gianbat-
tista Adriani. The one was betrayed or at least accused by her
bastard brother, the Earl of Moray; the other by his bastard
uncle Don John of Austria, of his own age and brought up with

him as a brother. Carlos was condemned by the Spanish Inquisition presided over by the Cardinal Espinoza, Mary by the
"inquisition" of the Scottish Kirk presided over by John Knox.
Schiller has enshrined the tragedies of both.

Ludwig von Ranke has brought together much information
regarding the unfortunate Spanish prince, and more lately a
Spanish historian, Don José Güell y Renté, has added to the
knowledge of the earlier writers; it is to be regretted that these
two were, apparently, ignorant each of the other's work, a combined effort might have produced a more complete solution.
The German tends to adopt the construction of the early Spanish
and Italian writers, and presents the prince as a wild, half-witted
youth, imprisoned by his father as unfit to succeed to the government, and attributes his death to his own act. The Spaniard,
on the other hand, takes the French and Flemish view that the
prince's characteristics were by no means contemptible, that he
was certainly sympathetic with the Netherlanders in their
opposition to religious persecution and had an important following in Spain, and it was on these grounds that he was imprisoned
and put to death by decision of the Inquisition, demanded by
Philip himself.

That Philip was quite fanatic enough to condemn his son for
proved luke-warmness towards "holy religion" can hardly be
denied. His letter to the Queen of Portugal, in which he said
the matter, that is the imprisonment, did not arise from personal
fault or insubordination, but that he had "chosen in this matter
to sacrifice to God my own flesh and blood and to prefer his
service to all other human considerations," leaves scarcely any
other interpretation possible. The elaborate precautions taken
to conceal the facts bear a strange resemblance to the precautions taken to conceal the facts of the murder of Montigny.
Philip was guilty of the one and quite capable of the other.

At the date of Mary's first widowhood, Carlos was in his
sixteenth year, she being just eighteen. It is clear that before
the period of mourning for the deceased Francis was ended,
negotiations were in hand for her remarriage with the Prince of

Spain. Catherine de Médicis did her utmost to prevent success; she was prepared to go to any length, even to offering her little daughter Marguerite, as a substitute, "Au moins," she wrote, "cela servira pour rompre l'autre coup[1]." By whom these negotiations were instituted is a point of interest; at the moment when the letter just quoted was on its way to the French Ambassador in Madrid, he was engaged in reporting to his Mistress the suspicious proceedings of a certain "Religieux" who had arrived in Madrid, to promote the match between Mary and Carlos. Some of the emissary's papers had *fallen* into his hands, but being in cipher he could not determine who the moving spirit was. The Religieux however used an infinity of arguments to show, "Combien, avec les Pays-Bas, l'une et l'autre pièce qu'il pretend seroient à propos[2]."

We have here something which appears to be the first whisper of plans to bring Carlos to the Netherlands as the husband of Mary, and to instal them as sovereigns of the Provinces, not perhaps, without exclusion of Philip who was already unpopular. It is usually held that Mary's uncle, the Cardinal of Lorraine, was the *deus ex machina* who moved the affair of the marriage, but the report just referred to seems to indicate some person or party in the Netherlands. Catherine herself, who was engaged in suppressing the Guises, held the former view, and expressed it to her daughter, the Queen of Spain, who replied that the King her husband knows of your opinion that, "Ceux de Lorene trestoit du mariage de leur nièce avec le prinse, et qu'il m'assuroit que non; que je vous écrivisse qu'il est bien aysé à connoistre d'où vient sela...." Without attaching too much importance to Philip's *dementi*, it seems to jump with the other

---

[1] *Negociations sous François II*, under date 3 March, 1561. It is worthy of remark that in this correspondence, Mary is always referred to under the sobriquet of "le Gentilhomme." It was a habit to adopt such methods as a thin veil to identity.

[2] *Ibid.*, 10 March, 1561. It is true that in a later letter, the Ambassador did not confirm his first suspicions; see under date 23 April, also *Papiers d'État de Granvelle*, vol. VI, p. 255, but this does not destroy the impression which his first idea creates.

evidence, and to exonerate the Guise faction in this instance.
There is a letter from a Lady in Waiting to the Spanish Queen,
addressed to Catherine in which she says, "The other marriage,
(that is Mary and Carlos) is not spoken of here, *except* that it is
persisted that she (Mary) is going to Joinville, it seems to me
that you should take care of this, *for it is very near Flanders*[1]."

There is also the remarkable confirmation of the interest
taken by the Netherlands, given by the Venetian Ambassador
in Paris, Suriano, writing on the 31 March (1561)[2], a date which
corresponds with the appearance of the "Religieux" in Madrid,
he says, "The Queen of Scotland left the court of Rheims...
they are treating to marry her to the Prince of Orange, and the
King (of Spain) favours the negotiation; but this proposal does
not please the Duke of Guise, who intends a greater marriage
for her. The Ambassador (of England) heard that the Duchess
of Arschot, sister of the Prince of Orange, went lately to Rheims
with the Queen, which causes a belief that the matter is far
advanced." Though the Venetian was not well informed as to
the relationship of the Duchess to the Prince of Orange and it is
doubtful if the Prince ever entered the lists as Mary's suitor,
there remains the fact that she (the Duchess) was, at this early
date, intriguing with Mary for a marriage in which the Netherlands certainly formed an objective. There is also the confirmation of the statement of Philip already referred to that the Guise
faction were not the moving spirits in this matter.

In August of the same year (1561) Mary returned to Scotland; Hubert Languet, a protestant writer of the time, described
her frame of mind, "Misera juvencula noctes et dies flere dici-
tur." Clearly the resolute, hard-hearted Queen was not yet in
being! It is not likely that during her first year she had much
time or opportunity to think of matrimony. There were numerous cross currents, which tended to delay and the Prince of Spain
was almost constantly ill at this time, yet the idea of the Spanish
marriage still remained uppermost, notwithstanding frequent

[1] *Negociations sous François II*, 6 February, 1561.
[2] *Venetian State Papers*, 1558–80, No. 249.

embassies from Lady Lennox in favour of her son, "She (Mary) does not dissemble about the Prince. She is determined to marry very highly[1]."

At this stage I must ask the reader to bear with me during a consideration of the state of affairs in the Netherlands, there is so much that is difficult to fathom in Mary's continued leaning to the Spanish match, that some attempt to gather the loose threads will, I hope, be useful. The seeds of dissatisfaction with the "old religion" had already been sown. Erasmus of Rotterdam, Martin Luther and John Calvin, had pointed the way, and their doctrines had found many adherents. The rule of Charles, afterwards Emperor, Philip's father, had been oppressive, but Charles was a Netherlander, born and brought up in the Provinces. He had, or could assume, the rough joviality of manner, which in spite of all left him not unpopular. The advent of his son, a Spaniard *par excellence*, haughty, unapproachable, sparing of words, ignorant of their language and customs, alien in all ways to the spirit of the country, produced an immediate change. If Philip had done nothing worse than his father there would still have been revolution against a system which would treat an hereditary appanage as a Spanish State and mould it to the pattern of Spain. An hereditary Prince was acceptable provided he was present; foreign domination was the reverse.

But Philip's action went far beyond his father's and, at the period with which we are dealing the Provinces were threatened with a measure which, quite openly, was intended to accentuate the already horrible cruelties of the Inquisition, and at the same time to override the civil rights of the people by the creation of ecclesiastical inquisitors not responsible to the civil tribunals. The leaders of the people were as much in opposition to these designs as the victims themselves; the names of William of Orange, of Egmont, of Montigny, began to be associated with the popular agitation. The horrors of the Netherlands and of the persecution for religion had re-echoed in many lands, not excluding Spain itself also groaning under the heel of the In-

---

[1] *Simancas Records*, 3 January, 1562.

quisition. Philip's boast that he had produced obedience was negatived by the *autos-da-fé* of Valladolid and Seville, an important party opposed the King's autocratic methods and fanatic views and was ready to take advantage of religious division to gain political ends.

It is an unsolved problem when the Prince of Spain first became the centre if not the leader of this party. Historians in general appear to attribute his disaffection to the promptings of the Baron Montigny when that unfortunate visited Spain as envoy of the States to become the victim of Philip's dishonour. But this *second* visit of Montigny did not take place until the summer of 1566, and there is very little doubt that Carlos was in sympathy with the Netherlands long before this. Two years previously (August 1564) Challoner, Ambassador in Spain, had reported to Elizabeth, "The Prince, as everybody affirmeth, hath a wit, but a strange wit, not removable from an opinion once caught...desirous of state and rule....Far diverse from liking all things that his father liketh. Notable tales have been told of his deeds and sayings."

Three quarters of a century before our period, the Flemish burghers had taken possession of the infant heir of the Imperial honours and set him up as ruler of the Provinces. They had defied the father who sought to regain his power; in due time the son of this infant became the ruler, and his son, our Philip, was inducted to the rule in his young manhood. When Philip left the Provinces, to return to Spain for good, he had left the promise to send his son, then aged 15 to represent him[1], a contract he failed to fulfil. Thus tradition, promise and personal desire were working in the mind of the young Carlos to impel him towards the Low Countries, and to these could be added a strong repugnance to the state of pupilage which his father

[1] See *Groen van Prinsterer*, S. 1, vol. 1, p. 301, note: "For a long time past it was more or less in question to send the Prince Royal. In 1559, in the reply of Philip II to a request of the Estates-General, the King gave it to be understood that it was very possible that on his return to Spain an early opportunity would be taken to send him." See also Gachard, *Doc. Inédits*, vol. 1, p. 328.

imposed on him in Spain and to all his father's works and ways.

In 1562, Mary's first year in Scotland, a definite cleavage began to take shape in the Netherlands. The Prince of Orange commenced his life-long labours for the freedom of the people, Montigny paid his *first* visit to Spain to lay before the King the grievances of the Netherlanders. It is probable, I think more than probable, that at this time Montigny, finding opportunity to ascertain the sympathetic views of the Prince carried back the idea of setting him up as independent sovereign, with guarantees of religious freedom and constitutional observance.

It is difficult to form a trustworthy picture of Carlos; sickly he certainly was, perhaps also malformed as stated by contemporary writers. Yet there does not seem to be sufficient reason to suppose that he had so far developed the hereditary taint of insanity which undoubtedly affected his father and grandfather and showed itself in both as a religious mania. There is clear evidence that he had a heart for warm friendship where his confidence was won, and his sympathy once aroused was not easily quenched. The stories told of his cruelty, gluttony, libertinism are told for the most part by those who can be suspected of a motive and are accompanied by details that carry their own condemnation. Brantôme, who had opportunity of seeing him does not give such impressions. At least it appears that the Estates of the Netherlands desired his presence and Mary Stuart, who had ample means of knowing more about him than we have, was ready to marry him; Elizabeth, the Queen of Spain and step-mother to the Prince was her closest friend and childhood's companion.

Mary had many suitors, the inevitable Archduke Charles of Austria among them, who seemed to be the *pis aller* to most of the eligible ladies of the time. Elizabeth of England had him up for choice twice or thrice, Mary would have none of him, for not only was his head as big as the Earl of Bedford's, which appears to be saying a good deal, but as a younger son he was without power or the means to procure it. Alphonso of Ferrara was another, he whose sister was the beloved of the poet Tasso, and whose other sister was Mary's close friend and "aunt," the Duchess Anne d'Esté de Guise. His mother was the pious and liberal patroness of the reformers, Renée of France, whom Mary also addressed as "aunt," and Alphonso himself had leanings, as had his uncle the Cardinal of Ferrara which were considered liberal. The Cardinal was suspected of friendship with the Chatillons and other chief heretics[1]. We may indeed regret that Mary did not go farther in this affair, but Alphonso was an extravagant youth with little power to help Scotland in those claims to the English succession which were at the time so much in debate.

This wooing of Ferrara brought into Mary's life the envoy, Bertino Solaro di Moretta, a Piedmontese noble, connected with the House of Savoy. He was a sinister and enigmatic individual whose movements are well worth study by those who follow Mary's later history. He left behind him a legacy in the person of David Rizzio, who combined the functions of intermediary and spy of the ultramontane party of which Cardinal Borromeo, the mainspring of the Papal policy, was the head.

We are often told by contemporary writers that such and such a person "ruled all," and frequently it is an expression rather of annoyance on the writers' part, than a statement of fact. Yet in the case of Mary Stuart, during the years that followed her assumption of Queenship in Scotland her remarkable lack of will power did in fact lead to the subordination of her action to the suggestion of stronger minds. The evidence of her weakness, or, perhaps we should call it, her want of the imperious will power that occasionally showed itself in young sovereigns, comes from so many sources, and is confirmed by so many facts of undoubted happening, that we must conclude that the training deliberately devised in France to keep her subject to French influence had left its effect. "The Queen of Scotland, is, I hear,

---

[1] Vargas to Philip, 7 November, 1561, *Papiers d'État.*

most governed by the Lord James (Stuart) and Lethington[1]."
"The Lord James is...commander of the Queen[2]." "The
whole governance rests with the Lord James and the Laird of
Lethington. The Queen quietly tolerates the reformed religion
through the realm, who is thought to be no more devout towards
Rome than for the contentation of her uncles[3]." "The Queen
seemed to have got some power by his (Moray's) absence[4]."
"No remedy will suffice while the Lord James rules all, both
Protestants and Catholics, the Queen's authority is nominal
only[5]." "The Queen herself he (Moray) held in his power as a
tutor doth a pupil[6]." "She having the name and calling and he
(Moray) having the very sway and regiment[7]." "I have requested him (Lethington) so to deal that...such resolution...
may appear to proceed from her own desire than led thereto by
persuasion as a child that ever dependeth on her pedagogrie[8]."
"He (Lethington) finds no such ripeness of experience or ma-
turity of judgment...as in the Queen's Majesty (Elizabeth)[9]."
"He (Moray) caused the Queen's Majesty become subject to him
as her Grace had been a pupil[10]." "The Lords will in no wise
think her at liberty albeit she be persuaded to say otherwise[11]."

Comments such as the above, from enemies, friends and
neutrals might be multiplied, but we have enough to serve the
purpose and to be of use for future reference.

Throughout the year 1562 there is no clear evidence that
Mary was pursuing the question of matrimony with much
interest. She was engaged in that series of acts which, cul-
minating in the destruction of the Gordons, indicate how entirely under the influence of the Lord James, now Earl of Moray,
she was. Lethington had been sent to London in the middle of
the year, but his business was connected with the meeting of
the two queens which Mary hoped for and not with any negotia-

[1] Cecil to Sussex, 7 Oct. 1561.   [2] Randolph to Cecil, 4 Nov. 1561.
[3] Cecil to Challoner, 7 June, 1562.   [4] Buchanan, *Hist.*
[5] *Papal Negs.*, Hay to Laynez, 2 Jan. 1563.   [6] Camden.
[7] Bishop of Ross in the *Defence.*   [8] Randolph to Cecil.   [9] *Ibid.*
[10] Mary's Commissioners in 1568.   [11] Melville to Cecil in May, 1567.

tions for marriage. During this period the Prince of Spain lay desperately ill from the result of a fall. Even the remedy of placing in his bed for a night, the dried corpse of a miracle working friar, had produced no immediate effect. Perhaps Mary thought it useless to pursue the matter! By the beginning of 1563 he had recovered and the English Ambassador reported him as "waxing bonito" and disposed to be fat.

"Men begin to dream here of this Queen's marriage with Spain," wrote Randolph on 30 December, 1562. We may fairly date Mary's active interest from about this date. It may be a coincidence, but the time was precisely that of Montigny's return from his first visit to Spain (see p. 37). It may be also that Mary was moved in the matter by the increasing bitterness of the conflict which was rapidly destroying the possibility of conciliation in the Church. Yet, it is necessary to emphasize that, Mary, entirely under the influence of the Earl of Moray and Maitland of Lethington, can hardly be said to have had sole guidance of the matter. In February 1563 Lethington was sent to London again. He had two missions to fulfil, the one to obtain Elizabeth's acknowledgment of her right to the succession, failing legitimate heirs, to be backed if possible by a declaration in parliament; the other secretly to negotiate with the Spanish Ambassador for a marriage with the Prince. In both these Moray and Lethington were certainly acting together.

We are then faced with the fact that Moray, a pronounced protestant, and Lethington, of more open mind but in general professing the reformation, were seeking to marry their Queen to the son of the great persecutor, Philip II. Were it not that the evidence points in the opposite direction one would conclude that, whatever Mary's own ideas were, her two ministers were not sincere, were, in fact, "bluffing" as a means to force Elizabeth to adopt the succession proposal. Yet this explanation does not fit the facts.

The state of affairs in Scotland at this time throws some light on the subject. The Earl of Moray was not treading the narrow plank which John Knox held to be the only approach to salvation and William Maitland was as usual "swimming between two waters" and earning his subsequent title of "The Chameleon!" A parliament had been summoned in May (1563) and to the disgust of Knox, no measure was brought forward to re-enact the laws confirmatory of the reformed religion, as passed by the illegal assembly of July 1560 before Mary's return to Scotland. The tendency of the Court was towards conciliation and the recognition of freedom of conscience, which did not suit Mr Knox. If we accept history as written by that personage, and especially such an interpretation thereof as that of Dr McCrie, we would assume that this state of lukewarmness towards reform on the Calvinistic basis was due to the machinations of the astute Queen, who, "Surmounted all opposition to her measures and managed so successfully the haughty and independent barons of her kingdom[1]." But in fact the Queen was rather dominated than dominating, and even if we see in the action of her protestant council, largely guided by Moray, the same result as she might have aimed at with unfettered power, we must still attribute the effect to the concurrence of her chief ministers. Knox had solemnly broken with Moray and denounced him and Lethington as backsliders.

In the light of this situation it is easier to understand the conversation between Lethington and the Spanish Ambassador, which the latter reported to his Master under date 18 March (1563). The Ambassador objected that the Scots would not accept a marriage with Spain on account of religion.

He (Lethington) answered, as regards religion they (that is, Moray and himself) thought they could find means to render the country peaceful and obedient. I asked him by what means. He said, several and amongst others he knew that the protestants would be willing to allow the catholics to live in their own way in their own houses and perform their masses peacefully and without molestation. ...Lord James had great influence with the preachers, and he also could do something with them and he thought they could manage it easily....He said he would send a courier to the Lord James in order to be able to tell me more about the business....I fancy there is not

[1] McCrie, *Life of John Knox*, p. 258.

much harmony between the Queen of Scotland and the Queen Mother and...it is very likely that what Lethington tells me is true, and the affair is more substantial than at first sight appears.

Lethington was on this occasion accompanied by Mary's French secretary, Raulet, and the Ambassador reported in another letter, "The Secretary Raulet tells me that the Lord James is extremely anxious for this marriage with the Prince."

To these reports, Philip replied on June 18, "I highly approve of your conduct...and seeing that this marriage may be the beginning of a reformation in religious matters in England, I have decided to entertain the negotiations." The utmost secrecy was enjoined, and the Duke of Alba wrote independently to the same effect, "Although his Majesty's letter will inform you of the extremely secret negotiations that are in progress about the Scottish marriage, I think it well to repeat the intelligence here to you as it is of so great importance."

There seems to be no doubt that the matter was genuine both on the part of the Scottish negotiators and of Philip, and there seems to be no doubt that it was not divulged by either of the former. Yet Elizabeth came to hear of it, though not the whole story; history attributes the information to John Knox who did indeed inveigh against foreign princes as a tribe, but does not appear to have had special knowledge as to Don Carlos. It is more likely that one Simon Renard, once the satellite of the Cardinal Granvelle but later his inveterate enemy, gave the information, "We have preserved on our part the most profound secrecy but Renard has, whether by conjecture or by other means, succeeded in penetrating the affair[1]."

Lethington returned to Scotland in June (1563) carrying back the message from Elizabeth that she had heard of the Spanish proposals and could on no account approve of them. He was disgusted with the result of his mission, both as to the question of the succession, on which he received only "fair words," and on the want of definition on the part of Quadra, the Spanish Ambassador. On his side Quadra evidently had

[1] Granvelle to Philip, *Pap. d'État*, 2 Jan. 1564.

some doubts as to whether he could trust Mary's envoy fully, and decided to send a special messenger to her. One Luis de Paz, a Spanish merchant residing in London, was chosen, he managed his mission very secretly, travelling via Ireland, and no one seems to have been the wiser at the time. He had, says M. Mignet, a conference with Moray and Lethington, and, it must be supposed with the Queen also, and returned to London on 24 August only to find that Quadra was dying. Six hours later the Ambassador departed with the words, "I can do no more." A month previously Quadra had summed up the situation in a letter to the Duke of Alba, "I fear that the Queen of Scots, losing confidence in the various marriages already offered and alarmed at this Queen's (Elizabeth) threats and the pressure of her subjects (Lethington among them) to marry a Protestant may be urged to some course that may lead to more harm than good, not only to religion but also to the preservation of the States of Flanders, which are in such a dangerous condition[1]."

This letter seems to contain contradictions, for while it affirms Lethington to have joined in pressing for a protestant marriage, in another part it alleges that failing the Spanish match he was preparing to prosecute other Catholic unions with France, or even Guise (Mary's cousin) himself. I read it as intended more as a spur to the vacillating Philip than as an accurate presentment of facts. There is, however, the same persistence in connecting Mary and this marriage with the affairs of the Netherlands which has been already noticed.

Here the first phase of the affair ends; on the part of Philip and of Quadra there is clearly the intention to sweep out heresy, to make Scotland the starting point of a new crusade to bring back Europe to the Roman faith. On the part of Mary, controlled by Moray and Lethington, it is impossible to suppose the same ambition. The two last named, recently emerged from the war—for it was no less—accompanying the expulsion of the French, could not desire domination of Spain; Mary herself, fresh from effects already described of her French environment, and

[1] *Simancas Records*, under date 17 July, 1563.

French to the core in her thoughts, could not have contemplated Spanish methods of compelling conscience nor accession to the power of Spain at the expense of isolating France. All three desired acknowledgment of the Scottish right to the English succession, but none of them would be foolish enough to believe that an acknowledgment, extorted by a threat, would be honoured if it became apparent that the power to enforce it did not exist, or, existing, was such that the English parliament would resist to the last.

Whatever the scheme was which secured the adhesion of both Moray and Lethington it must have contained at least two elements, sufficient strength to make it respected, and features not utterly antagonistic to English prejudices. Rather as a suggestion for further examination, than as advancing a truth established, I put it that the obscure facts are met by assuming a plan to marry Mary, already animated by the notion of healing the great schism, to Carlos, known or believed to have the same inclination, and to place them as rulers of the Netherlands and Scotland. What follows as to the second phase of the matter adds, I think, to the cogency of such a proposition.

At the time there was nothing unreasonable in such an idea, even if in the cold light of practical difficulties it was only a vision. The Augsburg Confession, or something like it, was not unacceptable to Mary's uncle or to those who counted most in her circle; to Lethington it would be congenial; to Moray not difficult. The Netherlands, wealthiest corner of Europe, was half way there already; England, Elizabeth at all events, was very near it; France had an important contingent; the Emperor Ferdinand, at this time was far from intolerant[1]. Savonarola had shaken Italy. If Spain and the Vatican held out it would not be for long, Pius IV was not deaf to compromise, or at least to political pressure. Here was a dream of concord arising from

---

[1] L'Empereur Ferdinand n'étoit pas intolérant, surtout dans les dernières années de sa vie....L'Ambassadeur d'Angleterre écrit 3 Oct. 1564, " Sub mortem aequior doctrinae nostrae fuit quam superioribus annis." *Groen van Prinst.* S. 1, vol. 1, p. 234.

Scotland, snatching the dominion to which Philip aspired from out his very house, combined too with material advantage which would accrue to the Scottish State.

The second phase of the affair includes its complete failure. There is an undated fragment of great interest, believed to be of Mary's hand, in the Record Office[1], which contains her own statement of what happened, a part of which translated, reads, "The marriage which she consistently favoured and negotiated with the Prince of Spain, which the Cardinal Granvelle, the Duchess of Arschot *and many notables*, and even her own subjects could testify to, seeing this broken off against her wishes by an agreement, made without her knowledge by her relations in France, with (the Archduke) Don Charles (of Austria), to which, apart from the displeasure of the rupture with the other (Don Carlos) she found no advantage for her kindgom...."

It is noteworthy that the principal persons named as parties to the negotiations are Granvelle and the Duchess of Arschot (see also p. 34), Philip himself is not mentioned. Ordinarily the most direct method of corresponding with Philip would have been, at least after the death of Quadra, through the Scottish and Spanish Ambassadors in Paris. In this second phase it would appear that, for some reason, the circuitous route via Flanders was chosen; possibly, so far as Mary was concerned, the correspondence was not intended to go beyond the persons named. Let us pause for a moment to bring together some of the elements which tend to establish the proposition.

If the estimate of Anthony Perrenot, Cardinal Granvelle, formed by Motley in his great work, *The Rise of the Dutch Republic*, is a true one, we find a man who was something more than Philip's *alter ego*, his was rather the contriving brain that Philip meekly followed. Yet it is not easy to get away from the feeling that the rose tinted spectacles through which Motley saw every act of the Prince of Orange cast too dark a shadow on the Cardinal. Granvelle was no Spaniard; born a Burgundian

[1] Printed in Labanoff, vol. I, p. 296.

and educated at Louvain, his natural sympathies were likely to
be with the Netherlanders where their interests clashed with
Spain. Brought up in the virile entourage of Charles V, one
may doubt if Philip's character would appeal to him; he
came of a large family many of whom were distinguished
in bold action. It was his younger brother, Champagny, who
twelve years later was Governor of Antwerp when the "Spanish
Fury" devastated the city, and he did his utmost, with no
thought of personal danger, to save the citizens. Motley describes Champagny as a sincere catholic and a still more sincere
hater of the Spaniards.

A complete study of Granvelle and his aims is wanting, but
it is impossible to set aside such a statement of his attitude
towards the Netherlands as he wrote to Vargas regarding the
approaching storm, "For my part I am deeply affected perhaps
more than others, though I say less, for I see the danger from a
nearer point. I foresee all the burden will fall on my head, for
his Majesty has put me in the forefront of this affair...Would
to God these new bishoprics had never been thought of[1]." In
the Council of the States he declared, "There is no one, be he
who he may, who has more boldly and resolutely ventured his
person and his life in maintaining the liberty and privileges of
this country, than I have done." Much the same thing occurs
in a letter from a friend and supporter, written after the Cardinal
had been forced to quit the Low Countries, "...Many of the
Lords could testify, if they chose, the language which you used
in Council, saying that you would be the first to oppose the
Spanish Inquisition and that you would guard the privileges as
much as any other[2]." At the least it is an historic fact, whether

[1] *Granvelle Corresp.* 14 Sept. 1561. The question of the creation
of the bishops is referred to at p. 35.

[2] *Ibid.*, Morillon to Granvelle, 10 Feb. 1566. See also note by
M. Edmond Poullet, at p. 111 of vol. 1, giving numerous references
in support of the view that Granvelle opposed the Spanish terror
in the Low Countries. Whether he shared the dislike of Spaniards in
general with other members of his family is not recorded, but at least
it is not improbable.

due to his restraining influence or not, that the persecution of the Netherlands became more acute after his departure than during his presence at the head of affairs.

He was a master of dissimulation it is true, as great a master as Philip himself. Yet, and again I am suggesting a case for further enquiry, there seems to be reason to suspect that all his verbal subservience to Philip hid plans of his own. He opposed the Prince of Orange-Nassau, but it may be that Granvelle aimed at other and more speedy results than were obtained by William the Silent after twenty years of war; it might be said, more *complete* results than William ever attained. Mary Stuart could claim the same blood of Gueldres as did William and in addition, that of the old Counts of Holland, through Philippa of Hainault, mother of the Black Prince. Her union with the descendant of the House of Burgundy had in itself much to recommend it to the Netherlanders. It may well be that Granvelle saw in a joint sovereignty of Mary and Carlos, a means to secure his own power which was already in jeopardy through Philip's absolutist assumptions in the Netherlands.

And of the other partner to the negotiations, the Dowager Duchess of Arschot; she was Anne de Lorraine and a first cousin of Mary's mother. Her first husband, René of Nassau, brought the principality of Orange to the Nassau family and was succeeded therein by William, surnamed "The Silent." Her second husband, Philip de Croy, Duke of Arschot, died in 1549; the Duke of Arschot who figures in the history of our period was her stepson. Her mother was Renée de Bourbon, whose marriage ceremony at Amboise was described by the historian du Boulay, as more splendid than had been seen for a hundred years. The splendour of the wedding was no doubt due to the splendour of her brother the famous Connétable de Bourbon, whose adhesion to the Roman Church was so little pronounced that when he advanced to the sack of Rome he is said to have carried a golden chain wherewith to hang the Pope! Renée herself was one of those noble ladies who was interested in the attempt to avoid religious quarrels, her niece by marriage was that Jacqueline de Longwie already noticed (p. 4) a strong supporter of reform and it was Jacqueline's daughter, Charlotte de Bourbon, who fled from her convent, embraced the protestant confession and became the third wife of William of Orange.

Thus, whatever may be said of many of the men folk of our Anne, Duchess of Arschot, and some of them had the reputation of harshness towards heretics or at least to Calvinists, the ladies, as often happened, were notable for holding the opposite opinion, and there is no doubt that Anne herself was in favour of compromise. Certainly her young womanhood in contact with the House of Nassau would tend in that direction, and at her mother's knee she was likely to have imbibed ideas more liberal than a strict Romanism would approve. Throgmorton, in a letter to Elizabeth, says that at a certain religious ceremony he continued to sit when apparently he should have knelt, and adds, "Right over against me *sat* the Duchess of Arschot," he seems to indicate that the lady did not agree any more than he did to the observance in question[1]. At a later date we find her sending for a friend of Granvelle to enquire if it was true that he approved of persecution of reformers, and receiving a reply that it was not true[2], from which it appears that she was also opposed thereto. Again there is the hint that she was not at one with her stepson who was a stout supporter of Philip, "It is rumoured that M. le duc d'Arschot has made it up with Madame sa Belle-Mère, but I am sure there is nothing in it[3]."

There are other indications that the Duchess occupied an antagonistic attitude to the Regent, Philip's sister, which might easily be accounted for by her disapproval of Philip's methods; she did not appear at a certain ceremonial, "Nor was she invited, this it is wisely said was on account of illness, but I know that she resents it[4]." On another occasion at her house, Egmont and others being present, "M. de Tournay said to them at

---

[1] *Cal. For.*, 10 Oct. 1560.
[2] *Gran. Cor.*, 10 Feb. 1566.
[3] *Ibid.*, 17 Feb. 1566.
[4] *Ibid.*, 9 Dec. 1565.

supper that they have now the power in their hands, and they should take care to use it carefully[1]."

Though one would wish for more complete information on all the circumstances which led to this strange conjunction of the Queen of Scots with the nominal leader of the Spanish party in the Netherlands and a lady who can perhaps best be described as a member of the nationalist or anti-Spanish section, there seems sufficient foundation for the suggestion that all three had the same ultimate object of bringing the Prince Carlos to rule the States as the husband of Mary. The correspondence which will presently be noticed adds some confirmation to this view.

When Lethington returned from London in June (1563) it was patent that he had cooled from his original enthusiasm. Elizabeth had found means to wean him from complete allegiance to his mistress. Whatever the cause which moved her, Mary seems to have become, more than previously, set on a prosecution of the Spanish affair. Possibly the disastrous state of things in France warned her that the voice of conciliation was fast being drowned by the clash of arms, and if her object was such as has been suggested, a speedy move was necessary. At all events, apparently on her own motion she sent Raulet to continue the negotiations arising from the communications already referred to of Luis de Paz.

Raulet left Edinburgh on the 29th or 30th August; there is every likelihood that Quadra's death which occurred on the 24th was known before he started, certainly he would have heard of it before he reached London. The point has this much interest, that Raulet's destination seems to have been from the first, Brussels and not London, and Cardinal Granvelle rather than Bishop Quadra was the person to whom he was addressed. He arrived at Brussels after an unusually quick journey on September 13. On the 14th the Cardinal wrote to Philip telling him of his interview with Raulet; there is something not entirely frank about the letter[2]; according to the Cardinal he, Raulet,

[1] *Pap. d'État*, 16 March, 1564, Morillon to Granvelle.
[2] *Ibid.*, Granvelle to Philip, 14 Sept. 1563.

was much embarrassed on arrival in London to find that Quadra was dead and he would have returned to Scotland but for want of an excuse to do so. The Cardinal then says that he imparted to Raulet some "information" which must have been stale, and the envoy returned with this meagre result of his long journey. The impression given is that the Cardinal was anxious to account for Raulet's visit, and, under show of a full statement, concealed other things of more importance. Raulet got back to Edinburgh after a very bad "crossing" on the 3rd October.

It is well to remember that the Cardinal's political position was at the moment threatened on all sides. The nobles had already addressed Philip demanding his removal; even the Duchess of Parma was not on his side, and Philip, who was ready enough to protect the horrible Inquisitor, Titelman, showed no effort on his behalf and had given him leave to go and see his mother, a visit from which he never returned to the Netherlands. Thus though the Cardinal's letters continued to breathe loyalty and devotion, one may suppose that he was sore and in a frame of mind to embark on designs of his own.

A considerable correspondence between Mary and the Cardinal followed Raulet's visit; a good deal of it is missing but this matters the less that those letters we have are very artificial and for the most part refer the recipient to the "Bearer" for the news and those missing were probably the same. There is one however, preserved, perhaps by accident, which seems to throw some light on the others and the nature of the negotiations. It is from Raulet to the Cardinal, written a day or two after his return to Scotland; it runs:

The man you know of is in doubt if you will take in hand yourself the action (*le procès intenté*) with his kinsman (parent), or at the least furnish the prosecution and support the cause of your cousin with money, friends and means (perhaps this may be translated, money, men and arms). So that the matter may come to agreement or at least appear to do so. Using this stratagem to gain time, which perhaps will bring him means to secure and strengthen himself. He fears you only, and dreads marvellously to take the affair in hand. To escape he will dissemble as much as he can (this is obscure).

I hear that he says nothing openly, yet gives enough to be understood; for before he became suspicious he was in no anxiety about the scheme undertaken by your said cousin, but since he has become aware of certain papers which have been sent to you, and others which you have sent hither, he thinks it better to reconsider the matter, the more so that he is without news, and has taken this fever (of anxiety). I thought it best to give you early warning, not doubting that you would find means to settle the affair[1].

The date of this document was October 8 (1563), and it was enclosed with other letters of the same date from the Queen to Granvelle, the packets being sealed with Mary's signet[2]. It is thus beyond a peradventure that the subject-matter relates to the Queen's affairs. It is a pretty riddle for the ingenious to exercise their wits upon; the semi-legal language employed is continued in other letters but the veil is very thin and typical of the naïve-cunning which seems to have passed for subtlety in those days. The "man you know of," who has become suspicious of the Cardinal, is I think certainly the Queen herself. He or "she" dreads the project in hand, which can hardly be negotiation for the marriage with Don Carlos taken by itself without any subsidiary intrigue, for in this, Mary was already fully

[1] The French of the above is not easy to translate accurately. I append it, so that the reader can form his own judgment:

"L'homme que scavez est entré en doubte que veullez vous-mesmes vous faire partye et prendre en main le procés intenté avec son parent, ou, pour le moins fournir à la poursuite et favoriser la cause de votre cousin, d'argent, d'amys et de moyens. Ce que le fait chercher accord, ou bien en faire semblant, et user de ceste ruse pour essayer de gaigner temps, que peultestre lui pourroit cy-après apporter moyen de s'asseurer et fortifier d'ailleurs. Il n'a peur que de vous et craint merveilleusement d'y avoir affaire; et pour éschapper se forera en tout ce qu'il luy sera possible. Et oyres qu'il ne parle ouvertement, si est-ce qu'il donne assez entendre; car devant qu'il fust entré en ce soupson, il n'éstoit point en peine de la poursuite que faisoit vostre dict cousin; mais depuis qu'il s'est apperçeu de quelques papiers que vous ont ésté envoyez et que avez aussi envoyé par deçà, il a pensé que estes pour consulter sur le faict du dict procés, encore qu'il n'en sust point de nouvelles, et est entré en ceste fiébvre; de quoi je n'ay voulu faillir vous donner incontinent cest avis, ne faisant doubte que ne vous en sachiez très bien accommoder." *Pap. d'État*, 8 Oct. 1563.

[2] *Ibid.*, Granvelle to Raulet, 26 Dec. 1563.

committed and had so to speak burnt her boats, with the knowledge and consent of Lethington and Moray. The identity of
the person referred to as "your cousin" is more obscure. He
or she has undertaken some activity which requires money and
friends. "Cousin" is of course a term applied between the Princes
of the Church and others of royal or equivalent rank; it may
refer to the Duchess of Arschot who was "parent" to Mary, and
who, as we have seen, was active in the affair.

It is remarkable that in all the letters addressed to Philip by
the Cardinal on the subject of the negotiations he omits any
mention of the Duchess, though we know that she was an active
participant in the correspondence between him and Mary. This
omission is accentuated by the fact that he was warned on no
account to impart the matter to anyone, "without exception[1]."
Even so late as 28 May (1564) when writing to the new Spanish
Ambassador in London, he not only does not mention the
Duchess, but while giving a full account of the proceedings,
says, "His Majesty desires that no one in the Low Countries is to
know anything about it except the Duchess of Parma[2]." We may
say with confidence that the Cardinal had something to conceal.

So far as the record goes the Duchess of Arschot entered
the correspondence on 6 January, 1564, but it is probable that
there were previous letters; her communication on this date
accompanied other letters from the Cardinal to Mary but unfortunately none of them are preserved. From Mary's reply we
gather that the main point was, if she, the Duchess, was assured
of a means of communicating secretly she would enter into
further detail[3]. In answer to this Mary sent a confidential
servant, whose name is spelt variously, Chesein, Shesum and
Hesum[4]. He was to pretend business affairs, and he carried

[1] *Pap. d'État*, Alba to Philip, 23 Oct. 1563.
[2] *Ibid.*, Granvelle to de Silva, 28 May, 1564. "It is remarkable that
in the great collection of documents edited by Gachard, there is no
mention of the Duchess."
[3] *Ibid.*, Mary Stuart to Duchess of Arschot, 20 Feb. 1564.
[4] There is very little doubt that William Chisholm is referred to.
He succeeded his kinsman of the same name as Bishop of Dunblane

letters both to the Duchess and the Cardinal. There followed a considerable correspondence in which very little that is tangible appears on the surface; on 20 May, Mary prays the Duchess to enquire "if those who make the offer are reliable," and this offer seems to bring us into touch with the other "notables" mentioned in the fragmentary memorandum already quoted (p. 45). There is also mention of one Francis Berty or Bertie, an English catholic resident in Antwerp, who had been taken into the confidence of the Duchess and the Cardinal, though there were some doubts as to his reliability.

In June there is a memorandum detailing a conversation between this Berty and "a Scottish gentleman," a faithful servant of the Queen, recommending that as much delay as possible should be brought about by pretending to listen to the proposal put forward on behalf of Lady Margaret's son (Lord Darnley); "By this means the said Queen can in the meantime do what she desires. Also the said B(erty) said to the gentleman that if the said Queen (Mary) had not a good claim on the crown (of England) *she need only to claim where you know and I* (Duchess of Arschot, see below) said the same thing myself. When taking leave of me he warned me to be on my guard as to a secretary named Rollez (Raulet) a Frenchman, given by the Queen Mother to that Queen...." The writer mentions that letters had been received from the Queen of Scots, in which "She made mention of her *claims* as follows, 'As to the other points about which you wrote by Hesum (see note p. 52), I beg you according to promise to send me news, for many reasons I must know the truth and cannot put off a resolution much longer about the affair you know of[1].'"

in the beginning of 1565. At this time, 1563–4, he held the position of Bishop Coadjutor. He was employed on many secret missions to Rome and elsewhere. Whether he was an uncompromising adherent of Rome is doubtful. On the occasion of a certain deputation intended to persuade Mary to take very drastic action against the protestants, he does not seem to have been trusted completely. "He is a true catholic very pious and honest, nevertheless...we are sending with him as an additional safeguard that Father Edmund who..." (*Papal Negs.*, 20 Oct. 1566).

[1] *Pap. d'État*, under date, 6 June, 1564.

This "memorandum" evidently forms part of a letter, and the editor of the Granvelle Papers apparently attributes it to the Cardinal himself, but it is clearly written by the Duchess of Arschot *to* the Cardinal. We have his reply dated 6 July (1564); he refers to Mary's claim to the English throne as resting chiefly on the support of the catholic party in England, and he says that this claim exists only on the death of Elizabeth without direct heirs (it is noteworthy that the claim is never otherwise asserted); he mentions that he has heard privately that Philip is still consenting to the marriage (of Carlos), he recommends her not to trust too much in F. B. (Francis Berty); if Raulet is false, he says, "nothing could be more contrary to the affair"; finally he says, "If you write (to Mary?) about this, I beg that this my letter may not be brought into the matter, and that it does not leave your hand...[1]." In the same letter the Cardinal adds what turned out a true prophecy, "If she speaks of Margaret's son she will cause his death, for already the Queen of England and the heretics have their tooth in the said Margaret and her son, on account of religion and the claim to the throne."

Here then is another riddle, what does the Duchess mean by the words, "she need only to claim where you know"? The Cardinal skirts round any direct comment on the remark; it can hardly refer to the reliance on the English catholics for this is openly stated elsewhere in the same letter, nor need Mary ask for resolution on this subject from the Duchess which she could get much better herself from England, nor was there any urgency in what would only arise on the death of Elizabeth. It seems to connect up with the enquiry already quoted on page 53, "if those who made the offer are reliable."

It is all very cryptic and it would be wearisome to grope further in the obscurity. What emerges is that Mary was counselled, both by the Duchess and the Cardinal, not to commit herself, to delay pending some event which was constantly expected to occur; that some offer had been put before her;

[1] *Pap. d'État*, Granvelle to Duchess of Arschot, 6 July, 1564.

that she dreaded taking something in hand; that she had "claims," which were under discussion.

As to all this we find, throughout the whole period with which we are dealing, the sending of the Prince to the Netherlands was on the *tapis* and Philip deferred it from time to time. In July, at the very time that Mary was being told to hold on a little longer, one of Granvelle's correspondents in Brussels mentioned that the Prince had attended the council and opined that this was a preliminary to his "coming hither." There are several indications that conditions were imposed from the side of Scotland as a part of these negotiations and it is likely that one of these was the instalment of the Prince as Governor of the Netherlands; so long as this hung fire no progress could be made.

The notion of an independent Netherlands was current even as early as this; a letter of June (1564) to the Cardinal says, "They (the French) are plotting, if the Spanish Queen has no children, to obtain the Low Countries and Burgundy, and if she has children they will guard the said countries for them. The Chief men of the said countries have promised and sworn the same.... There is a son of the late Emperor (Don John of Austria is meant) whom they intend to marry in France in order to make war (against Spain)[1]." Although this plot, if there was anything in it, has nothing to do with our case, it is yet noteworthy that the features of the two are very similar, and it is quite possible that two groups were formed or forming to effect the same result in different ways. In the years 1563–4 the excitement among the nobles against the Spanish autocracy was sufficient to create such schemes, in the one case to bring Don Carlos with the Queen of Scotland as a partner to rule the States, in the other to take Don John with a daughter of France for the same purpose.

A somewhat similar topic is contained in a letter to Granvelle

[1] *Pap. d'État*, 5 June, 1564.

from a certain Nicole de Savigny, whose principal claim to notoriety was alleged motherhood of a son by the late Emperor. "I have seen and heard recently from persons having close touch with the notables over there (Netherlands) that important enterprises are secretly being prepared against his Majesty, both on account of religion and to effect changes in the rule and government[1]." Granvelle expresses the opinion that this may be exaggerated but not purely invention.

Thus these loose threads seem to lead in one direction and to connect Mary's references to "notables," to the "making of offers," to the danger of the undertaking, to the necessity for delay, to the unspecified "claim," with a scheme which appears to have had more than one parallel. It may be a coincidence that the imprisonment of Prince Carlos (Dec. 1567) took place at the very time that the arrest of Counts Egmont and Horn (Sept. 1567) and the subsequent seizure and examination of their papers, may be supposed to have given Philip the evidence on which he sacrificed his son. Which evidence, if those who believe that the Prince was executed on account of his views on religion and government are right, may have originated in the schemes we have been discussing. The elaborate steps which Philip was accustomed to take to conceal his crimes would easily account for the absence of documentary proof.

Had it been possible to choose a leader from among the nobility, it is not likely that either Carlos or John would have been desired, but at this time Orange and Egmont were stars of equal magnitude, and there were others of a brilliancy not prepared to take second place. It may be objected that Granvelle, instrumental in supplying Philip with information as to events in the Low Countries, was little likely to be himself allied with either party, but indeed it would be rash to impose a limit to the powers of deceit of any personage of the time. Granvelle had a grievance, he would willingly ride back to power and would not be nice in his choice of the vehicle; Spain was far off; with Lorraine unfriendly, the sea alone permitted the passage of

[1] *Pap. d'État*, 2 June, 1564.

troops. We have seen that he was not quite frank, yet he was astute enough to keep his share out of the record.

On the other hand it was the action of the leading nobles that caused Granvelle's fall and it would be extravagant to suppose that he had any direct *liaison* with them, but it was here that the Duchess of Arschot would be useful. She stood well with Egmont (she was indeed related to him), and he was a political will-o'-wisp who would lead any forlorn hope; she was closely connected with Orange himself. Besides she was daughter, sister and aunt of successive Dukes of Lorraine; her sister-in-law, the Dowager of Lorraine, was niece to the late Emperor (Charles) and had been a candidate warmly favoured by the Nobles for the Regency of the States at the time when ultimately the Duchess of Parma was nominated. It would be impossible to select a person with greater influence of the kind required than she. If, as seems not unlikely, Philip became aware of the plot through the papers of Egmont it may well be that this was an additional reason for his execution, as also for that of Carlos; the Duchess of Arschot died conveniently at the same time. It is a strange synchronism which connects these events; Mary escapes from Lochleven, 2 May; Duchess of Arschot dies, 16 May; Egmont executed, 6 June; Carlos murdered, 23 July, all in the year 1568.

Whether due to doubts of the reasons which influenced Mary to seek union with his son, or because of other things, Philip, after his first intimation of agreement, became more hesitating. In October (1563) he sought the advice of the Duke of Alba, who, in a long document[1] gave his views couched in language so obscure that it could have been of little help in making up the royal mind. The light given on the tortuous policies of the day is interesting, but need not be quoted. He recommends Philip not to entrench himself behind the generalisation that the Prince was unfit to marry, which goes some way to falsify the rumours on that subject. Finally, Alba advises

[1] *Pap. d'État*, Alba to Philip, 21 Oct. 1563.

careful consideration of the age and disposition of the Prince, "if one wishes to get something out of the business," the "something" being the romanisation of England through Scotland.

Philip brooded long over this letter, and Mary's house of cards began to fall about her. "For two months she has divers times been in great melancholies, her grief is marvellous secret and she often weeps when there is little apparent occasion," wrote Randolph in December (1563). Every day increased the bitterness of the religious struggle and the gulf widened between the parties which, when she left France, counselled conciliation. She was importuned on all sides to marry, her pride was hurt by peremptory orders from Elizabeth as to whom she should not choose, she was treated as a child by her council. With but a little strength of character she would have ruled the situation and bided her time.

Not until August (1564) did Philip act, then he wrote simultaneously to Granvelle and the new Ambassador in London, "Considering the disposition of my son *and other things* which appear in him, I see that the fruit which I hoped for will not come of the marriage, that is to say the reduction of Scotland and England to the Catholic religion, for the sake of which I would expose myself to any consequence....I have decided to put an end to all new steps in favour of the Prince." They were to give as a reason that the Cardinal of Lorraine had definitely "offered" Mary to the Archduke Charles. To Granvelle he added that France was still to be led to believe that the match with Carlos was in hand in order to prevent the Queen Mother from attempting to engage Mary to her son Charles IX; should such a thing happen he, Philip, would renew the negotiations with Mary. Probably it was for this reason that Mary was not informed by Granvelle of Philip's decision; ultimately he decided to break the news through the Duchess of Arschot; his letter to her is dated 20 September, 1564. "You should give the Queen to understand the negotiations with the Archduke Charles have gone too far to be broken. At the same time if she will send a discreet person to the Spanish Ambassador (in London) she can hear the King's will. *Tell her that all this happened before the Emperor's death* (July) *which event may have caused a change....*"

This letter seems designedly to contain, first an irritant in the news that her affairs had been settled without her consent and against her wishes, and secondly a hint that the decision was not irrevocable. The Dowager wrote to Mary accordingly on 4 October; unfortunately the letter is not available, but we have Mary's reply written apparently shortly after its receipt and dated 3 January (1565), "I have your news, touching a certain marriage, I am glad to hear the decision, not because of the expectations that I had founded thereon but because it enables me to make up my mind without laying myself open to the blame of a too hasty decision." She goes on to say that those who assume that there had been acceptance on her part of the Archduke are mistaken, she had heard nothing of the matter for more than a year. Finally there is a paragraph partly in cipher which seems to indicate that she would have preferred the Spanish match for several reasons and if anything should happen regarding it she would let her, the Duchess, know and take her advice as her aunt and greatest friend.

The letter is very feminine, even to her "aunt and greatest friend," she would hide her disappointment, and give a hint that the Prince of Spain was not her only suitor and convey the idea that the rebuff is not wholly unwelcome. But it is clear that in addition to her letter, the Duchess transmitted the information, which she in her turn must have had from the Cardinal, that Philip was inclined to reconsider his decision if he saw danger of the French match materialising. Mary promptly took steps to "materialise" the French match. It was a foolish little plot, and it weighed nothing in the result. On 28 January she sent a letter to her Ambassador in Paris; he was to hasten to obtain on any pretext an audience with the Queen Mother, and give it the appearance of importance, to see to it that the English Ambassador should hear of it. The audience was to be prolonged and if possible repeated on the following day and then an express messenger was to be despatched to the Cardinal of Lorraine, to give the impression that the matter of the audience was in question, though in fact Lorraine was not to be admitted into the plot. An urgent reply as to the success of the plan was to be sent as soon as possible. Whatever reply was made by Mary's Ambassador is not recorded but the affair fell flat.

On 6 February (1565) Cardinal Granvelle took a fresh hand in the game and wrote to London, "It is a grave thing that there should be any thought of her marrying with the King of France. There is not the slightest appearance that it is merely a feint.... I am astonished that not even Luis de Paz has received any news from there...." Very evidently Granvelle was anxious that the negotiation should not be broken off with Philip. On the 24th March, Mary sent to the Ambassador in London to say that she had heard from France that he, the Ambassador, had received orders from Philip to reopen the negotiations. "I asked," says the Ambassador in reporting the matter to Philip, "from whom in Flanders his Mistress had received the information, and he replied from Marania...about a fortnight ago." "Marania" indicates Granvelle. Unfortunately there is nothing to show what, if any, correspondence had passed between "Marania" and Philip, but presumably he had some reason to suppose that the latter desired the matter to be further discussed; if this were so, Philip had neglected to inform his representative in London. In the end, de Silva sent to Mary asking that Lethington should be sent to him; in the meantime he begged for instructions from Philip as to what he should tell him (Lethington) on his arrival. Within a few days of receiving this message Lethington was sent to London and arrived there about the 17th April and on the 25th had his interview with de Silva. Here again we have the fact of the professing protestant, Lethington, discussing a marriage with Spain. He stated that Mary had awaited a resolution for two years and the pressure of her subjects had caused her to listen to certain proposals and conversations with the son of the Earl of Lennox and Lady Margaret. In this she had done her best to satisfy the English Queen. If, however, there was any hope of the Spanish negotiation proceeding, then, her own wishes and intentions on the subject were unchanged; she asked for information on the subject and had been informed by Cardinal Granvelle that Philip had issued some orders on the case.

To this, de Silva, who had received no fresh instructions, could only reply by the old fable of the negotiations with the Archduke Charles and Philip's delicacy about interfering with them. Lethington then made a *résumé* of the proceedings since the death of Mary's first husband. How the Queen Mother had induced the Cardinal of Lorraine and the Duke of Guise to act against their niece in the matter of the Spanish marriage, and how the former, without her consent, had interviewed the Emperor on the subject of the Archduke at Innsbruck and he, Lethington, had sent off in haste to beg him to desist because the Scots would not consent to it. He, Lethington, was convinced that she should only marry a foreign prince who was strong enough to hold his own. To this de Silva replied again stating the same reasons for Philip's action, and adding that he, Philip, would regard favourably a marriage with Lady Margaret's son; Lethington thought it the best alternative, but still hoped for the protection of Spain in case of Elizabeth objecting to the match. In this way he said great effects would be produced, and Mary desired to follow Philip's wishes.

Here the Spanish negotiations ended; probably a good deal of de Silva's description of the interview was tuned up to suit Philip's ears, but at least it was made clear to Lethington that nothing further could be done. A messenger was sent at once to inform Mary of the result; he arrived at Stirling on the 3rd May (1565).

We must now briefly detail the successive steps by which the Queen was finally entangled in the web spread for her by Elizabeth or her advisers. It is true that shortly after Mary's arrival in Scotland an enquiry had been instituted, by Cecil, into the steps taken by the Lady Margaret to urge Mary to marry

her son; this was in the early part of 1562; a number of charges
were made out of communicating without permission with a
foreign prince, but the affair passed without much difficulty.
We must assume that at that time the English court was genuinely
opposed to the idea, but it is also true that, then, there was no
immediate danger of a foreign alliance, and though the Lennox
family were cautioned there was no real cessation of the pressure
brought by them on the Queen of Scots to marry her cousin.
An enquiry was made at the same time into alleged irregularities
as to the marriage of Lady Margaret's mother, and in March,
1563, Quadra reported that the English council was secretly
debating on the subject, with its consequence that neither the
Lady Margaret nor her son Lord Darnley would be in the succession to the English crown. Cecil was thus taking every precaution to diminish the effect of a union which would add to
Mary's claim to succeed. Though Mary, as heir to her father,
stood a degree nearer to the throne than Darnley, her foreign
birth was a bar, but Darnley if legitimate was clearly next, and
both together would be irresistible. This was the danger and it
is obvious that it was clearly foreseen.

In July, 1564, negotiations were opened from the side of
England for the return of the Earl of Lennox to Scotland and
in September he went thither on a three months' "licence"
from Elizabeth, the ostensible reason being that he could within
that time settle his affairs in Scotland. Whatever point of view
may be taken of this permission, one cannot get away from the
fact that, with full knowledge of the *pourparlers* referred to in
the last paragraph, an Ambassador such as Lennox, was not only
permitted to come in contact with Mary, but she was even
pressed to receive him. She did receive him, she assembled a
parliament to restore him to his honours, forfeited twenty years
previously for treacherous desertion to the enemies of his country, and she declared publicly that his restoration was made at
the special "request of her dearest sister, Elizabeth of England."
So far as she could she made it clear that this sending of the father

was not due to her, but no doubt the intention was as patent to her as it must be to everyone.

Five months later, in February, 1565, Lennox, in the meantime having received an extension of his "licence" for another three months, was followed by his son. The reason given by him in his "Supplication" to be mentioned in the next chapter was that his heart yearned for a sight of the youth, but as normally he should have returned to England very shortly after, we may safely discount this exceptional affection, which would not have been seriously endangered if Elizabeth had refused the necessary permission for Darnley to join his father. It is, to say the least, remarkable that these occurrences took place at the very time that Mary's affair with "Spain" was going a-gley. No more favourable time to catch her, angry, disillusioned, bewildered, could have been chosen. "What to do or how to resolve she is marvellously in doubt," wrote Master Thomas Randolph on the 27th March, 1565, after Darnley had been some six weeks in Scotland.

Randolph was at this time Elizabeth's agent at Mary's court; he was a voluminous correspondent, he was also a widower, and in love with that Mary Beton who lives in song as one of the "Maries." It would be unnecessary to refer to this but that through this source it is to be feared that the lover received much information that he should not have had; it even seems to be the case that here, in her very nearest companionship, this poor queen could not count on faith and honour. Writing to Leicester a few months later, Randolph said, "The three Maries remain yet unmarried...but one (this must be Mary Beton) is most constant, stout and wise, and thinks her fortune so much the worse that mine is so evil. *She knows herself bound unto your Lordship* and ready to do what service she may. So was he lately required to signify unto him." It may be that the exaltation of spirit which accompanies the state of being "in love" induced an unwonted vein of plain speaking in Randolph; at all events he was shocked and disgusted at the idea of bringing Darnley to Scotland and he said so quite plainly.

In February (1565) he wrote to Cecil, "By your letter I perceive what earnest means hath been made both my Lord Robert (Dudley) and your Honor, for my Lord Darnley's licence to come to Scotland," and he expresses dread that one should come, "of whom there is so much spoken against." And again, "I would that Her Majesty were free of the suspicion that is here spoken openly that the sending of him was done of purpose to match the Queen meanly...." And again, "My whole care is to avoid the suspicion that the Queen's Majesty was the mean and worker hereof...as it was of his father's return at her Majesty's suit." But the plan seemed to hang fire; Mary took nothing more than a courteous interest in the young man; on the 15th March the Agent wrote, "I see no great good will borne to him. Of her Grace's good usage and often talk with him, her countenance and good visage, I think it proceeds rather of her own courteous nature than that anything is meant that some here fear may ensue."

Elizabeth—or shall we say Cecil, for his hand appears everywhere—had still cards to play. The game was age-old; the woman and the command, "thou shalt not eat"; Cecil could read Mary like a book; a command from the daughter of Anne Boleyn was an incentive to the Queen Dowager of France and Queen regnant of Scotland. On the 16th March, Randolph conveyed Elizabeth's ultimatum, "Till she was either married or determined never to marry she could not gratify her (Mary's) desire to have her title determined and published." As Mary had not asked for more than a declaration as to her rights "failing direct heirs," this was obviously a mere "driving of time," as the phrase went then, intended to indicate that the matter was closed. If there had been no thought of exasperating the Scottish Queen into taking the step which we are to suppose was the thing Elizabeth objected to, one would have expected that this announcement would have been deferred until Darnley was safely returned to England; but with Darnley on the spot, possessing in his person those additional claims to the English throne which Mary's foreign birth deprived her of, it seems beyond doubt that this *démarche* was carefully calculated to bring about the very catastrophe which ostensibly it was desired to avoid. To Mary it could not but be obvious that she was being fooled; it is small wonder that she was bewildered, unable to contend against the astute Philip, the Queen Mother, her trusted uncle of Lorraine, Elizabeth, and Cecil with his years of hard-won experience. All were jealous and using her as a pawn; her own two councillors, Moray and Lethington, were traitors playing their own hands. "She wept her fill," says Randolph, with his special means of knowing what went on behind the scenes. Foolish Mary! Why did she not bide her time following Granvelle's advice to copy Elizabeth's formula, "God has not yet disposed me to marry." "I am pressed from all sides, I can say no more," she had written, yet Elizabeth, under equal or greater pressure alternately laughed at or scolded her faithful Commons who dared to dispose of her against her wishes.

A correspondent in a well-known journal has recently told us that, "Mary Stuart was a typical *troublante*, almost a subject for comedy, in her self-assertion, her disregard for the standards of conduct, and her unfailing conviction that what she did must be right." No doubt he (or is it, she?) believes that Mary at a later date described herself as having a heart hard as a diamond, yet I am inclined to think that it must require a heart still harder not to pity her at this juncture[1]. She was a few months over 22, "She is alone, and has not a single protector or good counsellor....The men of power take advantage of her gentleness[2]."

The last act of the drama approaches. We have seen (p. 60) that Lethington reached London on 17 April. We know that he had several interviews with Elizabeth; and with the Spanish Ambassador on the 24th and 25th. What his story was to the

[1] "XY" in the *New Statesman*, 2 June, 1923. It is also stated that there exists a letter from Mary to Philip of this period that should have kept her for ever from claiming the hospitality of Elizabeth. I confess my ignorance. Where is the letter?
[2] *Papal Negs.*, De Gouda to Laynez, 30 Sept. 1562.

former we have no precise record, certainly he reported that his mistress was becoming entangled with Darnley. Elizabeth promptly sent a command that Darnley and his father should return at once. The order was sent to the Earl of Bedford at Berwick, for transmission to Randolph in Edinburgh, and it seems that some secret qualification was attached to it, at least it was not delivered with haste to the two delinquents. Elizabeth also expressed the intention of sending Throgmorton on a special mission to endeavour to prevent the marriage from taking place. It seems that having, as she believed, successfully traversed the various continental proposals, she was ready to withdraw the Darnley bait; perhaps this is to her credit; but mark the sequel.

Whether Lethington's conversations with the Ambassador caused fresh alarm or whether the intention was never serious, or perhaps was deemed too precipitate, may be left indeterminate; an urgent message was sent to Bedford to hold up the order of recall. Randolph reported on 28 April that he had received from Bedford the advertisement of the alteration of the Queen's mind and accordingly had stayed the letters; he regretted it because the recall would have served to abate "the suspicion which is now almost universal that the sending of Darnley was done of purpose." Throgmorton, the missioner to stay the marriage, was delayed from day to day, and when at last he left London on 5 May, he hastened very slowly and reach Stirling on the 15th; Mary refused to see him. I hardly think that anyone reading these facts, for they are just *facts*, can acquit Elizabeth of intention to entangle her cousin, of sending Darnley "of purpose." It is easy enough to argue in favour of the end which the Queen had in view, but there must be few who can approve of the manner of attaining it.

It was on 3 May that Mary received Lethington's report of his London visit (p. 61). He conveyed Elizabeth's thinly veiled commands as to who she should marry and who not, a hint that the succession would be settled in her disfavour, and also de Silva's cold reception of her approaches. She sat down to give herself the luxury of passionate repudiation of her "Sister's" authority. "I wish," says Randolph to Cecil, "you had seen the penning of the matter of her own hand..., you would have said there had neither wanted eloquence, despite, anger, love nor passion." The missive contained, "I am so long trained with fair speech and in the end beguiled of my expectations, (and now) do mind with the advice of my estates to use my own choice in marriage...and be no longer fed with yea and nay...." The messenger met Lethington at Newark on his return journey, he was to instruct him to retrace his steps and deliver the defiance to the English Queen, perhaps wisely, Lethington refused and continued on his way to Edinburgh. The die was cast; on 4 May, Moray was sent for to come to Stirling and the Queen put before him and other nobles her intention to marry the Lord Darnley; he declined to consent and produced a series of conditions which emanated from the Convention of the General Assembly under the leadership of John Knox, which by accident or design was at the moment sitting in Edinburgh.

It is not part of my purpose to follow the rebellion which ensued, most unquestionably it was fostered by the representatives of England, Throgmorton, Randolph and, later, Tamworth. Mary reiterated her decrees as to freedom of conscience for all men, she informed Elizabeth that should she succeed to to the throne of England there would be no innovation of religion, for herself she declined to change her confession. It is easy to say, as some do, that her promises were of no worth; there is no ground for this; on the contrary, the matter collected in these two chapters will, I think, show that in all probability she intended to ensure religious harmony. Driven to take arms for the defence of her crown against extremists to whom the idea of compromise was foreign, some of whom she had every reason to suspect were actuated by motives unconnected with religion, it may well be that she was embittered and forced gradually to part with the ideals which had formed her dreams in France. Peace was possible if Cecil had wished it, but Cecil was far from wishing it.

"A greater benefit to the Queen's Majesty could not have chanced, than to see this dishonour fall upon her, and her so matched where she shall be ever assured that she can never attain to what she so earnestly looked for," was Randolph's diagnosis of her situation. A little later (May 21) he described the effect that anxiety and disillusionment had had upon her.

I know not how to utter what I conceive of the pitiful and lamentable estate of this poor Queen whom ever before I esteemed so worthy so wise so honourable in all her doings and at this present find so altered with affection towards the Lord Darnley....To whom this may chiefly be imputed, what crafty subtlety or devilish device hath brought this to pass I know not, but woe worth the time that ever Lord Darnley did set his foot in this country....These things my Lord do move me much to lament her case, this is it that may move any man to pity that ever saw her, that ever loved her....What to judge of his home-coming many men know not, but the most part are persuaded that in sending of him there is other meaning than there was in utter show....One that ever I judged the most unworthy to be matched with such one as I have known her and seen her to be.

And in another letter.

...To remedy the mischief either he must be taken away, or those he hates supported, that what he intends for others may light upon himself....She is now so much altered from what she was that who now beholds her does not think her the same. Her majesty is laid aside, her wits not what they were, her beauty another than it was, her cheer and countenance changed into I wot not what. A woman more to be pitied than ever I saw....

It is perhaps necessary to explain that Leicester, to whom the above letters were written, was the patron of Randolph, and that between Cecil and Leicester there existed a deep feud. Evidently the person to whom the writer attributed Mary's undoing was Cecil, and there is no doubt as to his accuracy. Less reliable is his opinion that the cause of Mary's altered mien was love for Darnley. The whole course of the narrative in this chapter indicates that up to the last moment she adhered to her original hope of union with the prince Carlos, and, at least according to the view put forward here, a realisation of her girlish dream of being the agent of healing the schism in the church. Throgmorton, who was a cooler spectator of things as they were, described the matter differently: "When I consider the foundation of this matter, which was despite and anger, I cannot assure myself that such qualities will bring forth such fruit as the love and usage bestowed on Darnley shows." Yet, French fashion, having bestowed herself Mary would have made a good wife, had the husband permitted it. Despite, anger, the desire to defy Elizabeth had more to do with her marriage than the process we call "falling in love." Mary had seen the gallants of France, the half-fledged Darnley can hardly have stormed her heart.

It would hardly be possible to tell a story of which the heroine was less entitled to be described as bold, far-seeing, unscrupulous, resolute and all the rest of it, rather was she the antithesis of all these.

In his interesting chapter on the "Matrimonial Intrigues[1]" which affected Mary, Mr Henderson has come very near the suggestions made in the foregoing; he says, "It would further appear that Maitland and Moray had a Protestant scheme of their own: they deemed it possible that under the new arrangement Scotland might be governed, independently, as a Protestant kingdom....But whatever Maitland's real aims, and however far he and Moray were at one, it is plain that Maitland was doing his utmost to further the Spanish match." The Queen of Scots, says Mr Henderson, was to reside in Spain and Moray and Maitland were to divide the rule in Scotland, the one as Regent, or rather Viceroy, the other as chief Minister.

But the weak point of this is that it is impossible to suppose that Maitland could have viewed Philip in the light of a monarch who "Governed the different nations under his rule according to their own humour[2]." The happenings of the moment in the Low Countries were sufficient to stultify any such idea. The policy which guided Maitland, Moray and Mary was I feel convinced a much more practicable one than to include Philip as an influence in Scottish affairs.

[1] *Mary Queen of Scots, A Biography*, by T. F. Henderson, 1905.
[2] See Philippson, quoting a letter from Lethington to Mary.

Mary and the son of Philip, each with a quota of hereditary right, governing the Netherlands and Scotland on a religious basis akin to the Protestantism of England or the Augsburg Confession, supported by Lorraine and perhaps also Savoy, would be a combination secure from the vengeance of Philip. Possessing also the means to secure the right of succession to the throne of England, which was so close to Mary's heart, the centre of an organisation which would heal the schism in the Church; here was a dream which, however, beyond the small capacity of Mary to accomplish was at least a great one; had she possessed the resolution of Elizabeth or of Catherine it might have come true.

Was Philip's hesitation and ultimate refusal to send his son to Brussels due to knowledge of the scheme? There is only indirect evidence to show. Until this took place the plan hung fire. From the evidence also it appears that Mary herself was fearful of so great an undertaking, possibly, even probably, she dreaded a step which would place her even temporarily in conflict with the Church. Her constant reiteration of her faithfulness to the Papal supremacy and the Church of Rome gives the impression of one who protested more than there was need to do if her thoughts were wholly orthodox, and we must remember that in such protests she was not alone. Many of those who were definitely committed to reform within the Church made the same denial of heresy.

CHAPTER III

Consideration to the Lennox Bill of Supplication has been given by two writers, Andrew Lang and T. F. Henderson. But neither has remarked on the effect it has on the Official account of the Tragedy at Kirk o' Field. It is this omission that this chapter aims at supplying.

THE LENNOX NARRATIVE

THIS LENNOX PAPER would not in itself be worth a chapter were it not for the fact that it gives an *independent* account of the Darnley tragedy. It is this point that Andrew Lang misinterpreted; he thought the Paper to have been produced *after* communication with Scotland. Henderson in his Biography of Mary Stuart has exposed the error[1], but as there are some subsidiary points connected with the chronology of the Paper which Mr Henderson did not refer to it will be useful to gather together the circumstances leading up to the writing before dealing with the matter of it.

The story as told by Lennox differs in many details from the "official" version afterwards published from Edinburgh, and known to us as *The Detection* and thus we have ground to suspect the latter even if the former cannot be taken as infallible. At least, Lennox was in closer contact with the whole episode than any other witness for the prosecution, and to this extent his evidence should be more credible.

I. THE EVENTS PRECEDING THE WRITING

Mary escaped from Lochleven on Sunday evening, 2 May, 1568. Her subsequent movements were from the first unfortunate or ill-advised. If, as was said, the escape was premature and her friends not fully prepared, there was so much the more

---

[1] Before becoming acquainted with Henderson's *Biography*, I pointed this out myself in my *Indictment of Mary Queen of Scots*, p. 8. I think there is very little doubt that the Paper is a rough draft of the Bill of Supplication, yet in definitely assuming this to be the case, perhaps Mr Henderson has taken too much for granted.

reason that she should have been taken to a place of security while measures were developing for her restoration; in fact, this was not done. After spending some hours at Niddry she rode on the 3rd to Hamilton, some ten miles south-east of Glasgow. There is no hint in any contemporary record that she was molested on the way, though her company could not then have been numerous. There can hardly be a doubt that, then, she could have pushed on to Dumbarton without risk.

Reading between the lines of contemporary opinion, one must conclude that the unfortunate queen was a puppet, to be used by one or other of the contending parties in the State. Throgmorton, a shrewd observer, wrote a few days after, "Those who provided the means of escape, did so with no other intention than to seize the Government of the realm....[1]" Thus it was that she fell into the power of the Hamiltons and remained ten days at the castle of Hamilton.

The Earl of Moray, with all the resources of *de facto* Regent of Scotland, lay at Glasgow and with him many of the Lords. The Earl of Mar with the garrison of Stirling Castle was in communication with him. Nothing more convincing of the military ineptitude of the Queen's advisers or the Queen herself could be said. It is significant of the estimation of her liberty of action, held by her opponents, that, when on 4 May a notification of repudiation of the enforced abdication was sent into Glasgow, the Earl of Moray asked if the Queen herself had knowledge thereof[2]. There seems no doubt that the distressing events of the past eighteen months had sapped her intellectual vitality and left her more than ever a prey to the will of others.

It is unnecessary to sketch the course of the negotiations which preceded the final catastrophe at Langside. It will suffice for our present purpose if we take up the story on the morning of 13 May when Mary, in company of Lords Fleming and Livingston and about 20 persons, witnessed the disaster and believing it to be irretrievable, took flight.

---

[1] Teulet, *Relations*, Throgmorton to Melville, 6 (10?) May, 1568.
[2] Teulet, Drury to Throgmorton, 9 May, 1568.

Of Mary's intentions on the 13th when the flight commenced there is no record, there is nothing to show that she had then made any plan to throw herself on Elizabeth's protection. It is sometimes stated that she sent John Beton to announce her coming, but this is not so; Beton was sent off on the 4th, before the necessity for flight had occurred and his mission was to obtain aid either in England or France[1]. It is probable that the momentous decision to cross into England was taken at Thrieve Castle[2] on the night of the 14th and on the evening of the 16th she arrived in Cumberland, landing near Workington.

There is not the least doubt that the step was totally unexpected in London, and the news of it arrived with Sir Richard Lowther's letter of the 17th (see note 3 below) despatched at night of that date from Cockermouth, which arrived in London on the 20th, and it could not have been until the evening of that date or more probably on the 21st that Lennox, residing at Chiswick, heard of it.

In the meantime Moray after the fight at Langside contented himself with taking Hamilton Castle; he apparently made no attempt to follow the fugitive and returned to Edinburgh on the 18th. It is a curious fact that he did not receive news of Mary's whereabouts until the arrival of a message from Berwick, sent by Sir William Drury[3], probably on the 20th. He took prompt steps and despatched John Wood to London on the following day, the 21st May[4]. Despatched at 24 hours' notice, it is most

[1] Cabala, Cecil to Norris, 16 May, 1568.

[2] The facts as to Mary's flight into England and the route taken are so often misrepresented that I have added a note on the subject (p. 132).

[3] Drury, writing to Cecil on 26 May, 1568, says, "Having occasion to send to Edinburgh unto the Earl of Moray...by my messenger he *first understood* of her arrival there (in England)." As Drury himself had the news on the 19th we may assume that Moray had it on that date in the evening or on the 20th. There is very little doubt that the Queen was disguised and left Scotland without recognition, which may account for Moray's tardy information.

[4] It is necessary to be meticulous about these dates, for the argument depends on them to a great extent. It is extraordinary how frequently even the most reputable authors are mistaken in these apparently trifling matters.

unlikely that Wood took with him *any* of the incriminating documents, which afterwards became so famous, in fact Moray writing on the 22nd June seems to indicate that these were sent to him after his departure[1]. The exact date of Wood's arrival in London is nowhere stated; it would be on the 26th or 27th of May. We know that he passed through Berwick on the 22nd[2].

II. THE INCEPTION OF THE BILL OF SUPPLICATION

The brief sketch given of the events of the days immediately succeeding the Queen's escape from Lochleven will serve to give an accurate notion of why and when the Earl of Lennox began to move in her impugnment. It is worth while to recall that he was in the habit of appealing to Elizabeth for assistance in matters which concerned the death of his son. No doubt he regarded himself rather as the mouthpiece of his wife, Elizabeth's first cousin, than as having any special *locus standi* on his own account. Indeed as a renegade Scot who had but recently flouted Elizabeth's commands, it is not a little remarkable how easily he had obtained his reconciliation, and restoration in his English estates[3]. It is no doubt this attitude of relying on Lady Lennox's relationship that caused the petition which we are about to discuss to be made in their joint names.

The news of Mary's escape would have caused much excitement in the Lennox household and possibly some anxiety as to what revelations might take place if she should establish herself again on the throne. But as yet there was no anticipation of the final stroke of fate which was to bring the Queen in person

[1] Cecil, in a memorandum drawn up very shortly after the Queen's arrival in England, noted that the "proofs" of her guilt should "be had and sent hither." There is no doubt that a request for these was conveyed to Moray. The letter sent by Moray on 22 June contains, "And for our offer to make her Majesty (Elizabeth) declaration of our whole doings...we have already *sent* unto our servant Mr John Wood, *that* which we trust shall sufficiently resolve her Majesty of anything she stands doubtful unto....Our servant Mr John Wood has copies of the same letters...."

[2] Drury to Cecil, dated 22 May, 1568, Record Office.

[3] Simancas under dates 10 May, 4 June, 28 June, 1568.

within his influence; this unexpected news reached him, as we have seen, on the 21st May, possibly on the 20th. On the 20th Elizabeth summoned a hasty council of such of her privy council as were immediately available. Cecil was certainly present, and his opinion as to the proper action to be taken did not jump with that of his mistress. Elizabeth did all in her power to sustain her promises of succour[1], and it is pretty clear that she was opposed.

Cecil's action was prompt and characteristic; he wrote at once (20th) to Sir William Drury at Berwick directing him to place himself in immediate communication with the Earl of Moray. Drury received this order on the 25th and replied on the 26th, "I have received your advice and opinion touching the Queen of Scots and to aid of the Earl of Moray, to whom I have sent accordingly[2]." This is an important link in the chain of evidence: Moray, then in Stirling, would receive Cecil's message on the evening of 26 May. It is very unfortunate that Cecil's communication of 20 May is not preserved. Probably it was written after the meeting of the Council at which Elizabeth had shown signs of being "honour-bound" towards her sister queen and Cecil's first thought would be to provide evidence to satisfy his mistress that her unexpected "guest" could with propriety be relegated to the category of fugitive from justice. Evidently up to that time, whatever had been said as to Mary's guilt was confined to statements without proofs, and no doubt it was proofs as well as some person to represent him (Moray) in submitting these proofs to the Queen that Cecil now suggested should be sent. One gathers that there was no *written* communication for Moray, but a private message to be delivered by Drury telling him of the difficulty and its suggested remedy. At the time of writing Cecil was of course unaware that John Wood was about to start for London for the very purpose in question.

It is a remarkable fact that on the 27th May, that is the day

<hr/>

[1] Teulet, *Relations*, La Forrest to Charles IX, 22 May, 1568.
[2] Record Office, *Border State Papers*, Drury to Cecil, 26 May, 1568. There are two letters of the same date which bear on the subject.

after his receipt of Cecil's hint, a messenger with "closed writings" was sent to George Buchanan at St Andrews[1]. The conclusion can hardly be avoided that it was at this moment that the famous *Detection* began to take shape[2], and, that to Buchanan was entrusted the duty of preparing the "proofs" which Cecil required to present to Elizabeth. We know, from Moray's letter of 22 June, that the evidence had been sent, "We have already *sent* unto our servant Mr John Wood *that* which we trust shall sufficiently resolve her Majesty of anything she stands doubtful unto," but the exact date on which Mr John Wood was thus supplied is doubtful.

Sir William Drury occupied the position of Marshal of Berwick, or as we would call it Governor of the fortress. Through his hands passed practically all the intercourse between Scotland and England, and it was his custom to report to Cecil the movements of persons or the receipt of information connected with the more important affairs of the moment. We have a number of such reports dated in May and June but none of them make it certain when the fateful documents were passed on to Wood. Thus on 30 May he forwarded a packet, "From the Earl of Murray with his earnest request that the same might with all speed be conveyed unto you." This may have contained the copies of the letters for transmission to Wood, if so they would have reached him on or about 3 June, but it is not likely that Buchanan had had time to draw up the Latin summary, known now as the *Detection* for enclosure in this packet; at least, I think, this is the earliest date on which Wood is likely to have been in possession of the copies.

Again, on 6 June, there is a cryptic paragraph in a letter from Drury, "I send unto your Honor a book newly imprinted and also the 'fourme' of a conjuration used near unto Edinburgh, the form of the same as well of the letters as otherwise was also in like manner done in the ground. With a packet from the

[1] See printed *Accounts of the Lord Treasurer* under this date.
[2] A full account of the origin of this famous work is given in *The Indictment of Mary Queen of Scots*, Camb. University Press, 1923.

Earl of Moray[1]." This seems to be the latest date on which the documents may have been forwarded, for Moray left Edinburgh on the 10th and was carrying out his punitive operations around Dumfries until the 25th; it is probable that he would have completed these matters before leaving the Capital. It seems that the "book" newly imprinted *may* have been the Summary. There was a press at St Andrews, but printing was not a rapid business in those days and there would be no more than seven or eight clear days between the date on which Buchanan received the instructions, say 27 May and 4 June, when he would have sent the reply, which *via* Edinburgh reached Berwick on the 6th; within that period the Latin summary would have to be composed and perhaps printed. I confess that I have not hitherto thought that it was *printed*, but if it were so, the quibble used by Elizabeth at a later date might be condoned[2]. In any case the short time at his disposal would account for the "haste" with which Buchanan says the Paper was written.

Let us return to Lennox. In the dilemma in which Cecil found himself on the 20th May, due to Elizabeth's support of her cousin, he sent as we have seen to the Earl of Moray, but Moray's assistance could not be expected for many days; as an *ad interim* measure we may be pretty certain that he would call in the Earl of Lennox who was at hand. Had he known that Wood would be so soon on the way it is not likely that he would have done so, but this he did not know. Thus I suggest that on

[1] It is noteworthy that this messenger from Drury would have arrived in London on the 10th June, perhaps even on the 9th. On the 11th, Lennox, by the hand of John Wood, wrote to his friends in Scotland asking for certain information. He now for the first time betrayed knowledge of the real Casket Letters; see *Maitland Club Miscellany*, *Hamilton Papers*. In one of his letters Lennox says, "There is sufficient evidence in her own hand-write, by faith of her letters, to condemn her." Thus it looks as if it was on this occasion that the copies of the letters were sent to London.

I confess my inability to solve the riddle of the remainder of Drury's letter above quoted. Cecil was a collector of antiquities, and it may be that nothing more is meant than that Drury is sending him some new inscription or form of magic which he had come across.

[2] See *The Indictment of Mary Queen of Scots*, especially pp. 4, 5, 25.

the 21st or 22nd May, Lennox received his instructions to come forward with a demand for justice against the Queen of Scots for the murder of his son. To produce *something*, in short, which would serve to stay the generous impulse which at first seems to have affected Elizabeth. Possibly Lennox needed no prompting, but he had the reputation of being something of a fool and a slow mover, and a hint to him of the situation was a very likely step to be taken. An audience was fixed for the 28th and Lennox on behalf of himself and his wife was to plead his cause. We know that on another similar occasion when pleading before the Commission at Westminster, "Not being able to express his cause in convenient words, he put in writing, briefly and rudely, some part of such matter as he conceived to be true...[1]," and it is more than likely that he did so on this occasion also. He refers, in fact, in his letter to Cecil of 18 August, to the Bill of Supplication which he had submitted to Queen Elizabeth, and there is hardly a doubt that the audience of 28 May was the date of its submission.

As to whether the rough draft before us is that of the Bill there is no absolute proof. There is no official copy of it among the State Archives. On the other hand, it is a narrative and certainly drawn up by Lennox himself, for the first page and a part of the second are in his handwriting[2] and much of the rest is amended by him; it is obviously a first draft and it may have been altered materially before submission; this however is not of importance so far as its value to us is concerned. Furthermore it is a narrative so much at variance with those which were subsequently put forward that it is beyond doubt that it was composed *before* Lennox was in possession of the latest "facts." I propose to accept it as the genuine first draft of the Bill of Supplication.

[1] *Journal* of the Commissioners at Westminster on the 29th Nov. 1568.

[2] I have been able to find only a few scraps of Lennox's undoubted hand, but these and, especially Lennox to Elizabeth, 20 July, 1570, in the Record Office, leave no doubt as to the correctness of the above statement.

John Wood, passing through Berwick on his way to London on the 22nd May, could not have arrived there before the 26th; whether he came in contact with Lennox on that date or before the audience on the 28th, or whether his arrival caused any alteration in Lennox's Supplication we have no knowledge, nor, as said above, does it matter, our rough draft is certainly of pre-Wood period.

One more date and I think the reader will have as many pieces of the puzzle as is necessary to build upon. On the 29th May, as reported by Drury, "young Stewart, servant to the Earl of Lennox," passed Berwick on his way into Scotland. "Young" Stewart would have left London about the 24th, his journey was, I think we may assume, connected with the great matter which a day or two before his departure had been placed in his master's hands, and one can easily suppose that his mission was to collect evidence for Lennox's use. Very possibly it was from this "young Stewart" that the document emanated, which we now find among the Cambridge Papers[1] containing a medley of incredible stories to the detriment of the Queen of Scots. The last paragraph is the only one of any interest, "Further Your Honor shall have advertisement of, as I can find; but it is good that this matter be not ended until your Honor may have the copy of

---

[1] Univ. Lib. Press Mark, Oo. 7.47/5. In the British Museum, Add. MS. 35825, is a letter from the Earl of Lennox to John Wood dated 29 July, 1568, which is interesting in the above connection. It runs: "Whereas I received from you by the hand of my servant William Stewart, a letter from my Lord Regent unto me and have written unto his Lordship again together with another letter directed to my servant Thomas Crawford, being both enclosed within this packet. Wherefore I shall hereby desire you that with the first letter you despatch into Scotland you will send the same. Further I understand by my said servant Wm. Stewart that you think the Queen's Majesty will have this great matter tried, which I am very glad of. And if you be certain of the time and place I shall desire you to let me understand thereof. From Chiswick." I think "Young Stewart" and the William mentioned herein are the same person; he had evidently recently returned from Scotland, and it is more than probable that the Cambridge document was from his hand and that the "letter" mentioned was in fact the revised version of the "long" Glasgow Letter.

the letter which I shall have at (that is, send to) your Honor so soon as I may have a trust(y) bearer." If "young" Stewart were indeed the writer of this the date would be within the first few days of June; we shall have occasion to remark on this later. It certainly looks as though the writer said in effect, "Do not be in a hurry to complete your narrative until a copy of *the letter* is sent." In the meantime, however, perhaps under pressure from Cecil, the narrative was completed. Certainly it contains none of the memoranda collected, as we assume, by "young Stewart," nor is there any reason for supporting Mr Lang in his opinion that it contains any of the details which may have been supplied to him (Lennox) as result of his enquiries. As to what "young Stewart" referred to as "the letter" we have no certain information, but it is very probable, that on his arrival in Scotland, Stewart found that Lennox's version of the "long" Glasgow Letter was obsolete, and warned him accordingly.

It is well to recall that Lennox left Scotland at the end of April of the previous year (1567) and from that time onwards to the date of Mary's arrival in England (May, 1568) there is no reason to suppose that he was in the confidence of those who were the prominent actors in the events in Scotland of the intervening twelve months. I mention this to emphasize the fact that what Lennox wrote in the days between 21 May and 26 May, which we can take to cover the writing of our document, he was telling the story as he knew it at the time of leaving Scotland. The arrival of John Wood altered this state of affairs, but that is not the point at present.

Let us now consider the Narrative itself.

THE NARRATIVE

In his *Biography* of Mary Queen of Scots, Mr T. F. Henderson has printed the Paper from the MS. in the Cambridge University Library[1], in the Scottish vernacular. For con-

[1] Press Mark, Oo 7.47/8, consisting of fourteen pages of manuscript of which the last is a part repetition of the commencement. The first page and part of the second is in Lennox's hand, the remainder in a clerk's hand.

venience of reference I have appended a reprint in ordinary colloquial English of to-day. I have also divided it into numbered paragraphs.

PARAGRAPHS I AND II

Synopsis. Lennox ascribes his recall to Scotland as due to the good will of Mary, and the recollection of his services during her minority. The coming of his son he says was the result of his solicitations, he being unable to remain parted from him. The Queen falls in love at first sight and marries Darnley. The decay of their happiness due to the machinations of Rizzio.

The two first paragraphs require little comment. Lennox's recollection of his services in Mary's minority is somewhat highly coloured as is also the story of his homecoming. The inception of the marriage with Darnley has already been fully dealt with in the preceding chapter.

PARAGRAPH III

Synopsis. The inordinate favour shown to Rizzio, and the neglect of Darnley. The death of Rizzio. Darnley's pity and love for his wife and desire to please her in all things.

This paragraph opens the subject of the Rizzio affair, a subject which is altogether omitted in every document of the official account, emanating from Edinburgh. This alone marks this Paper as presenting an independent narrative. Even in the *Detection*, which in its original form as a Latin summary of the case, was written at practically the same time, there is no mention of Rizzio, though it is true such reference may have been excised after it left Buchanan's hands. One wonders what the reason was for such delicacy; not, we may be sure, on the ground that an aspersion against the Queen's honour prior to the birth of her son might affect his legitimacy, as has been suggested. Indeed, any idea of this kind would be more repugnant to Lennox than to anyone else, and he of all others would be most likely to resent it. As a fact the tenor of the preceding paragraph definitely precludes the idea, though in order to account for the murder he lays stress on the jealousy of his son, aroused by the favour shown to Rizzio.

M

Yet Lennox, who from October (1565) onwards saw these things or at least says he did, wrote to his wife two months later, "My Madge, we have to give God most hearty thanks for that the King our son continues in good health and liking and the Queen great with child, God save them all, for which we have great cause to rejoice[1]." Here is no shadow of the scandalous story which he has hinted at in his Supplication.

The return from Dumfries took place on 18 October, and it is true that at this time Darnley began to show himself in his true colours as a traitor to his country. There is no mystery about it; the English Agent, Randolph, was doing his utmost to support the rebellion headed by Moray, and without doubt Darnley had listened to suggestions involving the restoration of the rebels in return for their recognition of his rights to succeed to the throne. Mary had appealed for support to Spain and to France against the bellicose attitude of Elizabeth. As early as 12 October, the Pope had declared, "We hear that...certain persons are going to allay these tumults in a way which will be disadvantageous to the Catholic religion. We have therefore thought well to urge you (Cardinal of Lorraine) to endeavour ...to deter the King and Queen from such a compromise[2]."

Rizzio was the intermediary employed to keep the Queen up to the desired firmness of dealing drastically with the rebels, and Mary, fully aware of the treachery of England, though she diplomatically refused to include Elizabeth as a party, was as usual borne hither and thither on the cross currents. She "wept wondrous sore" at the words of Captain Cockburn who spoke in favour of the rebels. She knew well enough that the removal of Rizzio was planned in England and that Darnley was merely a tool. She had no real rancour against Moray, "She is better willing to accord than she would seem," wrote Randolph. How different, how much more effective in the preservation of

[1] Haynes, *Burleigh Papers*, dated 19 Dec. 1565, p. 443. On enquiry I find that the original of this letter is missing at Hatfield, though Haynes must have seen it.

[2] *Papal Negotiations*, p. 128.

authority, was the action of Elizabeth in the cases of Northumberland and Norfolk, neither of whom was more guilty than Moray and his confederates.

The real reason for the suppression of the Rizzio affair in all the documents sent to England from Edinburgh was the indefensible character of the action taken by Cecil, which was well known to many of the Council and especially to the Earl of Bedford[1].

PARAGRAPH IV

Synopsis. The Queen nourishes a desire to avenge the death of Rizzio which she suspects her husband of causing. He nobly risks his life to secure her safety. The King and Queen return to Edinburgh, outwardly reconciled. The rise in favour of Bothwell. The raising of an armed guard for the Queen. The birth of the prince. Darnley's unquiet life.

The story told of the escape from Holyrood, does not accord with fact. Darnley's share in it was by no means so noble as his father would have us believe. Buchanan, in the *Detection*, takes the story up at the point of the Queen's return to Edinburgh after the murder of Rizzio, but the two accounts are totally diverse; that of Lennox, though coloured from his own point of view, is likely enough to be correct in so far as the Queen's displeasure against her husband is concerned. She had indeed good reason, "She has now seen all the covenants and bands that passed between the King and the Lords, and finds that his declaration before her and the Council of his innocency of the death of David (Rizzio) was false, and is grievously offended that by their means he should seek the crown matrimonial[2]." Darnley was unquestionably guilty of high treason if not for seeking the Queen's life, at least for conniving at her imprisonment.

[1] See *Simancas Records*, under dates 13 April and 18 May, 1566; also *State Papers, Scotland*, Bedford and Randolph to Cecil, 6, 8 and 11 March, 1566.
[2] *State Papers, Scotland*, Randolph to Cecil, 4 April, 1566.

Synopsis. Darnley's sorrow at the Queen's neglect. The Queen accepts Bothwell as a lover. She concerts with him to avenge her for the death of Rizzio. She abandons herself to riotousness.

According to Lennox the Queen's infatuation with Bothwell began at the time of her residence in Edinburgh Castle, a very impossible situation all things considered. As a matter of fact Bothwell was not in the Castle at the time of the Queen's residence. The Earl of Moray seems by the correspondence to have managed her affairs during that time. Bothwell is not mentioned as enjoying special favour, though his services after the death of Rizzio naturally gained for him the Queen's confidence. Mary had hoped to get away to France for three months after her confinement, so Mauvissière reported[1], which in itself goes some way to dispose of these scandalous statements. Indeed, if Lethington is to be trusted she was anxious to retire to France altogether, presumably taking her child with her and leaving a regency to govern the kingdom[2].

Lennox in his story knows nothing about the visit to Alloa which Buchanan makes so much of, nor of the scandal of the Exchequer House which the latter writer relates with so many impossible details. There is not a hint of suspicion in the contemporary letters of any such happenings; on the contrary we find Mary doing her utmost to reconcile the feuds between the nobles, especially Moray, Maitland, Bothwell and Argyll. Nor does Lennox see fit to mention the story told by Buchanan of the Queen endeavouring to set Moray and Darnley in a quarrel, though if the report which reached the Venetian Ambassador was true there was cause enough for it; being very much to Darnley's discredit it is easy to understand why it is omitted[3].

---

[1] *Simancas Records* under date 18 May, 1566.

[2] *Tytler*, vol. VII, p. 47, Lethington to Randolph, 27 April, 1566.

[3] *Calendar Venetian State Papers*, under date 20 March, 1567. The rumour that Moray sought Darnley's death on account of this quarrel is no doubt the reason why Buchanan clothes the story in garments of his own making.

It may be argued that two persons telling a story would naturally remember different details, yet Lennox was much nearer the Queen in her movements than was Buchanan, he was anxious to make as bad a story as possible; had he known these tit-bits it is not possible to suppose that he would refrain from making use of them. The inference is that he did not know them and that they were not true.

PARAGRAPH VI

Synopsis. The Queen visits Jedburgh, and returns *via* Craigmillar to Edinburgh. At Craigmillar she invents the murder of her innocent and most loving husband, who had determined to quit the kingdom. Her dislike for Lennox himself. The nobles support Darnley on account of the Queen's neglect of him. The intention to murder Darnley is postponed until after the christening of the child. The Queen fears the effect of Darnley's good qualities on the Ambassadors assembled for the baptism, and keeps him in the background.

Lennox hints that the journey to Jedburgh was taken to get away from her husband and he has nothing of Buchanan's demonstrably mendacious tale of that incident. It is a curious instance of the working of a mind inexorably determined to find the accused guilty, to follow Mr Henderson in this matter. In many respects acute and fair in his presentation of the case, he says of this incident and that already referred to of the Exchequer House, "For the actual fact of the first admission of Bothwell into the house (The Exchequer House)..., Buchanan's authority is her confession to her brother Moray and his mother, *and though we have no corroboration of Buchanan's story* (my italics) it is at least possible that the confession was made when, as Nau[1] relates, Mary, at Lochleven gave birth to still born twins. *If* the Queen and Bothwell were thus intimate before the death of Darnley this would explain better than perhaps any other hypothesis the part taken by the Queen in luring Darnley to Edinburgh." On this slender foundation Mr Henderson gradually builds Ossa on Pelion and finally reaches a height which enables him, in perfect good faith, to slay the reputation of the Queen.

[1] See note concerning Nau, p. 133.

As a matter of fact there is a little point which I think escaped Mr Henderson, contained in the *Simancas Records*. De Silva reported, 30 August, 1567, that "Lady Margaret sends me word that the Queen had confessed (to Moray) that she knew of the plot to murder her husband." Out of this it would have been possible for Mr Henderson to make a better story; what the actual facts of Mary's alleged confession are it is impossible to say; Moray never alluded to it in his several statements made subsequently, but, that she told Moray, when he visited her at Lochleven, something about the events of that Sunday night, is probable. Something that it did not suit Moray's convenience to repeat.

This is not a place for medical details, but really, Mary's detractors should examine their dates and "facts" a little more carefully. The Exchequer House incident dates from 6 September, 1566, Jedburgh and its connected incidents was in October following. Nau's story said nothing of *still-born* twins, he merely says "a miscarriage" of twins, which took place at about the time when her abdication was forced upon her, that is 25 or 26 July in the following year. Father Stevenson goes one better and refers to "these children," but contemporary gossip says that the miscarriage occurred, if it occurred, at the seventh week! Medical science then, and even now, might be mistaken in such a case. Why Mary, married to Bothwell in May, should confess any such thing as is suggested above in relation to the previous September-October seems to pass imagination.

Lennox's statement that the time and manner of the murder was devised at Craigmillar may be dismissed as merely rhetoric, at least it is obviously impossible that the events of the ensuing two months could have been foreseen. The question of Darnley's threatened departure from Scotland is more interesting, one wonders why so much importance was attached to it. For one thing the presence of the father at the approaching baptism was evidently considered of importance, I do not mean of special importance in this particular case, but the laws of inheritance were keenly contested at the time and many safeguards were employed in royal births of which custom still retains some remains. For another thing the absence of a prince was regarded as causing the possibility of disaffection and rebellion; the case of Louis XI of France was often quoted at the time, and the threatened evasion of Don Carlos of Spain from his father's tyranny caused commotion. The idea expressed by Lennox of the love and devotion which his son had gained among the nobles must be taken with a grain of salt; the facts are quite the reverse, and the records are clear on the point. Bishop Keith, with his facility for consulting the records of the Scots College in Paris, now destroyed, quotes a letter from the Scottish Lords dated 8 October (1566) in which they thanked God for so wise and virtuous a princess and expressed themselves "utterly averse" from putting power into Darnley's hands, Moray, Argyll and Atholl being among the signatories. Unless they were dissembling greatly, for which there seems no reason, we have here a contradiction of much of the *subsequent* slander.

PARAGRAPH VII

Synopsis. Lennox having heard of the danger to the person of his son, advises him to come to him at Glasgow for safety. Darnley falls sick at Glasgow, which prevents him from fulfilling his intention of quitting Scotland.

It is noticeable that Lennox does not make reference to the conference at Craigmillar on the subject of divorce, which Buchanan includes in the *Detection*; he may, of course, have considered it unsuitable in a panegyric of his son, or he may have been ignorant of it. But Lennox mentions what Buchanan omits, namely the story that the Craigmillar Council resolved on the "warding," that is, the imprisonment, of Darnley. This question was evidently a rumour which had reached Darnley's ears and therefore his father's, and it is mentioned in the alleged "long" Letter from Glasgow, in words which I have no doubt are genuinely those written by the Queen, "He said that Minto sent him word that it was said that some of the Council had brought me a letter to sign to put him in prison and to kill him if he did resist...[1]." Mary in this "Letter" does not trouble to note the rumour as false, but this is inferable from her letter to the Archbishop of Glasgow dated 20 January[2] (1567), that is, several days before her conversation with Darnley noted above, "Only this far he (Heigate) confessed that he had heard a bruit how the King should be put in ward...." Heigate named another as the author of the story, who was also sent for and denied it, and Mary concludes, "In fine, amongst them all we find no manner of concordance...."

To my way of thinking this perfectly effortless letter of Mary's to the Archbishop, is the strongest possible confirmation of the genuineness of a part of the so-called *Letter* which looms so large in the volumes of argument on the subject of the Casket Letters[3].

Apart from the matter just referred to there is the other more important communication of Heigate, that Darnley had formed

[1] The last eight words are probably not genuine. Lennox does not go so far, he is content with "he should have been apprehended and put in ward." Mary's letter above quoted to the Archbishop, which is obviously frank, does not go beyond warding either. It seems certain that Lennox would have added this had it been part of the original "rumour."

[2] Reprinted by Keith from the *Records of the Scots College*.

[3] The German writer, Bernard Sepp, goes near the truth when he describes this Letter as a "Tagebuch," perhaps "Denkschrift-Notizen" would have been a better title. Very much of Sepp's work is wide of the mark, but there is, to my mind, scarcely a doubt that Mary scribbled notes of her days in Glasgow for subsequent entry in her diary; whether the elaborated diary or the notes only fell into the hands of her enemies, need not be guessed at. Mr Henderson has a very learned exposition of the difficulty of a forger in imitating a hand moved by various emotions, and I daresay he is quite right, but he seems to beg the question in assuming that the persons who examined the letters would have been capable of judging these niceties. But in any case Mr Henderson's argument carries its own condemnation, for we are expressly told that the Letters were "Duly conferred and compared, for the manner of writing and *fashion of orthography* with sundry other letters long since heretofore written and sent by the said Queen of Scots to the Queen's Majesty." It must therefore follow, either that the "sundry letters" exhibited all these emotions, which is absurd, or that the handwriting of the Casket Letters did not exhibit them, for in the collation "No difference was found" (*Proceedings at Hampton Court*, 14 Dec. 1568).

a plot *to crown the infant prince and assume the government him-self*, and, presumably, though not mentioned, do away with the Queen. Lennox omits this altogether, as does Buchanan, though both must have known all about it. Both the Casket Letter and the Queen's letter to the Archbishop refer to it, and the case was examined by the Council at Stirling. There seems no doubt that the whole enquiry took place at Stirling after the ceremony of the Baptism and *after* Darnley had fled to Glasgow, yet Lennox tells us that it was his warning on the subject that was the cause of Darnley's quitting Stirling. This is ingenious, and it may well be that knowledge of the Queen's intended enquiry into the Heigate disclosures had something to do with it, but without doubt another and more potent cause was the pardon of Morton, which the Queen had been persuaded to sign. Of Morton, Darnley stood not unnaturally in mortal dread, and he probably did not wait to hear the precautions taken for his safety, of prohibiting the Earl from approaching within seven miles of the court.

PARAGRAPH VIII

Synopsis. The Queen had no correspondence with her sick husband. She removes the baby prince from Stirling to Edinburgh. She then makes excuses to her husband for her inattention to him, and offers to come to Glasgow to visit him. Darnley sends an insulting message in reply.

Whether it is true that no correspondence passed between the Queen and her husband from the time of his leaving Stirling until her arrival in Edinburgh, that is, from 23 December to 13 January cannot be proved, but it is very unlikely. Bedford reported on 9 January from Berwick that she had sent a physician to see to the reported sickness of Darnley; as Bedford's news was not of quite recent date the sending may have taken place as soon as the sickness was known, and no doubt some communication passed at the same time[1]. Nau in his *Memoir*

---

[1] It is possible of course that the services of the physician may have been refused by Darnley, which would account for Buchanan's statement in the *Detection*, "The Queen would not suffer so much as a physician to come to him." That Buchanan should go out of his way to mention the matter seems to be a confirmation that there passed some question of sending one.

says that Darnley sent several times to the Queen, but does not say when. The "long" Glasgow Letter confirms this: "I enquired him of his *letters*, wherein he complained of the cruelty of some....And thus he said, it is of you alone that will not accept my offers and repentance." It is in fact certain that there had been an interchange of letters, but that Darnley ever sent the offensive message which Lennox refers to is so entirely out of accord with the statement just quoted as to "offers and repentance," that it must be rejected. Lennox omits it in his later narratives.

PARAGRAPH IX

Synopsis. Mary in reply sends loving messages, to drive suspicion out of his head. She visits Glasgow and persuades Darnley to return to Edinburgh with her. Lennox never suspected any sinister intention. Arrived in Edinburgh, she takes her husband to Kirk o' Field, already prepared for the murder, Darnley is unwilling to go there, but she induces him to obey her saying that she can see him frequently.

We are now coming to Lennox's account of the death of Darnley, and it is very interesting to note in how many respects this varies from the official narrative put forward by Buchanan, and the connected documents which were submitted to the Commission appointed by Elizabeth in the autumn of 1568. It is perhaps well to recall that the principal witnesses of the affair were servants of Lennox; Thomas Nelson was a survivor of Kirk o' Field and continued in Lennox's service after his departure from Scotland, Thomas Crawford was also his man though it is not clear if he was at any time in his household in England. Lennox must have discussed the events many times with these two. He was present in Glasgow during the Queen's visit to her sick husband in January (1567) and in the closest possible contact with the subsequent proceedings. His statement ought to take a high place in value, let me repeat that this document is independent of extraneous influences.

Lennox commences by asserting that *before* the Queen left Edinburgh she had prepared "all things ready for the execution of her horrible purpose," and a few lines further on he tells us what the preparations were, "The place (that is, Kirk o' Field) that was *already* prepared with undermines and trains of powder." There is not a word as to any alternative intention of taking the invalid to Craigmillar. Yet Thomas Nelson, Lennox's confidential servant, swore that he remembered that the first intention was that the King should go to Craigmillar, "But because he had no will thereof the purpose was altered and conclusion taken that he should lie beside the Kirk o' Field...." Nelson in short contradicts Lennox, for it is clear that he explains the going to Kirk o' Field to have been an afterthought.

We are then faced with the alternatives that Nelson was lying, or that Lennox was concealing something that he must have known, if Nelson knew it, for purposes of his own. My view is that Nelson was, on the 9th December (1568), when he gave his evidence before Elizabeth's Commissioners, permitted to tell the truth, because it fitted the scheme as it stood then. But Lennox, writing in the previous May, was confining himself to the story as devised up to that date[1].

Besides this, we have the extracts of the letter quoted by the Spanish Ambassador in London, de Silva, referred to below (Para. XIII), which clearly indicate Kirk o' Field, and omit all reference to Craigmillar, and thus provide evidence that this letter belongs to the earlier scheme. It is true that Mr Henderson, to whose argument it was necessary to show that the de Silva extracts are not essentially different from the corresponding parts of the "long" Glasgow Letter, as it has come to us, attempts to show that Craigmillar is referred to. He looks on the sentence, "She said she would stop at a house on the road, where she would try to give him (Darnley) a draught, but if this could not be done she would put him in a house where the explosion was arranged..." as meaning that Craigmillar was the "house on the road." But Craigmillar is not on the road of a party approaching Edinburgh from Glasgow, and it is too great a stretch of imagination to suppose that this place was in question.

[1] This matter is more fully dealt with in the next chapter and in Note G at the end of this volume.

However, neglecting this we have the remarkable plan, according to Mr Henderson, that Darnley was first to be carried to Craigmillar and after treatment there, the purified, purged and partly poisoned prince, was to be taken to Kirk o' Field, there to be comfortably blown up in the sight and hearing of the populace of the Capital—which is preposterous!

The ill-fitting conjunction of Craigmillar and Kirk o' Field which appears in the evidence, and which Lennox suppressed, is not to be explained in this way. In the next chapter I have ventured on a more simple solution, but for the moment let us pass on without touching on the evidence of the persons executed for complicity in the murder. This evidence, which clearly Lennox knew nothing about, effectually destroys his story of the *previous* preparation of Kirk o' Field, but it belongs to the consideration of what really happened at that place, and this cannot be touched on in this volume.

PARAGRAPH X

Synopsis. She visits him every night, uses him well and arranges the day when he shall return to Holyrood.

We have here Lennox's word for it that the day was "appointed" on which the quarantine should be considered complete and a return made, from Kirk o' Field, to the palace. A little further on (see Para. XI) we find, "The day before his death she caused the rich bed wherein he lay to be taken down and a meaner set up in the place, saying to him that that rich bed they should both lie in the *next night* in the palace...." By "day before" we must suppose Sunday 9 February is meant, and that Monday was the "appointed" day. This is a useful piece of information and it accounts for the choice of the day of the explosion as the last of his intended residence. It also serves to destroy the evidence given by his own man Nelson, who said that the bed had been taken away several days before to avoid soiling it with the bath. The *Book of Articles* says that the bed was removed on the Friday, but the discordancy is only of importance in that Lennox probably told the true reason for the removal, that is, that it should be used at the palace on the Monday. The Venetian, Giovani Correr, confirms this on the authority of Moretta, who was in Edinburgh, "The Queen having promised him that on the following night she would sleep with him."

PARAGRAPH XI

Synopsis. Darnley is entirely without suspicion of evil and writes to his father of his return to health and happiness. The Queen sees the letter and lovingly kisses him. She orders the bed to be taken down so that it may not be destroyed by the pending explosion, but tells him that he shall sleep in it at Holyrood the next night.

It is somewhat remarkable that this letter of Darnley describing his happy state, which Lennox reproduces, was written on the day when the Queen is supposed to have learnt from him that Lord Robert Stewart had apprised him of a plot for his murder[1]. The "guilty" Queen took the strange course of confronting the two on the following morning and of calling in Moray to listen to the story, in order, it must be supposed, to make the matter as public as possible. Was there ever so extraordinary a murderess? Lennox, perhaps wisely, omits the story and it is also noteworthy that, on the night of his death, Darnley, reminiscent of some words of the Queen regarding Rizzio's murder, which he and his servant discussed before singing their go-to-bed psalms, as Lennox tells us, no memory of the alleged plot seems to have disturbed him, though the scene had taken place but the day before.

It is a coincidence, if nothing more, that at the time these events were in progress rumours of a plot against the Queen of Scots were current in Paris. The Spanish Ambassador there, Don Francis de Alava, seems to have been more "in the know" than anyone else. We have two reports on the subject, the one

---

[1] See *Detection*, "About three days before that the King was slain she practised to set her brother, Lord Robert, and him (Darnley) at deadly feud....For matter to ground their dissension she made rehearsal of the speech that the King had had with her concerning her brother."

from the Archbishop of Glasgow in a letter to Mary dated at
Paris, 27 January:

> The Ambassador of Spain...specially required (me) to advertise
> you to take heed to yourself. I have heard some murmurings like-
> wise by others that there be some surprise to be trafficked in your
> contrary, but he (the Ambassador) would never let me know of no
> particular, only assured me he had written to his master to know
> if by that way he can try any further (Not clear what this means),
> and that he was advertised and counselled to cause me to haste
> towards you herewith. Further in this instance *and at his desire*
> (my italics) partly, I spake earnestly to know at the Queen Mother
> if she had heard any discourse or advertisement lately tending to
> your hurt or disadvantage, but I got no speed...

The other comes from the same source through the Spanish
Ambassador in London, "The Duchess of Parma writes to me
that Don Francis de Alava had advised her that he had news of
a plot being formed in Scotland against the Queen...."

If we are to understand from the above that after Don
Francis had his news he had time to write to Philip and to
receive his orders before 27 January it seems that the date of the
first intelligence must have been early in the month or perhaps
near about the time of the baptism. One is reminded that at
that time Mary was investigating the statement of Heigate that
Darnley had formed a plot to crown the infant and assume the
government, as stated above[1] (p. 89). It might also be supposed from the rather pointed remarks of the Archbishop that
he suspected the Queen-Mother of some knowledge of the
affair. Complete consideration of this matter does not belong
to our present subject.

Briefly reviewing these points it would seem that the avoid-
ance by Lennox of the confession of Heigate touching Darnley's
plot, and of the story of Lord Robert's accusation, was not
accidental but induced by the knowledge that the subject was

---

[1] See also the "long" Glasgow Letter, "As to the rest of Willie
Heigate's he confessed it, but it was the morn after my coming or he
did it." These words are, I think, undoubtedly a part of genuine
writings of the Queen.

not a safe one to handle. One can hardly avoid the suspicion that, in the Robert Stewart scene, the boot was on the other leg and that what the Queen learnt on that Friday night was not of a plot to murder Darnley, but of a plot which was some echo of that reported by Heigate. The calling in of Moray would be then quite understandable.

I must confess, too, to some doubts about the sincerity of Darnley's letter to his father, referred to in this paragraph. It is a little too effusive from a man whose plotting had already been made known and who was to be involved in further disclosures on that very day, a man too, who had offered repentance and ascribed his faults to his youth. This letter would have reached Lennox probably on Saturday; whether it contained a signal quite other than its words suggest cannot here be investigated.

PARAGRAPH XII

Synopsis. On the night of the murder (Sunday, 9 February) she remained with him until late; she would have stayed all night but for the persuasion of Bothwell and others, but this was only to deceive Darnley. After her departure Darnley orders his horses to be ready the next morning at 5 o'clock. He calls to mind some words of the Queen, which disturb him. After some conversation with his servants he goes to bed.

Here we have a very remarkable divergence from the Official Narrative and this part of the Lennox Paper deserves close attention. The frequently repeated reason for hurriedly quitting Kirk o' Field, which the Official documents put into Mary's mouth was her sudden recollection of her promise to attend the wedding party of one of her servants. But Lennox knows nothing of this; she was *persuaded* by Bothwell not to stay all night *because* she had arranged to ride early next day to Seton. Nothing about Bastian's marriage, nothing about that strong point of Paris coming in to give the signal that all was ready for the explosion, nothing about Paris at all, of whom so much is said elsewhere. Yet Nelson knew all about this, and Lennox could only have known about the ride to Seton, etc., from Nelson, who says something quite different in his " evidence."

Then comes the curious piece of information which occurs nowhere else and which must have come from Nelson, that Darnley had ordered his horse for five o'clock the next morning. A strange hour on a February morning for an invalid to take his first exercise after a dangerous illness. So strange that it would appear that Lennox had some reason for putting it in his story.

It is perhaps desirable to draw attention again to the curious fact that all this independent evidence is dropped by Lennox when, *after* his contact with Mr John Wood, he composed his second and third narratives[1]. In these he has learnt what he apparently knew nothing of previously, the examinations of Tallo, Powrie and the others; he cuts out the whole of the details of Darnley's last hours and gives Nelson a free run on his new recollections of the tragedy. It is impossible to suppose that if he had known of these examinations, he would not have coloured his document with some at least of their "confessions." The fact of his ignorance shows how extraordinarily secret these matters were kept, and how little foundation there is for the assumption that the contents of the Casket Letters were known through their exhibition in the Parliament of December, 1567. My personal opinion is that the untutored Lennox is a more reliable witness than the instructed Lennox of the later period.

PARAGRAPH XIII

Synopsis. Lennox digresses to recall the significant words of a letter which he alleges passed from the Queen to Bothwell while she was in Glasgow. He also recalls words alleged to have been used by the Queen to Darnley on the occasion of Rizzio's murder. Also some words that she let fall after her visit to Bothwell during the sojourn at Jedburgh, in the previous autumn.

We come to the Lennox quotation of the "long" Glasgow Letter. Very briefly the circumstances are these. In July of the previous year (1567) the Earl of Moray when passing through London on his return to Scotland, communicated to the Spanish Ambassador there, the contents of a (only one is mentioned)

---

[1] Both documents in Cambridge Univ. Lib., Press marks Oo. 7.47/11 and Dd. 3. 66.

letter, which he, Moray, had been told of (verbally?) by a man who had read it. The Ambassador wrote his recollections of Moray's communication to his master (Philip) and of this we have the original preserved in the Simancas Archives. Thus the Ambassador's version had passed through three memories, first of the "man who had read it" and taken the long journey between Edinburgh and France before repeating it, second Moray himself who in the meantime had travelled to London, thirdly, the Ambassador, who, unless he wrote from Moray's dictation, must have trusted to his memory.

From whom Moray received his information we are quite uncertain. On 21 June (1567), the very day of the alleged opening of the famous Casket, Maitland wrote to Cecil, but beyond saying that the bearer would explain his reasons for taking sides against the Queen, there is nothing to indicate that he had just become participant of such momentous information. His letter[1] would indeed be a strange one from a man who had just learned on irrefutable evidence that his Queen whom he had "reverenced," as he said in it, was an adulteress, a murderess and treacherous beyond description. Yet if Morton's story of the finding of the Casket is true, Maitland must have learned all this at the moment of writing. The bearer would have arrived in London about the 26th and on that day Cecil *did* send some packets to Moray, then in France, expressing the hope that he would return at once[2]. There were other urgent packets sent to Moray besides this one, on other dates, but in no case is there any indication that the bearer was one of the persons who was present at the opening of the Casket or the "sighting" of the contents. It seems extraordinarily unlikely that a verbal message conveyed by an unnamed person who had "read the letter" should have been sent[3].

[1] *Calendar of Scottish State Papers*, Maitland to Cecil, 21 June,1567.
[2] Cabala, Cecil to Norris, 26 June, 1567.
[3] Henderson and Lang are not at one on this point. The former nominates George Douglas as the messenger, but this is not likely, for he left Edinburgh on the 20th June, and he certainly did not go to France at once.

Then there is the language difficulty which I think our authors do not sufficiently consider. De Silva, the Ambassador, had no English, Moray is most unlikely to have spoken Spanish, French was probably the medium, Latin was not probable; then it amounts to this, a Scot told Moray something, Moray translated it into French, let us say, to the Ambassador, the latter put it into Spanish and told Philip, and Froude or Martin Hume has translated the Spanish into English which we have now in the *Calendar of the Simancas Records*.

With so much filtration, whether of memory or of translation, it is very improbable that we have the same ingredients as existed in the original sample. It seems more than likely that what Moray did was to quote from a letter which he had had from Maitland or Morton or some other of the principals, in which a general statement of the contents of the famous letter was given. Yet even so, and Mr Henderson notwithstanding, there are some items given by de Silva which do not exist in the "Letter" as we have it now, and which no statement, however general, could have woven into it. Andrew Lang seems to have justification in his argument that the "Letter" as quoted to de Silva was not precisely the same as when it emerged finally.

What we are especially interested in here, is that Lennox's quotations bear a strong family resemblance to those of de Silva, so strong that with confidence we may say that they were based on the same source. There seems no difficulty, such as occurred to Lang, in supposing that Lennox heard of these matters at the same time as de Silva, but had no occasion to use them until when he was preparing the "Supplication" a year later. The items used are practically similar, though clothed in different language, easily accountable by the translation difficulties of de Silva, and Lennox confirms de Silva in the radical (as I think) departures from the accepted "Letter[1]."

It is remarkable that out of eight letters supposed to have been found all together, only one should be quoted from or

---

[1] For easy reference I have printed the two quotations side by side at pp. 136-7.

referred to either by de Silva or Lennox. It might be argued that Moray's correspondent or messenger, whichever it was, told him of the whole discovery, but said that one of the letters contained so and so. Still it is odd that nothing is taken from the "short" Glasgow letter which is a pendant of the other. And it is odd that out of a "Letter" of some three thousand words, so many things are omitted; all reference to Craigmillar, and the bath and the secret invention by poison, and how her heart bled at her treachery and a score of other things which will occur to a reader who looks through the "Letter" in question. Oddest of all, that things should be quoted which are not in the "Letter" as we know it and that both de Silva and Lennox should quote them. In the following chapter I have dealt with a probable explanation of these discrepancies.

PARAGRAPH XIV

Synopsis. Lennox hints that the Queen was present at the murder of her husband dressed in man's apparel.

Lennox here tells us of the report that the Queen was present at the murder dressed in "man's apparel." This item is of course given up in his later narratives for it would not agree with the official story, but some attention to it is desirable. The Sunday of the murder was the last before Lent and given by custom to much festivity, masquerading and processions. The Queen, according to the evidence of Clerneau, went to Kirk o' Field, "Masked[1]," and this would probably mean in some sort of what we call "fancy dress" of which she had a number in her wardrobe. She was certainly given to amusements of this kind but whether it is true that she used to dance "secretly with the King her husband" in male attire or pass through the streets in any such costume, I cannot say; there would be no harm in it if she did. It is recorded that Catherine de Medicis used to walk masked through the streets of Paris and from the days of Harun al Raschid onwards it seems to have been a proclivity of royalty. I will leave the matter at this, that it is quite likely that Mary

[1] *Papal Negotiations*, Mondovi to Alessandria, Paris, 27 Feb. 1567.

7–2

was, on the occasion of her visit to her husband, disguised in some form of fancy dress[1], and this makes it not impossible that she was personated at the actual scene of the murder.

Synopsis. The quarrel between the Queen and her husband at Stirling at the time of the baptism is mentioned and the words that passed at the time.

The quarrel at Stirling between the Queen and her husband is pretty well authenticated. Lennox in his second and third narratives gives some further details of it; the former puts it:

When the King desolate of his servants was accompanied with certain honest men of the Lennox appointed by me (Earl of Lennox) to await on him at the christening time, she said to him, he come to do her spite, but she would spite him at the heart for it. Saying he had a goodly company of Lennox men with him, he asked why she should find fault therewith, she said there were too many Lennox men there and if they were without the Castle they should not come in again, he answered they should go where he went and if they were without the Castle and he with them, they should either enter with him or he would make an entry for them....

Lennox gives a good deal away; Buchanan is more circumspect in the *Detection* and merely says that his (Darnley's) servants were taken away. There seems every reason to connect the story with the enquiry which took place shortly after into the report of Heigate and Walker, that Darnley was aiming at a revolutionary movement in which the infant prince was to figure as nominal sovereign while the rule remained in his own hands. It seems certain that Darnley had backing which has never reached publicity[2]; the warning of the Archbishop of

---

[1] This small point may be of value when consideration is given to what actually happened at Kirk o' Field.

[2] We should not forget that the *Continuator* of Holinshed hints that the confession of Morton made years afterwards (1581) contained much more than was made public, and among other things he laid, "The cause, the contriving, and the execution of the murder on great persons now living." Nor should we forget the suspicious movements of those two harbingers of misfortune, the envoys Moretta and Du Croc, during and after the event.

Glasgow, already referred to, the letters of Sir Henry Norris at the time of the murder and his reiterated opinion, " As at first I thought thereof, I remain not to be removed, which was that the origin of the fact came from hence (Paris) for besides that their desire is (as I am advertised) to have the Prince hither, so do I see that all they that are suspected for the same fact make this their chief refuge and sure anchor[1]," all point the same way.

The matter belongs rather to the mystery of Kirk o' Field; for the present it will be enough to surmise that the true cause of the quarrel at Stirling was the suspicious behaviour of Darnley in bringing together a too numerous body of clansmen, a proceeding in which it is clear that his father was aiding and abetting. We may recall the words of the Casket Letter, "The Earl of Lennox...came not to meet me because he durst not enterprise to do so considering the sharp words that I had spoken to Cunningham (at Stirling), and that he desired that I would come to the inquisition of (enquiry into) the facts which I did suspect him (Lennox) of...I told him...he would have no fear if he did not feel himself faulty[2]."

PARAGRAPH XVI

Synopsis. Lennox returns to the murder. The king being asleep, Bothwell accompanied with sixteen others enter his chamber and strangle him, the house being in meantime surrounded. They then carry the dead body out into the garden, with that of his servant William Taylor, likewise strangled, laying beside the bodies the purple "night gown" used by Darnley. The conspirators then blow up the house with gunpowder. The Queen having waited to hear the noise went to bed. (Here the Manuscript ends abruptly.)

Lennox's account of the tragedy is obviously at variance with the official story. Fifty men surrounded the house, of whom sixteen were in company with Bothwell; this latter party entered Darnley's bedchamber and suffocated him there with a napkin

[1] Norris to Throgmorton, 5 April, 1567, in the Public Record Office. See also Cabala, Cecil to Norris, 21 March, 1567, "We heard before your writing of the French attempt for the prince."

[2] English translation of the "long" Glasgow Letter. *State Papers*, Public Record Office.

steeped in vinegar, after which they carried his body and his dressing-gown into "the garden" and likewise the body of William Taylor, "who suffered death in like sort."

All this must be at least partly imaginary, for if Nelson's story is true he and the other survivors were asleep, so that there were no eye-witnesses of the method employed, at least none who gave any account of it. It is interesting, however, to note that the house was surrounded; this is a matter which would probably be known at the time; Cecil on his first information, writing to Norris, mentioned thirty as the number employed[1]. The official account limited the number to nine. Dr Thomas Wilson (?) in the *Oration* says, "They thought it not enough to have set open the postern in the wall...nor to have set an ambushment before the door, that none should escape, but also, etc." The Venetian Ambassador in France, Giovani Correr, had a different story, derived from Moretta, who had exceptional means of knowing all that was said: "Towards midnight the King heard a great disturbance, at least certain women who live in the neighbourhood declare, and from a window they perceived many armed men round about the house, so he (Darnley) suspecting what might befall him, let himself down from another window looking on a garden, but he had not proceeded far before he was surrounded by certain persons who strangled him with the sleeves of his own shirt under the very window from whence he had descended, one of his chamberlains followed him...." Buchanan in his *History* has yet another version, that the body was carried through a door specially made for the purpose in the wall! There are other variations, but these are the principal accounts; the remarkable point is that the "official" account suppresses all mention of the wider ramifications of the plot and seeks to confine it to the work of Bothwell and a few of his servants acting on the instigation of the Queen.

The Lennox Narrative breaks off at this point; whether if he had completed it we should have been given any more hints than the above displays, cannot be said. One thing is certain,

[1] Cabala, Cecil to Norris, 20 Feb. 1567.

Darnley was not killed in the house, and Lennox and the compilers of the official narrative, and I think one may say the compilers of the official "evidence," apparently had their own reasons for concealing the facts. It does not belong to this section of the case to deal with the mystery of Kirk o' Field further; my object has been rather to draw attention to what may be learnt from this independent story, than to apply this knowledge, which must be combined with many other things, to arrive at a true conception of what happened on that tragic occasion.

CHAPTER IV

Consideration of the Casket Letters fills many volumes and I would avoid it if possible. Yet the authors, whether for or against the Queen, have followed each other in distressingly long dissections of the famous "long" Letter to the comparative exclusion of the "short" Glasgow Letter. The aim of this chapter is to bring the importance and significance of the latter into prominence, and at the same time to offer a very simple explanation of its origin.

THE GLASGOW LETTERS

I DO not wish to conceal, in fact I suppose I have not concealed, that my sympathies are with the Queen of Scots! Yet I have rather followed where reason leads, than started with formed convictions. My reason tells me that it is impossible that the Queen could have written such a " Letter " as the famous long epistle of three thousand words or so; every antecedent trait of her character, every scrap of accurate knowledge of her past life and environment, every one of the countless contradictions, chronological inexactitudes, and misstatements of historical fact which the "case" discloses, fortifies my reason in its conclusion.

Yet, at least to me, it is obvious that when, after several months, the rebellious Lords decided on their course of action, they did not set to work and forge the two Glasgow Letters. To do so as has been said would require an ingenuity beyond the possible devilishness of the human mind. But to weave into a plot the evidence of existing papers, which chance made suitable, required no great cleverness, and in truth the thing has been clumsily done. Forgery in those days was a fine art frequently practised; there are many instances of its employment, and, though I lay no great stress on it, I think that the first idea did not go beyond a *single* forged letter, based on the same genuine document which is the backbone of the "long" Letter as we have it. Whether this was so or not does not matter, for it is clear that the second idea of a *pair* of letters superseded it, and undoubtedly the first Letter, if it existed alone, required alteration to fit the new conditions; some of the points dwelt on in the previous chapter seem to give credence to this view.

The view that I shall put forward in this chapter is that No. 1 Letter, that is, the "short" Letter, is a genuine document, written and signed by Mary, and sent to Bothwell. It is, I say, the centre and main prop of the whole scheme on which the prosecution chiefly relied. Except in one respect it may be that the original was *entirely* unaltered, that one respect being the addition of the words "From Glasgow" in the date. There would be nothing unusual in the letter being simply dated, "This Saturday Morning"; instances of such could be quoted. I suggest that this is all that appeared on the original. As we have it, the date of course indicates 25 January, this being the only Saturday that the Queen was in Glasgow. I aim at showing in the following that the true date was Saturday, 11 January, and that the letter was written from Stirling and sent to Bothwell at Dunbar.

Before going further I would refresh the memories of readers on two points. That there is no trace of the *original* "Letters," written in French and exhibited to Elizabeth's Commissioners in 1568; we have only translated copies, in English, prepared for the Commissioners, and in Scottish. Of the latter there are at least three examples; in the main the variations between these three are unimportant and due perhaps to differences in copying. There is preserved in addition the first two or three lines of each letter in what is assumed to be the original French, and judging from this the English translation is more accurate than the Scottish. The second point concerns a matter debated by the disputants on one side or the other. The Letters when first mentioned were said to be signed, but later were said to be wholly in the Queen's hand but not signed. The explanation of this seems to be that it was Mary's custom to prepare drafts of her letters which were then copied by a secretary and signed by her; in very few cases did a letter issue in signed holograph. We have as an instance the long letter written by her to her uncle the

Duke of Guise, of which Father Pollen has given an interesting monograph; this is a draft and was not intended for signature.

In the case of Letter No. 1 it appears to me that both the signed copy which was not in her hand and the unsigned draft which was, fell into the hands of her enemies; they at first intended to use the signed copy but ultimately decided on the draft as being a better witness than the other, it was the draft only which was produced in London. A possible reason for this is that there never was a genuine signed Letter No. 2, but we need not waste time over this. Let us now proceed to put together the details relied on as a basis for the hypothesis advanced above.

I. THE ANTECEDENT EVENTS

It will be remembered that the Earl of Morton and some others were banished from Scotland for complicity in the murder of Rizzio. Notwithstanding Mary's representations to Elizabeth they remained in England, and at the time of the baptism, December, 1566, they were at Newcastle. Morton and his friends rightly attributed their misfortunes to the treachery of Darnley, and they entertained the bitterest animosity towards him. A letter written many years later by Archibald Douglas to the Queen narrates the circumstances:

...It may please your Majesty to remember that in the year of God 1566 the said Earl of Morton with divers others nobility and gentry were declared rebels by your Majesty and banished your realm...always such was the careful mind of His Majesty (of France) towards the quietness of that realm, that the dealing in that case was committed to M. de Mauvissière who was directed at that time to go into Scotland to congratulate the happy birth of your son...the careful travail of the said de Mauvissière was so effectual and your Majesty's mind so inclined to mercy that within a short space hereafter I was permitted to repair to Scotland...to make offer in the name of the said Earl of any matter that might satisfy your Majesty's wrath and procure your clemency...(the letter concludes) I returned to Stirling where at the request of the most Christian King and the Queen's Majesty of England, by their Ambassadors present, Your Majesty's gracious pardon was granted unto them all, under condition always that they should remain forth of the realm the space of two years, and further during your Majesty's pleasure. Which limitations was after mitigated at the humble request of your own nobility so that immediately after, the said Earl of Morton repaired to Scotland to Whittinghame, where the Earl of Bothwell and Lethington came to him...[1].

Now this Archibald, writer of the above, was without question a most unmitigated scoundrel. He was at the moment in seclusion, deeming the fate of Morton a sufficient warning, and he was endeavouring to ingratiate himself with Mary, in order to procure her mediation with her son for his return to Scotland. She had written to Mauvissière, "I promised him (Douglas) to do my best for him....However learn from him the main cause of his banishment, for if he is in any way connected with the death of the late King my husband, I will never intercede for him[2]." I think Mary was anxious to be persuaded of Archibald's innocence, for she must have known that he was far from spotless, but at the time, she thought that he would be useful to her son who was emerging from the Gowrie plot. However, the reply quoted above was his extenuation of his share in the affair, and he added the information, which may or may not be true, that Moray, Atholl, Bothwell, Argyll, and other lords entered into a "band" with the banished lords to have nothing to do with Darnley as King, and with this as a basis, it was agreed that Moray and company should intercede with Mary for the recall of Morton. This was in fact the basis of the famous conference at Craigmillar of which we hear so much, but there is no suggestion here or anywhere that Mary knew anything about this secret understanding at the time. The information tendered by Archibald Douglas of course dates from some sixteen years later than the Craigmillar affair.

The story given above of the pardon of Morton is in the main correct except that when the two years' banishment was remitted, a prohibition to approach within seven miles of the court was substituted. That Mary granted the pardon with great reluctance

---

[1] *Bannatyne Memorials*, Trial of Archibald Douglas, letter dated 1583.
[2] Jebb, vol. II, p. 535, Mary to Mauvissière, 12 Nov. 1583.

is, I think, unquestionable. In the previous August, the Earl of
Bedford wrote to Cecil, "Mauvissière worketh all he can for
the calling home of the Lords that are abroad, some thought
that he would not have done anything for them, much less thus
much as now he doth...." Finally it was not until 24 December
(1566) that Mary gave way. The time was just after the baptism;
she yielded to the united pressure of England and France;
Bedford recorded the result, "The Queen has granted the Earl
of Morton and the Lords Ruthven and Lindsay, their relaxation,
wherein Moray has done very friendly for them, *as I have done
by your advice*. Bothwell, Atholl and all the other lords helped
therein, else it should not have been so soon gotten[1]."

I have dwelt at some length on this subject, and more evidence might be adduced, in order to show that the recall of Morton
was permitted by Mary under pressure and against her better
judgment. Mr Malcolm Laing's suggestion that Bedford's inter-
cession was made at Mary's request, is positively malicious. His
object is to lead his readers to suppose that the subsequent
disasters were sought by Mary through the intervention of
Morton; Laing may base his assertion on Melville's *Memoire*,
but the above statement is irrefutable.

Undoubtedly Mary knew the serious nature of the step;
undoubtedly she disliked and distrusted Morton; undoubtedly
she knew that he would do all he could to revenge himself on
Darnley; undoubtedly she was weak and foolish to accede to
the pressure put upon her; but that is all there is to say. She
took such steps as were possible to minimize the effect by ordering Morton to avoid the court.

We must suppose that the document granting pardon to
Morton was duly drawn and registered and that it contained the
conditions under which the grant was made; unfortunately and
suspiciously it has disappeared. It was dated 24 December and
Morton did not enter Scotland until 10 January (1567); he made
his way first to Wedderburn and thence to Whittinghame, where

---

[1] *State Papers, Scotland*, under date 30 Dec. 1566, Bedford to
Cecil.

dwelt his cousin William Douglas, brother of Archibald afore-mentioned. Unfortunately we do not know the precise date of his arrival at the latter place; we have only Drury's report to Cecil dated 23 January: "The Lord Morton lieth at the Lord of Whittinghame's where the Lord Bothwell and Lethington *came of late* to visit[1]." It is pretty clear that Drury did not hear immediately of the fact mentioned; he was usually very precise. It seems probable that Morton had been at Whittinghame some time and I think he went there very soon after his entry into Scotland, say about the 12th or thereabouts.

Now let us return to the Queen; the ceremonies of the baptism were completed and the party broken up by the 24th December, 1566; the Earl of Bedford had departed to be fêted by Moray at St Andrews. Darnley fled on that day, whether alarmed at the danger from Morton or on account of the Heigate disclosures. Mary was in bad health and exhausted by the efforts of the past festivities. Du Croc wrote on the 23rd, "She continues to be so pensive and melancholy, she sent for me yesterday and I found her laid on the bed weeping sore, she complained of a grievous pain in her side...[2]." Hardly a doubt that the decision as to Morton, and Darnley's foolish behaviour affected her. In other matters there was cause for rejoicing; Bedford had brought proposals from Elizabeth which went some way to settle the question of the succession; a conference had been agreed on. Now of all times accord with her husband would have been desirable. There is not a hint in Bedford's letters or in any others of any unseemly conduct toward Bothwell.

Between the 24th December and the end of the month Mary paid two short visits to Tullibardine and "Drymen"; whether these were for change or in connection with State affairs is not known; Murray of Tullibardine appears to have been a friend of Darnley and the Lennox faction; it may well be that Mary's

[1] *Border State Papers*, Drury to Cecil, 23 Jan. 1567.
[2] *Scottish College*, Paris, printed in Keith, Du Croc to Archbishop Glasgow, 23 Dec. 1566.

visit was to obtain his assistance to bring her errant husband to reason. It is the more likely that Darnley's affairs and the safe-guards and assurances as to Morton were under discussion, that the Queen took Bothwell with her, possibly Lethington also, but this is not stated.

Mary returned to Stirling on the 31st December or 1st January and held a council there on the 2nd, the *sederunt* included; Huntly, Argyll, Moray and others and the Secretary Lethington, but *not* Bothwell. There is unfortunately no record of the matters discussed.

There is no absolute proof, but I suggest that there is every likelihood that after the discussion at Tullibardine, Bothwell was sent to open negotiations with Morton as to the question of reconciliation with Darnley, and the terms on which he would be received into favour again. Bothwell would undoubtedly take up his residence at Dunbar, within a few miles of Whittinghame, there to await the arrival of the culprit. Bothwell would arrive at Dunbar about the 3rd January; I suggest that he carried the "pardon" with him; if so the delay in the arrival of Morton into Scotland would be accounted for, but even so either Bothwell was slow in communicating with Newcastle or Morton was slow in responding, for some nine days elapsed before Morton came to Whittinghame[1].

Meanwhile Lethington was married in Stirling on the 6th January; he was also present there at a Council on the 10th. Again there is no absolute proof but I suggest that Lethington left Stirling with his bride after the Council and proceeded for a honeymoon to his paternal mansion of Lethington near Whittinghame; he would arrive there on the 11th or 12th. We have seen that he certainly was at Whittinghame on a date which Drury described on the 23rd as "of late."

One more date; Mary left Stirling probably on Sunday the 12th and arrived on Monday, 13 January, according to Birrel's *Diary*; the *Diurnal* gives the date as 14th; there are frequent differences of one day between the two journals.

---

[1] See note on the conference at Whittinghame, p. 138.

I think the reader will have no difficulty in seeing where we have got to, but let me summarize the situation; Mary in grave anxiety as to the outcome of the Morton pardon arrives in Edinburgh, *with the infant prince*, on Monday, 13 January, Bothwell has been absent since the 1st or 2nd on a mission to settle things with Morton, Mary is anxiously awaiting news, Lethington has gone to his home near Whittinghame, Mary sends a letter, from Stirling, to hurry Bothwell's news, to be delivered to Lethington for handing to Bothwell, she at the same time announces her return to Edinburgh (Craigmillar) on the Monday.

Now let us read the Letter; for simplicity I have divided it into consecutive paragraphs, and adopted the English translation.

THE SHORT GLASGOW LETTER

It seemeth that with your absence forgetfulness is joined considering that at your departure you promised me to send me news from you. Nevertheless I can learn none.

If Bothwell had acted promptly he might have had Morton's answer by the 7th or 8th January and transmitted it to Mary at Stirling. This sentence as applied to a letter from Glasgow dated 25 January is nonsense, for it is known that then Bothwell had gone to Liddesdale and could not send news.

And yet did I yesterday (the Cambridge copy has *yesternight*) look for that that should make me merrier than I shall be.

Yesterday or yesternight would be the 10th according to my hypothesis. It may well be that this was the date on which calculation would fix as the probable receipt of a communication from Bothwell after hearing from Morton. As applied to Glasgow, "yesterday" would be the 24th and according to the "Cecil" diary she had only parted from Bothwell the day before.

I think you do the like for your return, prolonging it more than you have promised.

It looks as if there was a mistake in the translation over the word "return," which is almost meaningless, whether in a letter from Glasgow or from Stirling. It is not easy to imagine what the original French was, but the word may have been "rencontre" contracted as to the middle syllable and taken for "rentrée." The idea may have been "You have prolonged (or perhaps "postponed") your meeting (*i.e.* with Morton) longer than you said you would." In any case as applied to a letter from Glasgow dated the 25th there is no sense at all, for Bothwell was even then *en route* for Jedburgh and Liddesdale which Mary must have known, and she could not have complained of his delay in returning from a journey only just commenced. Mr Malcolm Laing, zealous to prove the case against the Queen, saw this difficulty, but, *more suo*, got out of it by saying that the journey to Liddesdale was merely a blind and that Bothwell did not really go there at all. However we have, what evidently escaped Laing, the letter from Scrope, dated Carlisle, 28 January, "Yesterday the Earl of Bothwell...on the sudden did make a journey from Jedburgh into Liddesdale and did apprehend a dozen persons or thereabouts...." This quite unconscious evidence entirely destroys Laing's argument.

As for me, if I hear no other matter of you, according to my commission I bring the man, Monday, to Craigmillar, where he shall be upon Wednesday.

This is the sentence which I believe governed the whole scheme of the "Glasgow Letters" as we have them. If the letter was written from Stirling on the 11th, it means "If I hear nothing from you regarding your meeting with Morton, which might cause me to change my plans, according to the orders I have given I will, etc." The words "Bring the man" have been universally interpreted as a contemptuous reference to her husband, I think she refers to the infant prince. It is not unlikely that "*l'Homme*" was a little term used among her intimates. Let us remember that she was herself once called "*Le Gentilhomme.*" Besides there is in the *Balcarres Papers*, now in the Advocates' Library a letter from the "Old" Duchess of Guise to Mary's mother, and referring to the little son of the Duke of Guise, "*Le petit homme se porte aussi bien qu'il est possible.*" It is true enough that "*petit homme*" and "*homme,*" *tout court*, are not quite in the same category, yet I am inclined to adhere to the idea that "*homme*" was the word used, though an alternative is the substitution of this word for some other such as "*Prince*" or "*Monsieur.*" There would be little difficulty in altering "*prince*" into "*homme*"—the omission of one "m" was quite common at the time and would facilitate the change.

"*According to my Commission*" has been always held to mean, according to the orders you (Bothwell) have given to me, and in the spurious French copy it is put, "*Selon le charge que j'ai reçu.*" Mary's French would almost without doubt be "*Selon ma commission,*" or *comysion*, as she would spell it, and that would mean "according to the orders I have issued" or "the instructions I have given." "*To Craigmillar,*" round these two words centres much confusion. It was (I am giving my views) to preserve the sanctity of this precious genuine document that Craigmillar was introduced into the "long" Letter, which originally omitted it altogether; permitted to enter into Nelson's evidence which Lennox said nothing about in his Narrative; into Crawford's story; even into poor Paris's mouth, who I am sure said very little, if he said anything. I hardly think that any unprejudiced person can examine the allusions to Craigmillar in all these without noticing how "stuck on" they are, and how much better the story would be without them[1]. So much was sacrificed for "*Craigmillar*" that I cannot believe that "*Homme*" was not in the original! Do not let us forget that to Lennox, Craigmillar is, in connection with the death of his son, entirely unknown or, at least, unmentioned. Letter No. 1, as we know it, had arisen since his time, even Moray and the Spanish Ambassador knew nothing of it, when the former first communicated his version of the letter.

"*Where he shall be upon Wednesday,*" the Scottish puts it, "all Wednesday," probably the real French was "until Wednesday." It would be natural enough for the Queen to leave the child at Craigmillar for two or three days.

If one tries to weave these sentences into events connected

---

[1] See Note G at the end of this volume.

with a letter from Glasgow one comes to grief at once. I will not bore the reader by going through it.

And I to go to Edinburgh to be let blood, if I have no word to the contrary.

That Mary should go through the operation of blood-letting immediately on her return from Stirling is quite natural, it was a recognised cure for diseases of the spleen[1], and she had suffered severely from that complaint at Stirling. It is much more likely that she would have done this after the Baptism fatigues than that she should have waited until her return from Glasgow which did not happen until the beginning of February. "*If I have no word, etc.*"; this may be interpreted to mean that Bothwell's report might be such as to make it inadvisable to undergo the "cure," which necessitated lying up for a day or two. Applied to a Glasgow letter it is difficult to make any sense out of it. Why should Bothwell send word to Glasgow that she was not to be "let blood" after her return to Edinburgh?

He is the merriest that ever you saw, and doth remember unto me all that he can to make me believe that he loveth me. To Conclude, you would say that he maketh love to me.

It is really astonishing that any one can read these lines and suppose that Mary is writing of her husband, the same man of whom she wrote the previous day (or was it two days previously?) according to the Glasgow dispensation, "He desires nobody to see him...he sleeps not well....You never saw him better (that is, I suppose, in a "better frame of mind") nor speak more humbly...he has ever the tear in his eye...he has almost slain me with his breath...yet I came no nearer unto him but in a chair at the bed side and he being at the other end thereof...." Surely it must be patent that the baby is in question.

---

[1] There was a considerable controversy among physicians at the time as to which vein should be opened. In a work published in 1557, *Nova Constitutio Artis...per Venae Sectionem*, the practice of Galen of opening a vein in the left arm rather than the leg was upheld. The writer seems, however, to prefer the elbow to the hand, which was Galen's fancy!

Wherein I take so much pleasure that I never come in there but my pain of my side doth take me, I have it sore to-day.

It was a well recognised medical principle of the time that any emotion whether of pleasure or grief affected the spleen. The proper interpretation to be put on this passage is not in doubt.

To me, at all events, these extracts from this "murderous" letter indicate nothing worse than the exultation of a very loving mother. Let me recall that other letter sent later by Mary to her son then aged 3½ years, "Dear Son, I send this bearer to see you and bring me word how you do, and to remember you that you have in me a loving mother that wishes you to learn in time to love, know and fear God: and next that conform to God's command and good nature, to remember the duty anent her that has borne you in her sides....I pray God...that he will give you his blessing as I do heartily give you mine...your loving and good mother, Marie. R." And in the covering letter to the Countess of Mar, the child's governess, she says, "Also because we gave him the first coat he did wear so would we be glad he had his first doublet and long hose, likewise, of us." There are some aspects of the tragedy of Mary Stuart which no pen could pourtray!

If Paris doth bring back unto me that for which I sent, it should much amend me.

Read in conjunction with the previous clause, it can hardly be questioned that "Paris" was to bring back something to alleviate her pain. I see nothing sinister in the sentence, but I am inclined to think that it was this reference that brought poor "Paris" into the business. Again let me repeat that Lennox in his paper is ignorant of the activities of "Paris."

I pray you send me word from you at large, and what I shall do if you be not returned when I shall be there; for if you be not wise I see assuredly all the whole burden fallen upon my shoulders. Provide for all and consider well.

I read this to mean, "Send a full report of what has transpired, and if you are not returned to Edinburgh before I get

there next Monday, what should I do about going to Glasgow?
I cannot very well go there before matters are settled about
Morton. If you do not succeed in your embassy, I see that the
whole responsibility on account of the pardon (of Morton) will
fall on me. Leave no stone unturned to provide safeguards."
This is natural enough and falls into place, but it requires some
straining to fit this into a Glasgow letter, sent to a man who is
on his way to Jedburgh, whose return must be of a doubtful
date. The words seem to imply the expectation of an early
answer, but to catch Bothwell at Jedburgh or in Liddesdale and
get a reply was a matter of several days.

First of all, I send this present to Lethington to be delivered to
you, by Beton, who goeth to one day a (of?) law of Lord Balfour.
I will say no more unto you, but that I pray God send me good
news of your voyage.

In the Scottish versions the first three words belong to the
previous sentence, "*Discours first upon it with yourself.*" Moreover, the words "*present to Lethington to be delivered to you,*"
are omitted altogether in the Scottish. The former point is
unimportant, probably the Scottish is correct, but the latter
point is more interesting. It has been suggested that the reference to Lethington was purposely left out of the Scottish copies
to avoid involving him, but as the original was sacrosanct
nothing was allowed to interfere with it. I would suggest this
explanation: John Beton was almost certainly the bearer (some
writers give Archibald Beton); he was Master of the Queen's
household, the Laird of Balfour was also John Beton, and uncle
of the John in question. It has been tacitly accepted that "the
day of law" between these two Betons took place in Edinburgh,
but this is very unlikely, it is much more probable that it would
be in the Sheriff's court at St Andrews, or if it was some minor
matter, even at the family house of Balfour, or quite possibly
at Haddington. At all events, John Beton proceeding in advance
of the Queen and probably stopping in Edinburgh to settle
matters in connection with her approaching arrival, was to go
on to attend his family matters and to hand the Queen's letter

to Lethington at his home for delivery by the latter to Bothwell when they met as was probably arranged at Whittinghame. It is likely that the superscription included words to the effect that Lethington was to pass the letter on. This may account for the inclusion in the English version. Beton having completed this mission went, let us say, to Haddington or by boat to St Andrews.

In this we have a perfectly natural course of events, but it would not be possible without serious straining of the possibilities to suppose, in the first place, that Beton would have been taken to Glasgow if he had business necessitating his return to Haddington or some other place in the east of Scotland[1], and in the second place it is more than unlikely that the Queen would entrust Lethington with an incriminating document, to send on to Bothwell on an expedition in Liddesdale. Nor is it likely that she (in Glasgow on the 25th) could have been expecting early news of his "voyage" to Liddesdale whither he started on the 24th. It is also noteworthy that there is not a hint that she is anxious about Bothwell's well-being in the hasards of the business of rounding up the rebels, which I think would have been natural in so violent a lover as the Queen is supposed to have been.

Is it possible that the woman who had sat up half the night preceding to tell Bothwell that she was the most faithful lover that ever he had or ever shall have, who ended her letter by kissing his hands, and asking him to love her as she did him, etc., etc., could have written the very measured document under examination within a few hours after? Really the idea is fantastic!

From Glasgow, this Saturday Morning.

It was quite a common thing for a letter, especially one that might be described as a "note," to be simply dated, for example, "this Saturday Morning," without any place, nothing could

[1] Balfour is in Fife, three or four miles inland from Wemyss on the north shore of Forth. The direct route from Edinburgh would be *via* Leith to Kinghorn and thence ten or twelve miles by road. Fife roads in winter were troublesome, and the longer road to Aberlady and thence by water would be preferable. It may be mentioned that a return journey from Glasgow to Balfour would not pass anywhere near Edinburgh if taken by road.

have been more simple than to add the two words "From Glasgow." The date would probably have been in a separate line, and ample space would exist.

There are several things regarding this Letter which seem to mark it as in some degree placed on a different level to the others; it was the *first* exhibited at the public exposure before the Commissioners at Westminster on 7 December, 1568, though as coming later in date one would suppose it would come after the "long" Letter. It looks as if this obviously genuine article was the *pièce de resistance* intended to produce a favourable leaning to possible doubts arising from the others. Again, though it is clear that the Bishop of Ross when writing his *Defence* of the Queen's honour, had heard of bits of the other Letters he gives no hint of any knowledge of this one, he goes so far as to say, that no one of the letters is dated or contains the name of the bearer, or the place whence sent, all of which are in this Letter.

Again, both Lethington and John Beton were available to relate their knowledge of the matter, yet neither was questioned; there is no hint that the least effort was made to enquire into any of the numerous points which would occur to a modern judge. We know that Beton was in France in June of the following year (1569) in favoured contact with the Queen-Mother and the King, if there is any truth in the statement that copies of the Letters had been sent to them (and I think there is none[1]) he would surely have been questioned, or if he had known anything about such a Letter he would have told his brother the Archbishop what he knew. The facts could not have been kept quiet. Mary, in a letter of June 1568, says that Beton was canvassed by the other side to join them, but resisted temptation. He died somewhat suddenly in October 1570, "solemnised by my tears and accompanied by my prayers," as she wrote. Could the publication of the Casket Letters have taken place in Beton's lifetime? It is strange how lucky Mary's enemies were, in the removal by death of several persons whose evidence might have been inconvenient.

[1] See note F, p. 143.

As to what happened when Beton handed the Letter to Lethington for delivery to Bothwell, we need spend little time in surmising. The Whittinghame conference, between Morton and Archibald Douglas on the one part and Bothwell and Lethington on the other, took place the next day or within a couple of days, say on the 12th or 13th of January. Lethington may have retained the Letter or Bothwell may have given it to him after reading it, or, and this seems to me to be the most likely, it fell into the hands of Douglas. Whatever Douglas was then, we know that years after he had developed the art of concocting forged correspondence, witness the notorious plot against the life of the *then* Earl of Lennox in 1581[1].

Before the "brain-wave" of using this genuine Letter as the central item of a correspondence occurred to the conspirators, it would seem that a less ingenious plot had been evolved, of which the extracts quoted by Lennox are the remnant. At first the "long" Letter stood by itself and was somewhat different in its form; at a later date, and unknown to Lennox, this new "evidence" was brought in, some parts of the first idea being abandoned and some additions being made to weave in the new "facts."

Acceptance of the explanation proposed destroys the principal evidence produced against the Queen, but it does not prove the Queen guiltless. The rebel lords were in a desperate position, and it is quite understandable that they would create evidence of a sort without attention to its quality. The Queen's innocence must rest on arguments of a different nature, unconnected with the fraud of the Letters. In such an argument the independent Lennox Narrative will be found to furnish valuable matter.

[1] See Tytler, *Hist.* vol. VIII, and the Bowes Correspondence.

APPENDIX A

The Lennox first Narrative. Transcribed from the original in the University Library at Cambridge. Colloquial English of to-day is used instead of the original language, partly Scottish and partly English. The Paper is divided into sixteen paragraphs for easy reference.

THE LENNOX NARRATIVE
(Cambridge, Press Mark, Oo . 7 . 47/8.)

PARAGRAPH I

AFTER the Queen of Scots' arrival in her realm out of the parts of France first to note, the Earl of Lennox, perceiving by the intelligence of his friends in that realm, the good will of the said Queen towards him for his faithful service done to her in her minority, not unknown to the face of the world. The said Earl procuring his licence of the Queen's Majesty here for his passing into Scotland, purposely to the erecting and setting up of his house again, that had been so long asunder. At his voyage thither he was so honourably received and used of the said Queen and Nobility of that realm that shortly after there ensued a parliament only for the said Earl's restitution. At which time the said Queen declared openly to all the Nobility his good service done to her and to her mother in bringing them out of captivity and setting the crown upon her head.

PARAGRAPH II

The said Earl being established there, for the paternal love and steadfast affection he bare unto his dear son, Henry, the first of Scotland of that name, and the languor of heart he had by reason of his son's absence from his being one of his chiefest solaces, entered into earnest suit to the Queen's Majesty of England for his said Son's coming into Scotland. Shortly after his arrival into Scotland (by this I mean this Henry of most worthy memory) the Queen of that realm upon his sight being struck with the dart of love by the comeliness[1] of his sweet behaviour and personal (illegible) with herself, the

[1] The alternative reading of the above runs as follows:
"Comeliness of his sweet behaviour, personage and virtuous qualities as well in languages and letters, sciences, as also in the art of music, dancing and playing on instruments and especially, she also considering with herself the blood he was come of both by the father and mother, resolved in her heart, etc."

blood he was come of, resolved in her heart the consummation of their marriage and from that time forth agreed in such sort as shortly after their marriage took effect. The which being finished their loves to other increased more and more every day, so that shortly after by the grace of God was the said Queen conceived with child. Now their loves were decayed till their return from the journey of Dumfries[1], at which time by the means of wicked David, her secretary, who began to grow in such favour with her that she brought in a pardon, without the consent of the King her husband, to sundry persons being those banished. Whereupon the said King perceiving the Queen his wife beginning to take upon her the doing directly of all things without him, otherwise than she was wont, began not only to muse thereat....

PARAGRAPH III

...But perceiving every day more and more how she was abused and carried away by particular council and in especial by the said David whom the said King might see increase in such disordinate favour with his wife, as he being in his lusty years, bearing such great love and affection unto her, began to enter into such jealousy as he thought he could not longer suffer the proceedings of the said David, she using the said David more as a lover than a servant. Forsaking her husband's bed and board very often, liking the company of David, as appeared, better than her husband's. Whereat sundry of their Council and Nobility, of that realm, perceiving the misusage of the King their Sovereign, contrary to the honours of them both and also their own, if it should be suffered, began to increase the fire that was already kindled in the King's heart in such sort as by the King's sufferance the said David was apprehended, but not slain by his consent. After which death the King's heart being moved with pity and love towards his wife, whose lamentable tears were to him insufferable, began to give himself so wholly to please her and follow her will in all things.

PARAGRAPH IV

And she craftily perceiving the same began to restrain her tears and bridle herself in making it seem to him that she had from her heart forgot him, and cast away the suspicion that she had conceived of him touching the death of the said David, keeping still in store the venim and poison in her heart towards her most loving and faithful

[1] The alternative reading of this runs:
"And their loves never decayed till their return from the journey, etc."

husband, who by her fewer tears and amiable using of him, thinking himself more sure of her love than ever he was before, sought all the means and ways he could to set her to liberty from the place which she was in then, and with great hazard and danger of his life, with six in number and himself, conveyed her from the place where she was, by night, to the Castle of Dunbar, without the knowledge either of his father or any other. And having remained a certain time in the said Castle, the doers of the said fact being fled out of the realm, the Nobility thereof being come in to them, returned to Edinburgh again to their great contentation and heart's ease, as outwardly it did appear.

Where they were not long till the superfluity of the Queen's venim so abundantly impostumed within her heart against her loving and dear husband began by little and little to burst out by using him now and then with taunting and sharp words, and therewith immediately raised certain bands of soldiers by the advice and drift of Bothwell, whom she made General of the said bands, besides the force of the Hamiltons which she called into her service to wait upon her, being the ancient enemies of the King her husband's house. Then having remained a few days in the town of Edinburgh they passed to the Castle where they abode till she was brought to bed. During which time although they accompanied at bed as man and wife, yet that innocent lamb who meant so faithfully unto her his wife, had but an unquiet life.

PARAGRAPH V

Insomuch that he being overcome with inward sorrow of heart by her most strange and ungrateful dealings was forced to withdraw himself out of her company oftener than he himself would have done. In the meantime Bothwell waxed so great that he, supplying the place of the aforesaid David, was her love in such sort that she, forgetting her duty to God and her husband, and setting apart her honour and good name, became addicted and wholly assotted unto the said Bothwell. Not only for lust of the body, but also to seek the blood of her dear husband in revenge for the death of her servant David. Although she daily forgave and pardoned sundry of the deed doers and yet continued still in her deadly hatred towards her husband till she had his life.

After her deliverance she passed from the Castle of Edinburgh to Stirling before her month was out being a green woman[1], only to absent herself from the company of her husband, taking her pleasure in most uncomely manner arrayed in homely sort, dancing about the

---

[1] A curious term; I have come across it elsewhere meaning a wet-nurse.

Market Cross of that town. In such sort as abandoning herself to all riotousness, forgetting her princely state and honour, her husband keeping house one way and she another, thought not herself satisfied in using her self in that manner at home.

PARAGRAPH VI

(She) thought she would yet find the way to be further from her husband and so under colour invented a journey to Jedburgh for keeping the Justice Ayres. Where at that time and shortly after at her coming to Craigmillar she with her complices invented and resolved the time and manner of the most cruel and horrible murder of her most innocent and loving husband, who by reason of her unnatural and ungrateful usage of him, using her so obediently and lovingly as he did waxing so weary of her strange dealing towards him, having before her journey to Jedburgh determined his departure out of the realm, but his careful and loving father was the stay thereof, thinking by his labour and counsel to bring them to their former Godly love and agreement together. But alas all in vain, for such love as she bare to the son, she likewise bare the father. Yet proving by all the means that could be to win her and by the advice of his father and other his friends he did not only visit her in her sickness at Jedburgh but also at Craigmillar. Where at both times she used him but strangely. And although she travailed in procuring the Nobility of that realm so far as she could to use him as strangely as she did in not frequenting his company and waiting on him as they were wont, yet the worse that her usage was towards him, they, perceiving her cruel and ungodly dealings towards him her husband and their sovereign Lord, inflamed their hearts the more against her. So that his case being so lamentable to the face of the whole realm, won thereby the whole hearts of the Nobility and Commons thereof. So that she perceiving the same, began to grow in such fear, as she thought to have shortened the time in laying hands on him and satisfying of her devilish intent, if the Ambassadors of France and England had not come in at that present time. But perceiving that she was disappointed at that time by the coming of the said Ambassadors, the christening of their son drawing so near, she thought to defer the matter till the triumph was finished and done and the Ambassadors gone, and in the meantime to dissemble and cloak the matter as she could well enough.

And fearing the King should have spoken with the Ambassadors before they had been with her, and so have informed them of her unnatural proceeding towards him, she after her accustomed famed manner, knowing him of so good nature, that she could not so soon show him good usage, but he would as soon receive it in such good part as he would think she meant good faith, whereas inwardly her meaning was most false and cruel towards him, that after an amiable and gentle manner she desired him that he would neither see nor speak with the said Ambassadors till both she and he were at Stirling where they both together should receive them, desiring him that he would repair to Stirling before, and she would follow shortly after. So after both their coming thither at that time, she, fearing that the comeliness of his personage, his princely behaviour, modesty, qualities and language which God had endowed withall should have not only allured the hearts of that assembly towards him at that time, but also the hearts of the Ambassadors, and for avoiding thereof and preventing all things that might have been the let of that most devilish and horrible murder which lay fostered and hid in her heart, she feigned to be in a great way and choller against the King's tailors that had not made such apparel as she had devised for him against that triumph. So she desired him even as tendered her love and honour that he would absent himself from the said triumph and sight of the Ambassadors. And although it was much contrary to his nature and will, yet to follow her mind in all things, thinking thereby still to win her love, being counselled also by sundry Noblemen so to do granted her request.

PARAGRAPH VII

In this meantime his father being advertised that at Craigmillar, the Queen and certain of her Council had concluded an enterprise to the great peril and danger of his Majesty's person, which was that he should have been apprehended and put in ward, which rested but only upon the finishing of the christening and the departure of the said Ambassadors. Which thing being not a little grievous unto his father's heart, did give him warning thereof. Whereupon, he, by the advice of sundry that loved him, departed from her shortly after the christening, and came to his father to Glasgow, being fully resolved in himself to have taken ship shortly after and to have passed beyond the seas, but that sickness prevented him, which was the cause of his stay.

PARAGRAPH VIII

During which sickness she never sent to him till she went to (was at) Edinburgh, purposing to take the Prince her son with her and to prepare the place of sacrifice for his father according to her wicked invention. Then she sent unto the King her husband making her excuses and letting him understand the occasion of her stay from him all that while. Which was by reason of her want of health, and also the care that she had of the Prince their child to see him safely brought to Edinburgh[1]. But now finding herself in health better than she was, if it pleased him she would come and visit him. He answered her servant saying that he never gave her just cause to think otherwise on him but that her company should be most comfortable unto him. Therefore she was wise and knew well enough the duties that the wife owed to the husband, and especially in such time of sickness. Wherefore if she would come she should be most heartily welcome. Her servant answered demanding whether it were his pleasure or not that she should come. The King replied saying I have told you that she is wise and is not ignorant of her duty towards me, like as I know my duty towards her if she were in like case that I am presently in. Wherefore I remit her coming or tarrying to her self. If she come it shall be to my comfort and she shall be welcome. If she tarry, even as it pleaseth her so be it. But this much you shall declare unto her that I wish Stirling[2] to be Jedburgh, Glasgow to be the Hermitage and I the Earl Bothwell as I lie here and then I doubt not but she would be quickly with me undesired.

PARAGRAPH IX

Within certain days after the return of her servant from the King having concluded and prepared all things ready for the execution of her horrible enterprise she sent very loving letters[3] and messages unto him to drive all suspicions out of his head, that he might have of her, and shortly after came unto him herself to Glasgow, where she tarried certain days with him.

[1] This statement is not to be found elsewhere. It tends to confirm the interpretation of the "short" Glasgow Letter given in Chapter IV.

[2] In making up this precious story, Lennox has forgotten the opening lines of this paragraph, "She never sent to him till she went to Edinburgh." One must assume that the Queen was yet at Stirling when the above message was sent.

[3] It is remarkable that there is no mention made of these "loving" letters in the Glasgow Letter, rather one would gather that the letters which passed were not of this nature. In any case it is strange that "loving" letters should pass immediately after the insulting message of the last paragraph. If such were the fact Darnley must have been thick-headed not to suspect something. But I think Lennox must have been ignorant of the words, "He suspects of the thing you know and of his life" which occur in the Letter.

During which she handled the matter so craftily with sweet words and gentle using of him that contrary to his father's mind and consent he granted to go with her to Edinburgh according to her fetch and desire, although neither he nor his father never thought that she meant any such cruelty as shortly after came to pass, but that all controversies past between them were clean forgotten and buried. Finally they set forward on their journey towards Edinburgh, he being as yet not whole of his disease, where to the great rejoicings of the people they were honourably received[1].

And lighting at the place that was already prepared with undermines and trains of powder therein for his persecution. The locks and double keys of all the gates and doors thereof in her custody. He looking upon the said house which was so little in his sight, as he in no wise liked of, and beholding another lodging near by which seemed fairer in his sight, said that he would lodge in that house, for that he misliked the other that she prepared for him[2]. The Queen took him by the hand and said that, although that house was fairer in his sight, yet the rooms of the other were more easy and handsome for him and also for her for that there passed a privy way between the palace and it, where she might always resort unto him till he was

---

[1] According to the *Book of Articles* (Hopetoun MS.) the route taken was: Kilsyth, about 12 miles, Linlithgow, about 20 miles, Edinburgh, about 16 miles. A horse litter, in which Darnley was carried, would travel slowly. Probably the first night was spent at Kilsyth, that is, Monday night the 27th January. The Lennox-Cecil also gives Callander, about midway between Kilsyth and Linlithgow, as a stopping-place, which is likely enough. If the night of the 28th was spent at Callander House, the arrival at Linlithgow would be on the 29th. There she spent the 30th and perhaps the 31st, and arrived at Edinburgh on the 30th, 31st or 1st February, all three dates are given. Bothwell to whom she is supposed to have written from Linlithgow, was certainly at Hermitage or Jedburgh on the 28th, and *en route* for Edinburgh on the 29th, where he arrived on the 30th. One need only read Scrope's letter to see that Bothwell was about his ordinary business of keeping order on the border without any thought of the momentous *coup* that he was supposed to be engaged in. (See Scrope to Cecil, 28 Jan. 1567, in *Border Papers*.)

[2] The "fairer house" was the Hamilton residence, it was not in the precincts of Kirk o' Field, but it is true that the travellers would pass it after entering the town by the Potteraw Port, as no doubt they did. But Lennox has apparently forgotten what he had said, see Para. IV, about the enmity of the Hamiltons; to have thought of lodging in Hamilton house would be the last thing that Darnley would do.

whole of his disease[1], and he, being bent to follow her will in all things, yielded to the same and so entered the house, where he continued unto the time of his death.

PARAGRAPH X

During which time she visited him every night and used him in every sort as well as he himself could wish, and appointing the day that he should remove from thence into the palace. Taking such pains about him that being in his bath would suffer none to handle him but herself.

PARAGRAPH XI

Whereupon he assured himself so much of her favour that to comfort his father, who then remained at Glasgow, sick by the pains he took in tending the King his son in his sickness, wrote his letter unto him a little before his death to the effect as follows:

My Lord, I have thought good to write unto you by this bearer of my good health, I thank God. Which is the sooner come to, through the good treatment of such as hath this good while concealed their good will, I mean of my love the Queen. Which I assure you hath all this while and yet doth, use herself like a natural and loving wife. I hope yet that God will lighten our hearts with joy that have so long been afflicted with trouble. As I in this letter do write unto your Lordship so I trust this bearer can certify you the like. Thus thanking Almighty God of our good hap, I commit your Lordship into his protection.

From Edinburgh the vii of February, your loving and obedient son Henry, Rex.

As he was writing this letter the Queen his wife came unto him and seeing the contents thereof seemed to be so well pleased withall that she took him about the neck and kissed him as Judas did the Lord his Master. This tyrant having brought her faithful and most loving husband, that innocent lamb, from his careful and loving father to the place of execution, where he was a sure sacrifice unto Almighty God. The time thereof approaching now at hand, the day before his death she caused the rich bed wherein he lay to be taken down and a meaner set up in the place, saying to him, that that rich bed they should both lie in the next night in the palace, but her

[1] A certain amount of mystery has been made of the "privy" or "secret" way by which the Queen could visit Kirk o' Field, but there is nothing in it. It merely means that coming from Holyrood she could pass privately through the grounds of the Black Friars Monastery, and thence by the lane to Kirk o' Field.

meanings were to save that bed from the blowing up of the fear of powder.

PARAGRAPH XII

The present night of his death she tarried with him till eleven of the clock. Which night she gave him a goodly ring entertaining him still with very loving words, and seemed that she would have tarried all night with him, but both he and she were persuaded to the contrary by Bothwell and others, who seemed to bear a good countenance, appointing for that she had appointed to have ridden the next day in the morning to Seton. And all to abuse him that he should take no suspicion of his most cruel murder that was prepared for him, which ended within two hours after.

Then after her departure from him, remaining but a few of his own servants within his chamber (he?) commanded that his great horses should be in readiness by five of the clock in the morning, for that he minded to ride them at the same hour.

Yet nevertheless he began to wax somewhat pensive, remembering a word which the Queen his wife told him a little before her departure that night, which was that she called the King to remembrance that David her servant was murdered about that same time twelve months. So casting the same in his mind, demanded of a servant of his whom he loved, what he thought of the same words or why she should call the death of that man to remembrance at that time, which she did not of long time before, who answered that he was sorry she called the same to remembrance or yet that he should take any unrest therein, wishing his Master to take no thought thereof but get him to bed, for that he had appointed to be up early in the morning.

This man having a book in his hand the King asked him what book it was he answered it was a psalm book, then said the King let us go merrily to bed in singing a song before. His servant desired him that he would play on his lute, and they would sing. He answered, that his hand was not geve (inclined?) to the lute that night, and so appointed the fifth psalm of David, and after he and his well beloved servant had sung the same, called for his wine and drank to his servant bidding him farewell for that night and so went to bed. Which other wise might be called the scaffold or place of execution.

PARAGRAPH XIII

But before we proceed any further in this matter, I cannot omit to declare and call to remembrance her letter written to Bothwell from Glasgow before their departure thence, together with such cruel and strange words unto him (Darnley) which he, her husband, should have better considered and marked than he did but that the hope that he had to win her love did blind him, together that it lieth not in the power of man to prevent that which the suffering will of God determineth.

The contents of her letter to the said Bothwell from Glasgow was to let him understand that although the flattering and sweet words of him with whom she was then presently, she meaning the King her husband, had almost overcome her, yet she remembering the great affection which she bare unto him, there should no such sweet baits dissuade her or cool her said affection from him, but would continue therein, yea though she should thereby abandon her God, put in adventure the loss of her dowry in France, hazard such titles as she had to the crown of England as heir apparent thereof, and also the crown of her realm. Wishing him then presently in her arms. Therefore bade him go forward with all things according to their enterprise, and that the place and everything might be finished as they had devised against her coming to Edinburgh which should be shortly. And for the time of execution thereof she thought it best to be the night of Bastian's marriage, which indeed was the night of the King her husband's murder[1]. She wrote also in her letter that the said Bothwell should in no wise fail in the meantime to despatch his wife and to give her the drink as they had devised before[2].

And to the cruel and strange words that she had at sundry times (used?) to the King her husband. First the night he had her to Dunbar, adventuring his life to save her and to content her, at the place where they took their horse in the churchyard of Holyrood House, near to the place where David was buried, she asked the King whose grave it was, he answered that it was David's, she replied saying it should go very hard with her but a fatter than he should lie near by him ere one twelvemonth were at an end. At her coming to Edinburgh from Dunbar, where she began to misuse her husband, as is aforesaid, sometimes in her sharp and taunting words to him she would say that she never trusted to die till she might revenge the death of her servant David with her own hands. And that she

---

[1] Taking this at its face value, Mary writing on the 24th or 25th of January, says in effect "We will get through the unpleasant business on the night of Feb. 9th, while Bastian's wedding is going on." How this fits all the other statements about the original idea of going to Craigmillar, the reader will be able to judge (see p. 113).

[2] Only the most vivid imagination can bring in anything about "despatching" Bothwell's wife into the real Casket Letter, yet both de Silva and Lennox have this item.

feared the time should come that he himself might be in the like case as David was and ask mercy many a time, when it should be refused unto him. She also said at Jedburgh openly after her coming from Bothwell, who then lay sore hurt, in the Hermitage, her servants saying unto her that they marvelled how she being but a woman could take the pains that she did, having wearied all them that were her servants in that journey, she answered and said, "Troth it was she was a woman, but yet was she more than a woman, in that she could find in her heart to see and behold that which any man durst do, and as her strength would serve her thereto."

PARAGRAPH XIV

Which appeared to be true, for that some said she was present at the murder of the King her faithful husband, in man's apparel, which apparel she loved oftentimes to be in in dancings secretly with the King her husband, and going in masks by night through the streets.

PARAGRAPH XV

In Stirling at the Christening time before his coming to Glasgow, in using certain sharp words to the King, whereupon the colour of his face began somewhat to change, she said to him that his face was somewhat red and for remedy thereof to abate his colour if he were a little daggered and had bled as much blood as my Lord Bothwell had lately done, it would make him look the fairer[1].

PARAGRAPH XVI

Now to return to this most dolorous and woeful matter. The King had not lain one hour and half, being in sleep, till fifty persons in number environed that house, whereof XVI of them, Bothwell being chief, came the secret way which she was wont herself to come to the King her husband, and with their double keys opened all the locks of the garden and house and so quietly entered his chamber, who, finding him in bed, finally did suffocate him with a wet napkin steeped in vinegar. After which being done, bare his body into the garden, *laying by him* (erased in the MS.) his night gown of purple velvet furred with sables....(The Manuscript ends here, but on the

---

[1] It is noteworthy that not one of the stories retailed in this part of the paper is contained in the collection of "Young Stewart" referred to at p. 79, and Andrew Lang is mistaken in supposing this to be the case.

last page there is the following, apparently intended as substitution for part of the foregoing.)...his night gown laid by him and his servant Wm Taylour in like manner, who suffered death in like sort. Whose souls the Lord recalled into his glory. All which being finished the house being blowed up with powder. Upon the crack and noise thereof which the Queen waited for to hear, she went to bed....

(There is in addition to the foregoing a page and a half of matter which is in the main repetition of parts of the Manuscript; this is not copied, but reference to variations from the above transcript is made at pp. 120–121.)

APPENDIX B

In this section I have added a few notes on matters referred to in the text, but which it was not desirable to expand there. I hope they may be of use in clearing up some misconceptions which have grown into the history of the Queen of Scots, or of suggesting further enquiry by those interested.

A. THE ROUTE TAKEN BY MARY STUART IN HER FLIGHT FROM LANGSIDE

IT is a matter rather of sentiment than of historical importance to attempt to trace the route taken when Mary, believing her disaster at Langside to be irretrievable, fled to Dundrennan and thence to England. It appears from the absence of any mention of a pursuit (except in a French account which may be neglected) that she got away unobserved, and from the curious delay in ascertaining her whereabouts which thè Earl of Moray experienced, we may be sure that at an early stage she assumed some disguise. Nau's *Memoir*, which was probably in this matter well informed, has a significant memorandum, "How she caused her head to be shaved."

The generally accepted idea that she passed by Sanquhar to Terregles the home of the Maxwells near Dumfries is based on Camden and the *Abridged Scottish History* of Lord Herries (a descendant of the Herries who accompanied the Queen) but a glance at the map will show how unlikely so long a detour from the objective would be, besides it is not probable that proximity to a large town would be sought.

There are two items of information which give the true line of the journey. The first is again in the Nau *Memoir*, "How the Laird of Lochinvar gave her some clothes and a hood." The residence of Gordon of Lochinvar was Kenmuir Castle, situated near the head of Loch Ken. The second is given in a letter from Sir Willam Drury, which says, "I am come to understand, the Queen here, if the Earl of Moray's power draw anything towards her where she now is, which is at Thrieve, that standeth in a loch in Galloway, she minds to draw into England."

Thrieve Castle stands on an island in the Kirkcudbrightshire Dee and is the traditional scene of the first appearance of the great cannon called Mons Meg, which carried a ball as big as a Carsphairn Cow. Its first discharge cut off the hand of Margaret Douglas, the "Fair Maid of Galloway," who held the place against King James II.

The two points, Kenmuir and Thrieve, are in a more or less direct line to Dundrennan, and if it is literally true, as Mary stated in her letter to Elizabeth that she travelled 60 miles the first day, it must mean that Thrieve was her first stopping place, perhaps with a short rest at Kenmuir. Assuming that the flight commenced at about 11 o'clock on the 13th May and allowing an average speed of say six miles an hour including stops, she could not have arrived at Thrieve until about 10 at night. For a delicate woman, who had just emerged from a year's incarceration at Lochleven without possibility of exercise, to undergo this exertion must have reduced her physically to complete collapse, and mentally to a condition of incapacity to make any decision. No doubt she remained at Thrieve on the 14th, and probably there the fatal plan of trusting to England was made.

Claude Nau has some memoranda which gives us a little insight, "How she drank some sour milk at the house of a poor man."... "How she borrowed some linen."..."How she was 24 hours without eating or drinking." The last may be a little exaggerated but at least some notion of her discomforts may be gathered.

The Lord Herries makes the statement that he and others endeavoured to dissuade her from the plan but in vain. In her state she was indeed incapable of connected thought, one can hardly blame her for a foolish decision. Nor should we blame Elizabeth too much for failing her; "In the affairs of nations, particular friendships can have no place," such was the remark of the French Ambassador, La Forrest, when he heard of Mary's simple trust in her sister Queen.

From Thrieve I think she went direct, on the night of the 14th or early morning of the 15th, to Dundrennan Abbey, and thence on the morning of the 16th took her dangerous passage in a small boat across the Solway Firth.

B. THE MEMOIRS OF CLAUDE NAU

The Manuscript preserved in the Cotton Library and described as *An Historical Treatise...* is attributed to the pen of Claude Nau, by the Rev. Father Joseph Stevenson, S.J., who has edited it in a very interesting volume. Nau was appointed to Mary's service as Secretary for her foreign affairs, in 1575. That is some seven years after she had come to England. The Manuscript is but a fragment and contains a number of memoranda which the writer evidently intended to develop; some of these are quoted in the preceding note. Father Stevenson expresses the opinion that the narrative of Nau is derived directly from the Queen herself, but it is this point to which I would direct further attention.

Whether it be the case or not that the pen was Nau's, I think there is little doubt that the matter is not Mary's but contributed by her surgeon, one Arnault, also described as Arnauld Colommius. It was he who attended her during her serious illness at Jedburgh in the autumn of 1566; he who was with her in Lochleven during her imprisonment; he who most probably accompanied her during the flight into England after Langside, for among the persons who arrived with her at Carlisle was "Mr Nawe a Secretary."

It is a curious fact, which may be only a coincidence, that Arnault was frequently described as "Mr Nawe," thus Bishop Leslie so calls him in writing an account of the Queen's illness at Jedburgh; see Keith, vol. III. Again, the Bishop writes his name as Renauld in a letter to Cecil in May, 1569. Both these names are evidently the result of the French pronunciation of Arnault, which a scribe might take down as R. Naw; possibly he was called Naw or Nawe for "short"; they were fond of such petits noms in those days.

The intimate details given of the Queen's illnesses and of various facts as to occurrences at Lochleven make it very clear that the narrator was a person in close contact with what he describes, and no one more in a position to know of such things than Arnault could be named. If he were indeed the author of these Memoirs or at least of that part of them which is referred to above it could only add to their value.

It is remarkable that in October, 1577 (Labanoff. v.), Mary wrote asking that one Arnault might be obtained as her secretary, and he appears to have been appointed later; whether this person is the same as her former surgeon, I cannot say, nor is it clear when Arnault left her service in his former capacity.

C. WHETHER DARNLEY HAD PREVIOUS ACQUAINTANCE WITH MARY

The assertion that Darnley had visited France and met Mary both during her reign as Queen of France and afterwards when a widow, has been made by several modern writers. His uncle, John Stewart, Seigneur d'Aubigny, was of course a resident there and the holder of several offices and titles. His father had spent some time in France and there is no doubt that this branch of the Scottish royal family was considerably courted there in the hope of favours in the future. In Lady Elizabeth Cust's work *The Stewarts of Aubigny* it is stated (p. 75) that in spite of Cecil's precautions, Darnley more than once visited his uncle and that he was received on one occasion by Francis II and Mary at Chambord. In Fraser's well-known work, *The Lennox*, a similar statement is made with circumstantial detail,

"After the death of Francis in Dec. 1560, young Darnley was the bearer of a letter from his mother to Mary Stewart which he delivered to her at Orleans...."

I have been unable to find confirmation of these statements in contemporary records, but they may rest on family papers not made public. The last quotation seems to have a resemblance to the evidence of one Forbes when examined in connection with an enquiry into the proceedings of the Lennox family, see *Cal. For. Eliz.* 9 May, 1562, "Forbes deposes that he knows of the despatch of letters to the Queen of Scots from the Lord and Lady Lennox and Lord Darnley, and of their delivery at Orleans, and of an answer of the Queen's hand in French." This indicates that Darnley was not the bearer but the sender of a letter.

More hopeful is the rumour circulated at the time of the Earl of Bedford's visit to the French Court in Feb.–March, 1561, to express condolence on the death of the late King and to felicitate his successor, "It is bruited lately that the Earl of Lennox' son had gone over with Bedford..." (Randolph to Cecil 26 Feb. 1561). Almost at the same time Bishop Quadra wrote to Philip, "Lady Lennox is trying to marry her son to the Queen of Scots." Again on the 16 March of the same year one Thomas Stewart wrote to Lady Lennox from Edinburgh, "The common bruit of Scotland is that my Lord Darnley is gone to France to be a suitor to the Queen of Scots.... Whereof my answer was that I am ignorant."

All this is inconclusive, but there is another and a better evidence that Darnley had visited France, contained in the *Simancas Records* under date 29 June 1566, "The Secretary of the Scottish Ambassador in France said that the English Ambassador was surprised at the friendship the King of Scotland (Darnley) had with Don Francis d'Alava, and that he had replied that they were intimate friends in Paris." Unfortunately the record does not show *when* this friendship existed. Alava was not appointed as Spanish Ambassador until February, 1564, but there is evidence that he was employed on missions which took him to Paris before this date. The Director of the Archives at Simancas has been so good as to find one date so early as November, 1562, but it is quite possible that this was not the first.

Against the supposition, is the report of one Arthur Lynhart, who was Darnley's tutor, and sent secretly to Mary after her return to Scotland by Lady Lennox: he represents Mary as making enquiries as to Darnley's stature, qualities, etc., which if the story be true would indicate that she could have no personal acquaintance with him. But the story is not very likely to be genuine and does not help much either way.

It has been asserted[1] that Darnley did not speak French; I know of no reason for this. On the contrary, I should say it is almost certain that he did, as a well educated young man, frequenting the Court of Elizabeth and with a good deal of French connection, it is more than probable. We have the statement of Lennox himself that one of his son's many attractions was his gift of "Languages" (see p. 120, footnote), and in such a statement I think Lennox can be relied on. This seems sufficient proof that his language with Mary would be French. She knew little English, while her Scottish was not fluent and Darnley had as little of the latter[2].

D. THE DE SILVA-LENNOX QUOTATIONS

Placed in parallel columns below are the two independent quotations said to be part of a long letter sent from Glasgow, by Mary to Bothwell. The Lennox extracts are placed out of their order so that they may compare with the corresponding clauses in the other.

As quoted by the Spanish Ambassador in his letter dated 2 Aug. 1567, to Philip. Translated from the Spanish, by or for Mr Andrew Lang and printed in his book, *The Mystery of Mary Stuart*.	As quoted by the Earl of Lennox, in his Narrative referred to in Chapter III of this work.
I. She says in substance that he (Bothwell) is not to delay putting into execution that which he had been ordered, because her husband used such fair words to deceive her, and bring her to his	I. To let him understand that although the flattering and sweet words of him with whom she was then presently (she meaning the King her husband) had almost overcome her, yet she remember-

[1] Henderson, *Casket Letters*, 2nd Ed., p. 57.
[2] The effect which this matter has on the question of Thomas Crawford's evidence has been overlooked. It has frequently been pointed out that the epitome in Scottish given by Crawford of the conversation between Mary and Darnley at Glasgow, agrees with extraordinary verbal accuracy, with the same conversation recorded by Mary in the "Letter." If, as is almost certain, the conversation was in French, we have an incredible accident: Darnley translates his recollection of the matter to Crawford; Mary writes down in French her recollection of the same matter independently; some third party translates Mary's French into Scottish; the two Scottish translations agree as to sequence of items and largely as to verbal similarity. Credat Judaeus! Mary's story is probably genuine, but I fear Thomas Crawford as a witness must be condemned.

will that she might be moved by them, if the other thing were not done quickly.

II. She said that she herself would go and fetch him, and would stop at a house on the road where she would try to give him a draught, but if this could not be done she would put him in the house where the explosion was arranged for the night upon which one of the servants was to be married.

III. He, Bothwell, was to try to get rid of his wife either by putting her away or poisoning her.

IV. Since he knew that she, the Queen, had risked all for him, her honour, her kingdom, her wealth which she had in France and her God, contenting herself with his person alone.

V. Omitted in this version.

ing the great affection which she bare him (Bothwell) there should no such sweet baits dissuade her or cool her said affection from him.

II. Therefore she bade him go forward with all things according to their enterprise, and that the place and everything might be finished as they had devised against her coming to Edinburgh, which should be shortly. And for the time of execution thereof she thought it best to be the night of Bastian's marriage (which indeed was the night of the King her husband's murder).

III. She wrote also in her letter that the said Bothwell should in no wise fail in the meantime to despatch his wife and to give her the drink as they had devised before.

IV. But would continue therein (her affection) yea though she should thereby abandon her God, put in adventure the loss of her dowry in France, hazard such title as she had to the crown of England as heir apparent thereof and also the crown of her realm.

V. Wishing him then presently in her arms.

Mr Henderson, following J. A. Froude, considers that the above extracts are a reasonably near imitation of the Casket Letter as it has come down to us, after making allowances for the differences arising from faults of memory or of translation. The following are the corresponding extracts from the letter in question.

I. As to me he says he would rather give his life or he did any displeasure to me. And after this he show me so many little flatteries so coldly and so wisely that you will abash thereat....But fear not the place shall hold unto death.

It may be agreed that this is not very dissimilar from the Lennox version.

II^a. He spake even of the marriage of Bastian.

The two extracts can hardly be said to have much in common with this or even with each other.

II^b. Advise too with yourself if you can find out any more secret invention by medecine for he should take medecine and the bath at Craigmillar.

This is relied on to cover the idea of poisoning on the road.

III. See not her (Bothwell's wife) whose feigned tears should not be so much praised nor esteemed as the true and faithful travails which I sustain for to merit her place.

The extracts indicate that Bothwell was to see his wife to some purpose! It is extravagant to suggest similarity.

IV. Seeing to obey you my dear love I spare neither honour, conscience not greatness whatsoever.

Somewhat similar, but remarkable that both extracts are nearly similar and more full than the original.

V. I cannot sleep as they do and as I would desire that is in your arms my dear love.

The Lennox extract is near enough to this.

E. THE WHITTINGHAME CONFERENCE

It may have escaped the notice of readers, not intimately acquainted with the story, that no hint of the nature of the discussion at Whittinghame came to the surface during the period when Mary's guilt in respect of the death of her husband was under investigation. It was not until the execution of the Earl of Morton in 1581, that is some fourteen years later, that any information on the subject transpired, and even then Morton's "Confession" was known to few until the publication of Holinshed's *History*, which contained a copy; this was in 1587, after Mary's death.

There is a good deal of uncertainty as to what Morton really "confessed" and the documents which we have are in any case not official, but admittedly the work of certain ministers of the Kirk who attended him to give him comfort in his extremity. The writer of the *History* admits having left out some parts of the confession which involved "great persons now living." The manuscript copies which are available supply what *may be* the omissions in Holinshed, and, in them, the Queen of Scots is certainly involved as well as Archibald Douglas. I say "may be," because it is by no means certain that the

MS. story has not been garbled; it is at least the case that Mr John Durie, one of the ghostly ministrators referred to above, was quite capable of colouring the "Confession" with matter damnatory to the Queen. He was at the time ordered to quit Scotland for uttering abuse of the King's (James) mother, and following the footsteps of his predecessor, John Knox, he was accustomed roundly to admonish the young sovereign on his supposed leanings towards the Roman Church, which at the moment were pronounced.

Whether the omissions of Holinshed were intended to shield the Queen of Scots, which at the time seems unlikely, or whether he found that some other persons, perhaps including a Queen who was not Mary, were named, cannot be said with confidence. We have Mary's letter to Elizabeth of the 21st November, 1582, in which she says, "By the Agents, spies and secret messengers, sent in your name into Scotland, while I was there, my subjects were corrupted and encouraged to rebel against me...and in one word to speak, do, enterprise and execute that which has come to the said country during my troubles. Of which I will not at present specify other proof, *than that which I have gained of it by the confession of one* who was afterwards amongst those that were most advanced for this good service."

This does not look as though Mary had seen or even heard of a "confession" in which she herself was named as the "doer," but it does look as if England had been brought into the question in some degree or other.

The statement attributed to Morton so far as it relates to Whittinghame, is:

In the yard of Whittinghame after long communing, the Earl of Bothwell proposed to me the purpose of the King's murder...seeing it was the Queen's mind that the King should be taken away....My answer was that I would not in any ways meddle in that matter....After this answer Mr Archibald Douglas entered into conference with me for that purpose, persuading me to agree to the Earl of Bothwell. Last of all the Earl of Bothwell, yet being in Whittinghame, earnestly proposed the same matter to me again, persuading me thereto because it was the Queen's mind and she would have it done. Unto this my answer was, I desired the Earl of Bothwell to bring the Queen's write to me....Which warrant he never reported unto me.

If any such conversation occurred it is truly astonishing that no use was made of it by the "prosecution" at Westminster and Hampton Court. The retort that it would have involved Morton himself as an accessory or of foreknowledge, is not sufficient, for Morton and his friends were quite equal to putting such slight variation to the affair as would avoid any trouble. When we remember the favour shown to Morton in England during the time of his exile immediately preceding the Whittinghame affair, and all the circumstances surrounding the murder of Rizzio, in which English influence was unmistakably present and the immense efforts made to save Morton at the time of his downfall and much else that showed no hesitation to employ the darkest methods for maintaining the reformed religion in Scotland, in which Morton was a principal agent, then it is not unreasonable to suggest that the conference at Whittinghame has been twisted into a sense the precise reverse of the truth. Perhaps it was not Bothwell who made the proposal, but Morton; perhaps it was not Mary whose warrant was awaited but Elizabeth, or at least Cecil; perhaps it was not the King who was to be taken away, but the Queen.

For what it is worth I will quote from the statement attributed to Bothwell still preserved in Sweden, "They (Morton and others) promised to forget all that was passed and by the good offices of friends to satisfy those whom they had formerly offended and bore hatred to...." This seems to me to have been the subject of the long communing at Whittinghame and the purpose for which Mary sent Bothwell from Stirling; whether a different direction was given to the talk by one or other of the disputants we need not discuss, but if it were so, Mary was not responsible.

THE AFFAIR OF JOSEPH LUTYNI

The reason why I add a brief note on this episode as a pendant to the Whittinghame Conference is partly that it supplies some confirmation of the suggested date on which the latter took place and partly because there seems to be a link between the three subsidiary mysteries of the Heigate-Walker incident, the Whittinghame incident and this one of Lutyni.

In the *Quarterly Review* of March, 1841, Lord Mahon has thrown some light on the case, but he has made the error of antedating the letter which will presently be referred to and this has confused the result of his research.

On 6 January (1567), Mary, being then in Stirling, signed a passport for one Joseph Lutyni, an Italian in her service, to proceed to France.

On 17 January, for reasons to be mentioned, she sent, or there was sent in her name, a letter addressed to Sir William Drury at Berwick, asking that the said Joseph might be arrested and sent back to Edinburgh on a charge of theft. Drury was not at Berwick at the time, but he arrived there within a few days, probably on the 21st or 22nd.

On 23 January, Drury wrote to Cecil, "At my arrival here, I found here one Joseph...." How long the said Joseph had been in Berwick is not stated, but it is mentioned that he was stopping in Berwick on account of his health not enabling him to proceed.

On 13 January, the Queen had returned from Stirling to Edinburgh, so it must be concluded that the misdemeanours of Joseph came to light between that date and the 17th, which by the way, was the precise time of the Whittinghame meeting.

Drury sent a copy of the passport and of the Queen's letter to Cecil; he seems to have had suspicion that the demand for Joseph's "extradition" contained more than met the eye; he asked for orders how he should proceed, in the meantime he did not acknowledge the letter from Scotland.

Some days later a letter was sent by Joseph Rizzio (a brother of the murdered David), another Italian in the Queen's service, to his friend Lutyni, which, abridged, ran as follows:

I have told the Queen that you have taken my money, and the reason why I said it and for whom (or, on whose account, "e per quel") you will understand (intenderete)....Then Bastian told the Queen that I asserted you were going on her affair....They all began to say that it was some knavery, and that you have put your hands to the Queen's papers, and not wishing (you) to be suspected (I) said that you have carried off six "Portuguese" and five "nobles."...The Queen suddenly asked me "Where are my bracelets" and I said you had taken them with you...and then they made such a to do, that the Queen ordered Lethington to write a letter to cause your arrest....In the meantime M. de Moretta arrived, who says that you told him yonder (that is, in Berwick) that I was the cause of your making this journey. Take care how you speak, for if you mention on whose account (per quello che) you are going, we shall all get into trouble. I have said that the money which you have taken of mine, you would restore to me when you return from France....For the love of God...say that the money, I said you have taken, that you have taken it....If you say what I suggest you will be excused as well as I....She (the Queen) has said that she will speak to you in secret, take care of your speech as I have written to you and not otherwise....I pray you have pity on me. Write to me by an express man what you will say....I pray you burn this letter as soon as you have read it. Edinburgh, this Sunday.

The first point arising from this letter is that Lethington, writer of the request for arrest on the 17th, must have even then returned from Whittinghame, which confirms the date suggested for the meeting as between the 12 and 15 of January. A date later than the 17th is unlikely, for the Queen left Edinburgh *en route* for Glasgow on the

20th or 21st, and we are expressly told that she was in Edinburgh when Lethington in company with Bothwell and Douglas returned; besides we gather from Drury's letters that there was another letter from Lethington on the subject of Lutyni, which presumably was later than that of the 17th.

The other point is one over which the writers on the subject have stumbled, and even the *Calendar of the State Papers* is wrong. Moretta did not leave Berwick on his way to Edinburgh until the 23rd; he stayed a night in Dunbar and was presumably in Edinburgh on the 24th. Hence, "This Sunday," the date of the above letter, must, at earliest, be Sunday 26 January. We must conclude that Moretta on arrival sought out and had a conversation with Rizzio say on the 25th which put that worthy in such a taking that he felt constrained to send off his letter of warning on the following day. How or when it fell into Cecil's hands we have no knowledge, but it is endorsed by Cecil himself.

This late date of the letter gives rise to some conjectures: Joseph Rizzio had seen his friend off and known of the subsequent question of arrest, and of the perturbing circumstances nine or ten days before he thought of taking any steps. It was the arrival of Moretta, always a bird of ill-omen, which apparently caused a change in his equanimity. And at Berwick the other Joseph was apparently taking no particular thought of the morrow until the passage of Moretta put him in fear of a "prepared death" should he return to Edinburgh. All the movements of Moretta at this time are mysterious, but we cannot follow them at this stage.

It would naturally be supposed that when Rizzio relates about the Queen's demand for her bracelets he was referring to something that had just occurred, but the Queen had been away at least five days when he wrote. His writing seems to show no sign of agitation, it is clearly written without mistakes or erasures in a bold roman script.

One sees a shadowy connection with Darnley in the No. II Letter, "The questions he asked...of Joseph," and again, "He asked that (why?) I would send Joseph away," and then there is the strange reference to bracelets in the letter which seems so meaningless, but finds a corresponding "excrescence" in the Glasgow Letter.

In the end we are told that Drury sent Lutyni back to Edinburgh but not until after the Kirk o' Field explosion, and then though the Queen did not see him, Bothwell entreated him very courteously and gave him *thirty* pieces of silver and sent him on his way rejoicing.

It is a strange story redolent, I think, of the residuum of a plot that died young and was replaced by something better. It gives me a *sensation* that other "vestigials" of the same conception are to be found in the de Silva-Lennox extracts (see note D), "She said she would *go* and fetch him...," "Bothwell should in no wise fail...to despatch his wife," and other things. The despatch of poor Lady Bothwell appears to have been put in hand, or at least in writing, at once, for we have Drury's report dated 28 February, "Lady Bothwell is, I am by divers means informed, extremely sick and not likely to live, they will say that she is marvellously swollen"; as "Mary" says in the famous letter, guess what presage that is! It is remarkable how frequently Drury took the *rôle* of Chorus between the acts of this drama.

F. WHETHER THE CASKET LETTERS WERE SHOWN TO THE FRENCH AGENT DU CROC

Considerable importance has been attached by several writers to the supposed handing to the Frenchman Du Croc, of copies of the alleged Letters between Mary and Bothwell. Mr Henderson states it as a fact discovered in 1892, and Mr Lang also accepts it and gives the fact as an objection to the existence of an early version of Letter II, for, argues Lang, if such a copy had been given to Du Croc he would have been in a position to condemn the published version when the latter was issued some years after.

The idea seems to be based on several contemporary letters:

I. "Du Croc carries with him matter little to the Queen's advantage, and the King (of France) may therefore rather satisfy the Lords than pleasure her." See *Calendar Scottish State Papers*, p. 351, Throgmorton to Elizabeth, 14 July, 1567.

II. "Of further circumstances and of the whole affair, your Ambassador M. du Croc, can more fully advise your Majesty. As...we have fully informed (him) of the justice of our cause." See letter addressed to French King by the Lords, quoted in Melville's *Memoirs*.

III. "There is here that the Queen had a box wherein are the practices between her and France wherein is little good meant to England...." See Drury to Cecil, 25 June, 1567, in *State Papers, Scotland*.

IV. "The Queen's adversaries assert positively that they know she had been concerned in the murder of her husband which was proved by letters under her own hand, copies of which were in his possession" (presumably in the French Ambassador's possession, that is, M. de la Forrest). See *Simancas Archives*, de Silva to Philip, 12 July, 1567.

V. "They mean to charge her with the murder of her husband whereof they say they have the proof by the testimony of her own hand writing." *State Papers, Eliz. For.*, Throgmorton to Elizabeth, 25 July, 1567.

On the face of it, I should imagine it very unlikely that the Lords would have given copies of the incriminating documents to the Frenchman at that time. He left Edinburgh on 29 June, that is, within a week of the alleged finding of the Casket and the Letters (see *Diurnal and Cal. Scottish St. Prs* No. 549) and he was the bearer of the letter addressed by the Lords to Charles IX of which No. II above is an extract. This letter does not mention the matter of the incriminating letters or of any copies having been handed to du Croc, though it does say that he has been "fully" informed. But there is no suggestion anywhere that Throgmorton was similarly favoured or Villeroy who had been sent especially from France to enquire into the whole affair, and had been sent empty away. Then again there is no hint that du Croc carried the "copies" to France, he apparently gave them to the French Ambassador in London, M. de la Forrest, which would be a strange thing to do. Strangest of all, to Moray, who one would suppose to be best entitled to receive "copies," nothing more was sent than extracts from one letter.

The main "proof" rests on No. IV above, but what does this amount to? The Spaniard, de Silva, writes in cipher on the 12th July that the French Ambassador says he had "Copies," the original Spanish decipher given in *Documentos Ineditos* puts it, "Y que este tenia las copias." I am inclined to think that a small mistake in the cipher or the decipher could easily have distorted this from a similar statement as that made in No. V above, that, "they, that is, the Lords, have proof by the testimony of her own handwriting" of which *they* have copies.

Extract No. I certainly gives the impression that what du Croc carried was the copy of certain political papers, and No. III confirms this.

En passant let us note what a curious coincidence it is that in No. III above Drury is telling of the ransacking of the Queen's private papers contained in a "box," that is, on 25 June; his information must have emanated from Edinburgh not later than the 24th, and more likely the 23rd or 22nd of June, which is the day or the second day, after the opening of the Casket, which contained, as is said, nothing about "practices" with France, but other matters of a more discreditable character!

G. THE CONNECTION BETWEEN THE TWO GLASGOW LETTERS

The explanation given in Chapter IV of the origin of the "short" Letter, which we will call No. I, is rather more than a theory; it seems so completely to fill the conditions required, and to fall naturally into its place, that I accept the hypothesis as proved. It remains then to endeavour to reconstruct the course of events which led to the completed scheme of the *two* Letters alleged to have been sent to Bothwell from Glasgow.

The presence of Archibald Douglas at Whittinghame at the moment of the delivery of Letter I in January, 1567, and his presence also at the moment of the alleged finding of the Letters in the Casket in June following—for let us remember that it was he who was closely concerned in the capture of Dalgleish and his associates—is a guarantee that an active mind, unquestionably inclined to forgery and underhand tricks, was in contact with the affair from the beginning.

The treacherous seizure of the Queen at Carberry Hill on 15 June (1567) created the necessity for justification of the act. Up to that moment there had been no official accusation of the Queen; on the contrary, Bothwell alone was dubbed the murderer, and the release of the Queen from his "thrall" was the ostensible object of the Lords. Even at the Council held on the 21st June, the very day of the alleged opening of the "Casket," there is only mention of the guilt of Bothwell, in unlawfully holding the Queen's person, and the same is the case at the Council of the 26th June. The imprisonment of the Queen which occurred on the 16th was an act of indisputable high treason and the conspirators had burnt their boats. The first idea of justifying the act by alleging the Queen's refusal to break with Bothwell was obviously insufficient to cover the culprits from subsequent prosecution. It was at this juncture that the peculiar genius of Douglas probably came into activity, aided perhaps by others. At any time subsequent to the 16th the Queen's private papers were at the disposal of the rebels.

The fair copy of Letter I may have been in Douglas's possession since the Whittinghame meeting, or alternatively it may in fact, as alleged, have been among Bothwell's papers when these were taken from Dalgleish or some other person on 19 June. The draft, in Mary's hand, was no doubt with her private papers. In neither case, as I think, was the future usefulness of the letter discerned.

Archibald Douglas and his helpers, did not, I am stating my views, go beyond a single letter, and this had as its backbone, matter extracted from the loose leaves of the Queen's rough notes of her sojourn in Glasgow. The *whole* of these notes was not brought into service. Matter which certainly would have been in them was omitted. The entire absence of Morton's name, for instance, would not have been possible in a conversation between Mary and her husband at that time.

As to the practical difficulty in adding paragraphs or pages to the existing pages or perhaps merely scraps of paper, there was probably none. That the original *was* on scraps, on which memoranda intended to be expanded later had been jotted down at some moment of leisure, seems not to be in doubt. The additions seem rather to be complete paragraphs than interlineations or verbal alterations. As to the *matter* of the additions it is for the most part not of a nature to cause any difficulty on the score of super-intelligence of the writer, and in the few points to which this criticism does not apply, there is nothing unreasonable in supposing that the original provided the necessary lead, in parts which were not themselves produced.

In the "long" Letter, or Letter II, as we have it, there are two references to Craigmillar. One, I regard, as an undoubted addition: "Advise too with yourself if you can find out any more secret invention by medecine for he should take medecine and the bath at Craigmillar." The other is, I think, genuine: "I answered, that I would take him with me to Craigmillar, where the mediciner and I might help him, and not be far from my son." There is no reference at all to Kirk o' Field, other than the *last* item of the Memoranda, which is, I think, an obvious addition: "Remember you, of the lodging in Edinburgh." If Mary's French was "Souvenez vous," it means of course, in this connection, Remember or "make a note of," not an address to some other person. There were six "Notes" at this part of the Letter, and the penultimate one was, "Remember about the Earl of Bothwell," which would be an odd thing to put in a letter addressed to that individual!

The first conception of Letter II was, judging from the excerpts given in Note D, much coarser and more direct than the Letter as we have it, and it seems clear that Craigmillar could not have been mentioned in it. Moreover, it appears to have been a complete forgery, for it was, we are told, written on three double sheets of paper and signed. All the telling scrappiness and scribbleness of the original was apparently foregone, in order to make a regular letter out of what in the end is only a letter by courtesy, containing a great part of the genuine notabilia.

When and why was a change made? The original plan held good up to the time of Moray's return to Scotland in August (1567) and likely enough it was then pigeon-holed, for the Queen was safely shut up in Lochleven and no very inconvenient questions had been asked. The deposition of the Queen, and the crowning of the Prince had been arranged with Cecil's approval. There was no reason for anxiety on the score of the high treason and probably nothing was done to alter the evidence. Lennox who left Scotland in April (1567) and resumed his residence in England, remained in possession of whatever notions had been imparted to him as to the mode of thought on the subject.

The Queen's escape from Lochleven changed the whole aspect of the case, and at the time of receiving Drury's message (see p. 75) that documentary proofs were wanted in a hurry to convince Elizabeth, a hasty re-examination of the evidence took place. The documents would have to pass scrutiny which *might* be impartial, and this was never anticipated at first. Genuine originals became of the utmost value, subtlety replaced mere craftiness. The idea of using genuine Letter I came into the conception and assumed the chief place; partly genuine Letter II was reconstructed, bringing in the genuine reference to Craigmillar with some addition, and making use of the original sheets as far as they would serve, omitting Kirk o' Field, the poisoning of Lady Bothwell and some other extravagances of the first edition. Letters I and II now became a connected pair, both of them referring to Craigmillar as the King's first destination.

But inevitably confusion occurred, time did not admit of all the threads being taken up, and recollection of some of them had passed away. Buchanan wrote the Indictment in evident want of complete knowledge, and uses the old style Letter as his guide at St Andrews, while at Edinburgh the new style is under issue, both processes being in hand at the same time. Lennox is equally, and as it turned out, unfortunately, left in the dark and he too is synchronously at work on the old story as we have seen, probably it was not foreseen that he would be called in. It must be remembered, however, that both " Buchanan " and " Lennox " were suppressed, that is, their first efforts did not appear before Elizabeth's Commissioners, but were transmuted into the final Indictment known as the *Book of Articles*.

Having embarked on what we may call the "genuine" stunt, it became necessary to colour the evidence of the two witnesses called, Thomas Nelson and Thomas Crawford, so that the points should be emphasized. The Prosecution seems to have been a little nervous as to whether the traces of the first dispensation were sufficiently removed, hence Nelson is made to say: "The Deponar remembers, it was devised in Glasgow, that the King should have lain first at Craigmillar, but because he had no will thereof, the purpose was altered, and conclusion taken that he should lie beside Kirk o' Field." On the same day, Crawford rubbed in Craigmillar in three different places in his statement: "She answered that she would take him to Craigmillar, where she might be with him and not be far from her son"; and again: "She minded to give him the bath at Craigmillar"; and again: "I liked it not because she took him (would take him) to Craigmillar, for if she had desired him with herself...she would have taken him to his own house[1]."

In all probability it is perfectly true that Mary had chosen Craigmillar as a place suitable for her husband's convalescence, and also true that for reasons of his own Darnley refused at the last moment to go there and preferred Kirk o' Field. It gave, no doubt, satisfaction to the Prosecution to be able to offer evidence that was at least true in parts. The point, however, that we are concerned with for the moment is that Nelson, in close touch with Lennox, and most likely present at the compilation of his "Supplication," allowed him to go so far astray as to neglect Craigmillar altogether and to pin himself to Kirk o' Field and its preparation for the murder *before* the Queen went to Glasgow, he (Nelson) knowing all the time that Kirk o' Field was not in the picture until shortly before the party arrived there.

The independent testimony of one Servais de Condé, *valet de chambre* to the Queen, who made an entry in the inventories of the goods of Holyrood House, with no thought of its having any bearing on the tragedy, goes far to confirm the evidence of Nelson; this entry runs: "Discharge of the furniture which I, Servais de Condé... delivered at the lodging of the King in the month of February 1567, which articles were lost without recovery...." Here we have trustworthy evidence that the House at Kirk o' Field was only fitted up just before the King arrived there.

A consideration of the foregoing, I think, justifies the conclusion that Letter I was the pivot on which the final scheme of evidence was framed. Before it came into the plot, Kirk o' Field *only* was mentioned; afterwards, this place came in as a late thought and the idea of *previous preparation*, which had been a strong point, falls to the ground.

[1] Among the Cambridge Papers there is a valuable draft of Crawford's evidence, press mark Dd. 3. 64. No. 36; it has been reprinted by Henderson in his work *Mary Queen of Scots* (1905). The document contains many corrections and erasures, and was evidently the subject of much thought. The quotation above is prefixed by the words, "The King asked me what I thought of his voyage (that is, his journey to Edinburgh with his wife). I answered that I liked it not, etc. (as above)." These words apparently gave ground for consideration. The first draft was "The words that the King spoke unto me at his departing" which are scored out. There is also, "At his departure out of Glasgow." This, too, is scored out and "At this present time" substituted. The writer seemed to be in trouble as to how far it was desirable to assert *when* it was that the destination of Craigmillar was still spoken of.

Mesmerism, Spiritualism, &c.

Historically & Scientifically Considered

William Benjamin Carpenter

CAMBRIDGE
UNIVERSITY PRESS

CAMBRIDGE UNIVERSITY PRESS

Cambridge, New York, Melbourne, Madrid, Cape Town, Singapore,
São Paolo, Delhi, Dubai, Tokyo, Mexico City

Published in the United States of America by Cambridge University Press, New York

www.cambridge.org
Information on this title: www.cambridge.org/9781108027397

© in this compilation Cambridge University Press 2011

This edition first published 1877
This digitally printed version 2011

ISBN 978-1-108-02739-7 Paperback

MESMERISM, SPIRITUALISM

&c.

LONDON : PRINTED BY
SPOTTISWOODE AND CO., NEW-STREET SQUARE
AND PARLIAMENT STREET

MESMERISM, SPIRITUALISM, &c.

HISTORICALLY & SCIENTIFICALLY CONSIDERED

BEING TWO LECTURES

DELIVERED AT THE LONDON INSTITUTION

With Preface and Appendix

BY

WILLIAM B. CARPENTER, C.B.

M.D. LL.D. F.R.S. F.G.S. V.P.L.S.

CORRESPONDING MEMBER OF THE INSTITUTE OF FRANCE
REGISTRAR OF THE UNIVERSITY OF LONDON
ETC.

LONDON

LONGMANS, GREEN, AND CO.

1877

PREFACE.

THE recent direction of the public mind to the claims
of what is called ' Spiritualism,' partly by the discussion which took place in the Anthropological Section
of the British Association at its Meeting in Glasgow,
and partly by the Slade prosecution which followed,
having led the Directors of the London Institution to
invite me to deliver two Lectures on the subject, I consented to do so on the understanding that I should
treat it purely in its Historical and Scientific aspects:
my purpose being to show, first, the relation of what
seems to me essentially an Epidemic Delusion, to Epidemics, more or less similar, which have at different
periods taken a strong—though transient—hold on
the popular imagination ; and secondly, to point out
how completely the evidence adduced by the upholders
of the system fails to afford a scientific proof of the
existence of any new Power or Agency capable of an-
tagonising the action of the known Forces of Nature.

In consequence of many representations made to me that these Lectures might be advantageously brought under the notice of a wider circle than that of their original auditors, I was led to prepare them for publication in *Fraser's Magazine,* with the addition of passages which want of time prevented me from including in their oral delivery. And in now reproducing them in a separate form, with an Appendix of *pièces justificatives,* I have no other motive than a desire to do what I can to save from this new form of Epidemic Delusion some who are in danger of being smitten by its poison, and to afford to such as desire to keep themselves clear from it, a justification for their 'common sense' rejection of testimony pressed upon them by friends whose honesty they would not for a moment call in question. Among these *pièces,* there are none which seem to me of more value than the extracts I have given from the writings (long out of print) of the late Mr. Braid; whose experiments, which I repeatedly witnessed, not only contributed essentially to the elucidation of what is real in the phenomena of Mesmerism and the states allied to it, but furnished (by anticipation) the clue to the explanation of many of the curious psychical phenomena of *honest* Spiritualism.

In the discussion to which I have just referred, Mr. A. R. Wallace, speaking from the Chair of the Anthropological Section, addressed me in the follow-

ing words :—' You expect us to believe what *you* say,
'but you will not believe what *we* say.' And the
same distinguished Naturalist has since publicly accused me of ' habitually giving only one side of the
'question, and completely ignoring all facts which tell
' against [my] theory.'—The reader of these Lectures
will see that my whole aim is to discover, on the
generally accepted principles of Testimony, what *are*
facts ; and to discriminate between facts and the in-
ferences drawn from them. I have no other 'theory'
to support, than that of the constancy of the well-
ascertained Laws of Nature ; and my contention is,
that where apparent departures from them take place
through Human instrumentality, we are justified in
assuming in the first instance either *fraudulent* deception, or unintentional *self*-deception, or both combined,—until the absence of either shall have been
proved by every conceivable test that the sagacity of
sceptical experts can devise.

The two different modes in which Spiritualists and
their opponents view the same facts, according to their
respective predispositions, is well brought out in cases
of the so-called 'materialization.' — A party being
assembled in a front drawing-room, the ' medium' re-
tires into a back room separated from it by curtains,
and professes there to go into a trance. After a short
interval, during which the lights are turned down so
as to make ' darkness visible,' a figure dressed in some
strange guise enters between the curtains, and dis-

plays itself to the spectators as an 'embodied spirit.'
Precluded from any direct interference with the performance, a sceptic among the company slyly puts
some ink on his fingers, and, whilst this is still wet,
grasps the 'spirit-hand,' which he finds very like a
mortal one. The 'spirit' withdraws behind the curtains, after a short interval the lights are raised,
and the 'medium' returns to the company *in propriâ
personâ*. The sceptic then points out inkstains on
one of the 'medium's' hands, and tells what he has
done.

These are the *facts* of the case.—Now, the 'com-
mon-sense' interpretation of these facts is, that the
'medium' is a cheat, and the 'embodied spirit' a vulgar ghost personated by him; and until adequate
proof shall have been given to the contrary, I maintain that we are perfectly justified in holding to this
interpretation, confirmed as it is by the exposure of
the trick in every instance in which adequate means
have been taken for its detection.

But the explanation of his inked fingers given by
the 'medium' is, that the impress made on the hand
of the 'embodied spirit' has been transferred 'according to a well-known law of Spiritualism' to his
own; and this assumption is regarded as more probable, by such as have accepted the system, than
that their pet 'medium' is a cheat, and their belief
in him a delusion!

That such an assumption should not only gain

the acceptance of minds otherwise rational, but should be stoutly upheld by them with unquestioning faith, seems to me a striking exemplification of the strength of the hold which a 'dominant idea' may gain, when once the protective safeguard of 'common sense' has been weakly abandoned. And I would further deduce from it the educational importance of that *early* Scientific training, of which a disciplined and trustworthy judgment on such subjects is one of the most valuable resultants. For that training—which essentially consists in the formation of habits of accurate observation, and of correct reasoning upon the facts so learned—pervades the *whole* mind, and shapes its general forms of thought in a degree which is rarely (if ever) equalled by the direction of its powers at a later period of life to the culture of some limited field of scientific investigation. Any such specialization leaves the wide domain of thought which lies outside, untouched by scientific influences ; and thus it happens that men who achieve high distinction in particular lines of scientific enquiry, may not only have no special competence for the pursuit of an enquiry of a totally different kind, but may be absolutely *dis*-qualified, by preformed tendencies, for its thorough and impartial prosecution. A remarkable case of this kind, incidentally noticed in the following pages (pp. 7 and 69), I have elsewhere more fully discussed.[1]

---

[1] 'The Radiometer and its Lessons,' in the *Nineteenth Century* for March 1877.

CONTENTS.

LECTURE II.

APPENDICES.

CONTENTS.

MESMERISM, SPIRITUALISM, &c.[1]

LECTURE I.

THE aphorism that 'History repeats itself' is in no case more true than in regard to the subject on which I am now to address you. For there has been a continuity from the very earliest times of a belief, more or less general, in the existence of 'occult' agencies capable of manifesting themselves in the production of mysterious phenomena of which ordinary experience does not furnish the *rationale*. And while this very continuity is maintained by some to be an evidence of the real existence of such agencies, it will be my purpose to show you that it proves nothing more than the wide-spread diffusion, alike among minds of the highest and of the lowest culture, of certain tendencies to thought, which have either created ideal marvels possessing no foundation what-

[1] The Lectures, as here presented, include several passages which were necessarily omitted in delivery.

* B

ever in fact, or have, by exaggeration and distortion, invested with a preternatural character occurrences which are perfectly capable of a natural explanation. Thus, to go no further back than the first century of the Christian era, we find the most wonderful narrations, alike in the writings of Pagan and of Christian historians, of the doings of the Eastern 'sorcerers' and Jewish 'exorcists' who had spread themselves over the Roman Empire.[1] Among these, the Simon Magus slightly mentioned in the Book of Acts was one of the most conspicuous ; being recorded to have gained so great a repute for his 'magic arts,' as to have been summoned to Rome by Nero to exhibit them before him ; and a Christian Father goes on to tell how, when Simon was borne aloft through the air in a winged chariot, in the sight of the Emperor, the united prayers of the Apostles Peter and Paul, prevailing over the demoniacal agencies that sustained him, brought him precipitately to the ground. So, in our own day, not only are we seriously assured by a nobleman of high scientific attainments, that he himself saw Mr. Home sailing in the air (by moonlight) out of one window and in at another, at a height of seventy feet from the ground ; but eleven persons unite in declaring that Mrs. Guppy was not only conveyed through the air in a trance all the way from Highbury Park to Lamb's Conduit Street, but was brought by invisible agency into a room of which the doors and windows were closed and fastened, coming 'plump down' in a state of complete unconsciousness

[1] *Appendix A.*

and partial *déshabille* upon a table round which they were sitting in the dark, shoulder to shoulder.

Of course, if you accept the testimony of these witnesses to the aerial flights of Mr. Home and Mrs. Guppy, you can have no reason whatever for refusing credit to the historic evidence of the demoniacal elevation of Simon Magus, and the victory obtained over his demons by the two Apostles. And you are still more bound to accept the solemnly attested proofs recorded in the proceedings of our Law Courts within the last two hundred years, of the aerial transport of witches to attend their demoniacal festivities : the belief in Witchcraft being then accepted not only by the ignorant vulgar, but by some of the wisest men of the time, such as Lord Bacon and Sir Matthew Hale, Bishop Jewell and Richard Baxter, Sir Thomas Browne and Addison ; while the denial of it was considered as virtual Atheism.

The general progress of Rationalism, however, as Mr. Lecky has well shown, has changed all this ; and to accept any of these marvels, we must place ourselves in the mental attitude of the narrator of Mrs Guppy's flight ; who glories in being so completely unfettered by scientific prejudices, as to be free to swallow anything, however preposterous and impossible in the estimation of scientific men, that his belief in ' spiritual ' agencies may lead him to expect as probable.

If time permitted, it would be my endeavour to show you by a historical examination of these marvels, that there has been a long succession of epidemic

Delusions, the form of which has changed from time
to time, whilst their essential nature has remained the
same throughout; and that the condition which
underlies them all is *the subjection of the mind to a
dominant idea.* There is a constitutional tendency in
many minds to be seized by some strange notion
which takes entire possession of them ; so that all the
actions of the individual thus 'possessed' are results
of its operation. This notion may be of a nature
purely intellectual, or it may be one that strongly
interests the feelings. It may be confined to a small
group of individuals, or it may spread through vast
multitudes. Such delusions are most tyrannous and
most liable to spread, when connected with religious
enthusiasm ; as we see in the flagellant and dancing
manias of the Middle Ages ;[1] the supposed Demoniacal possession that afterwards became common in
the nunneries of France and Germany ; the ecstatic
revelations of Catholic and Protestant visionaries ;
the strange performances of the *Convulsionnaires* of
St. Médard, which have been since almost paralleled at
Methodist 'revivals' and camp-meetings ; the preach-
ing epidemic of Lutheran Sweden ; and many other
outbreaks of a nature more or less similar. But it is
characteristic of some of the later forms of these epidemic delusions, that they have connected themselves
rather with Science than with Religion. In fact, just
as the performances of Eastern Magi took the strongest hold of the Roman mind, when its faith in its old
religious beliefs was shaken to its foundations, so did

[1] *Appendices, B, C.*

the grandiose pretensions of Mesmer,—who claimed the discovery of a new Force in Nature, as universal as Gravitation, and more mysterious in its effects than Electricity and Magnetism,—find the most ready welcome among the sceptical votaries of novelty who paved the way for the French Revolution. And this pseudo-scientific idea gave the general direction to the doctrines taught by Mesmer's successors ; until in the supposed ' Spiritualistic ' manifestations a recur-rence to the religious form has taken place, which may (I think) be mainly traced to the emotional longing for some assurance of the continued existence of de-parted friends, and hence of our own future existence, which the intellectual loosening of time-honoured beliefs as to the Immortality of the Soul has brought into doubt with many.

I must limit myself, however, to the later phase of this history ; and shall endeavour to show you how completely the extravagant pretensions of Mesmerism and Odylism have been disproved by scientific inves-tigation : all that is genuine in their phenomena having been accounted for by well-ascertained Physiological principles ; while the evidence of their higher marvels has invariably broken down, when submitted to the searching tests imposed by the trained ' experts ' whom I maintain to be alone qualified to pronounce judgment upon such matters.

Nothing is more common than to hear it asserted that these are subjects which any person of ordinary intelligence can investigate for himself. But the Chemist and the Physicist would most assuredly demur to any such assumption in regard to a chemical or physical enquiry ; the Physiologist and Geologist would make the same protest against the judgment of unskilled persons in questions of physiology and geology. And a study of Mesmerism, Odylism, and Spiritualism extending over more than forty years, may be thought to justify me in contending that a knowledge of the physiology and pathology of the Human Organism—corporeal and mental—of the strange phenomena which are due to the Physical excitability of the Nervous System, of the yet stranger results, the possession of the Mind by dominant emotions or ideas, of its extraordinary tendency to self-deception in regard to matters in which the feelings are interested, of its liability to place undue confidence in persons having an interest in deceiving, and of the modes in which fallacies are best to be detected and frauds exposed, is an indispensable qualification both for the discrimination of the genuine from the false, and for the reduction of the genuine to its true shape and proportions.

I hold, further, not only that it is quite legitimate for the enquirer to enter upon this study with that ' prepossession ' in favour of the ascertained and universally admitted Laws of Nature, which believers in Spiritualism make it a reproach against men of science that they entertain ; but that experience proves that a prepossession in favour of some ' occult ' agency is almost sure to lead the investigator to the too ready acceptance of evidence of its operation. I would be among the last to affirm that there is not ' much more

in heaven and earth than is dreamt of in our philo-
sophy ; ' and would be as ready as anyone to welcome
any addition to our real knowledge of the great
Agencies of Nature. But my contention is that no
new principle of action has any claim to scientific
acceptance, save after an exhaustive enquiry as to the
extent to which the phenomena can be accounted for,
either certainly or probably, by agencies already
known ; an enquiry which only 'experts' in those
departments of science which deal with such agencies
are competent to carry out. The assumption of a
new agency, and the interpretation of phenomena in
accordance with it, is a method which has proved so de-
ceptive as to be now universally abandoned by men
of truly philosophical habits of thought ; being only
practised by such as surrender their common sense to
a 'dominant idea,' and deem nothing incredible which
accords with their 'prepossession.'

The recent history of Mr. Crooke's most admirable
invention, the Radiometer, is pregnant with lessons
on this point. When this was first exhibited to the
admiring gaze of the large body of scientific men assembled at the soirée of the Royal Society, there was
probably no one who was not ready to believe with
its inventor that the driving round of its vanes was
effected by the direct mechanical agency of that mode
of Radiant Force which we call Light ; and the
eminent Physicists in whose judgment the greatest
confidence was placed, seemed to have no doubt that
this mechanical agency was something outside Optics
properly so called, and was, in fact, if not a new Force

in Nature, a new *modus operandi* of a Force previously known under another form. There was here, then, a perfect readiness to admit a novelty which seemed so unmistakably demonstrated, though transcending all previous experience. But after some little time the question was raised whether the effect was not really due to an intermediate action of that *mode* of Radiant force which we call *Heat*, upon the attenuated vapour of which it was impossible entirely to get rid ; and the result of a most careful and elaborate experimental enquiry, in which nature has been put to the question in every conceivable mode, has been to make it (I believe) almost if not quite certain that the first view was incorrect, and that Heat is the real moving power, acting under peculiar conditions, but in no new mode.

No examination of the phenomena of Spiritualism can give the least satisfaction to the mind trained in philosophical habits of thought, unless it shall have been, in its way, as searching and complete as this. And when scientific men are invited to dark *séances*, or are admitted only under the condition that they shall merely look on and not enquire too closely, they feel that the matter is one with which they are entirely precluded from dealing. When, again, having seen what appears to them to present the character of a very transparent conjuring trick, they ask for a repetition of it under test conditions admitted to be fair, their usual experience is that they wait in vain (for hours it may be) for such repetition, and are then told that they have brought an 'atmosphere of incredulity' with them, which prevents the manifestation.—Now

I by no means affirm that the, claims of Spiritualism
are *dis*proved by these failures ; but I do contend that
until the evidence advanced by believers in those
claims has stood the test of the same sifting and cross-
examination by sceptical experts, that would be applied in the case of any other scientific enquiry, it has
no claim upon general acceptance ; and I shall now
proceed to justify that contention by an appeal to the
history of previous enquiries of the like kind.

MESMERISM.

It was about the year 1772, that Mesmer, who had
previously published a dissertation *On the Influence of
the Planets on the Human Body*, announced his discovery of a universal fluid, 'the immediate agent of
all the phenomena of nature, in which life originates,
and by which it is preserved ;' and asserted that he
had further discovered the power of regulating the
operations of this fluid, to guide its current in healthy
channels, and to obliterate by its means the tracks of
disease.   This power he in the first instance professed
to guide by the use of magnets ; but having quarrelled
with Father Hell, a professor of astronomy at Vienna,
who had furnished him with the magnets with which
he made his experiments, and who then claimed the
discovery of their curative agency, Mesmer went on
to assert that he could concentrate the power in, and
liberate it from, any substance he pleased, could
charge jars with it (as with electricity) and discharge
them at his pleasure, and could cure by its means

the most intractable diseases.[1]   Having created a
great sensation in Bavaria and Switzerland by his
mysterious manipulations, and by the novel effects
which they often produced, Mesmer returned to
Vienna, and undertook to cure of complete blindness
a celebrated singer Mdlle. Paradis, who had been for
ten years unsuccessfully treated by the court physician.
His claim to a partial success, however, which was in the
first instance supported by his patient, seemed to have
been afterwards so completely disproved by careful
trials of her visual powers, that he found himself
obliged to quit Vienna abruptly ; and he thence proceeded to Paris, where he soon produced a great sensation.   The state of French society at that time, as
I have already remarked, was peculiarly favourable to
his pretensions.   A feverish excitability prevailed,
which caused the public mind to be violently agitated
by every question it took up.   And Mesmer soon
found it advantageous to challenge the Learned
Societies of the capital to enter the lists against him ;
the storm of opposition which he thus provoked
having the effect of bringing over to his side a large
number of devoted disciples and ardent partisans.
He professed to distribute the magnetic fluid to his
congregated patients, from a *baquet* or magnetic tub
which he had impregnated with it, each individual
holding a rod which proceeded from the *baquet* ; but
when the case was particularly interesting, or likely
to be particularly profitable, he took it in hand for
personal magnetisation.   All the surroundings were

[1] *Appendix D.*

such as to favour, in the hysterical subjects who constituted the great bulk of his patients, the nervous
paroxysm termed the 'crisis,' which was at once recognised by medical men as only a modified form of
what is commonly known as a 'hysteric fit;' and the
influence of the 'imitative' tendency was strongly
manifested just as in cases where such fits run through
a school, nunnery, factory, or revivalist meeting, in
which a number of suitable subjects are collected
together. And it was chiefly on account of the
moral disorders to which Mesmer's proceedings
seemed likely to give rise, that the French Government directed a Scientific Commission, including the
most eminent *savans* of the time—such as Lavoisier,
Bailly, and Benjamin Franklin—to enquire into them.
After careful investigation they came to the conclusion
that there was no evidence whatever of any special
agency proceeding from the *baquet* ; for not only
were they unable to detect the passage of any influence
from it, that was appreciable, either by electric, magnetic, or chemical tests, or by the evidence of any of
their senses ; but on blindfolding those who seemed
to be most susceptible to its supposed influence, all
its ordinary effects were produced when they were
without any connection with it, *but believed that it existed.* And so, when in a garden of which certain
trees had been magnetised, the patients, either when
blindfolded, or when ignorant which trees had been
magnetised, would be thrown into a convulsive fit if
they believed themselves to be near a magnetised tree,

but were really at a distance from it; whilst, conversely, no effect would follow their close proximity to one of these trees, while they believed themselves to be at a distance from any of them. Further, the Commissioners reported that, although some cures might be wrought by the Mesmeric treatment, it was not without danger, since the convulsions excited were often violent and exceedingly apt to spread, especially among men feeble in body and weak in mind, and almost universally among women; and they dwelt strongly also on the moral dangers which, as their enquiries showed, attended these practices.[1]

Now this Report, although referring to a form of Mesmeric procedure which has long since passed into disrepute, really deals with what I hold to be an important principle of action, which, long vaguely recognised under the term 'imagination,' now takes a definite rank in Physiological science;—namely, that in individuals of that excitable nervous temperament which is known as 'hysterical' (a temperament by no means confined to women, but rare in healthy and vigorous men), the *expectation* of a certain result is often sufficient to evoke it. Of the influence of this 'expectancy' in producing most remarkable changes in the bodily organism, either curative or morbid, the history of Medicine affords abundant and varied illustrations; I shall presently show you that it can generate *sensations* of a great variety of kinds; and I shall further prove that it operates no less remarkably in calling forth *movements*, which, not being

[1] *Appendix E.*

consciously directed by the person who executes them, have been attributed to hypothetical 'occult' agencies.

I shall not trace the further history of Mesmer, or of the system advocated by himself; contenting myself with one ludicrous example of the absurdity of his pretensions. When asked in his old age by one of his disciples, why he ordered his patients to bathe in river-water in preference to well-water, he replied that it was because river-water is exposed to the sun's rays; and when further asked how these affected it in any other way than by the warmth they excited, he replied, "Dear doctor, the reason why all water ex-"posed to the rays of the sun is superior to all other "water, is because it is magnetised—since twenty years "ago *I magnetised the sun !*"

In the hands of some of his pupils, however, Animal Magnetism, or Mesmerism (as it gradually came to be generally called), assumed an entirely new development. It was discovered by the Marquis de Puysegur,—a great landed proprietor, who appears to have practised the art most disinterestedly for the sole benefit of his tenantry and poor neighbours,— that a state of profound insensibility might be induced by very simple methods in some individuals, and a state akin to somnambulism in others; and this discovery was taken up and brought into vogue by numerous mesmerisers in France and Germany, while, during the long Continental war and for some time afterwards, it remained almost unknown in England. Attention seems to have been first drawn to it

in this country by the publication of the account of a
severe operation performed in 1829 by M. Cloquet,
one of the most eminent surgeons of Paris, on a female
patient who had been thrown by mesmerism into a
state of somnambulism ; in which, though able to converse with those around her, she showed herself entirely insensible to pain, whilst of all that took place
in it she had subsequently no recollection whatever.
About twelve years afterwards, two amputations were
performed in our country, one in Nottinghamshire,
and the other in Leicestershire, upon mesmerised
patients, who showed no other sign of consciousness
than an almost inaudible moaning ; both of them ex-
hibiting an uninterrupted placidity of countenance,
and declaring, when brought back to their ordinary
state, that they were utterly unaware of what had
been done to them during their sleep. And not long
afterwards, Dr. Esdaile, a surgeon in Calcutta, gave
details of numerous most severe and tedious operations performed by him, without the infliction of pain,
upon natives in whom he had induced the mesmeric
sleep ; the rank of Presidency Surgeon being conferred
upon him by Lord Dalhousie (then Governor-General
of India), 'in acknowledgment of the services he had
" rendered to humanity." The results of minor experiments performed by various persons desirous of testing
the reality of this state, were quite in harmony with
these. Writing in 1845, Dr. Noble, of Manchester
with whom I was early brought into association by
Sir John Forbes in the pursuit of this enquiry,) said:

" We have seen a needle thrust deeply under the

nail of a woman sleeping mesmerically, without its exciting a quiver; we have seen pungent snuff in large quantities passed up the nostrils under the same circumstances, without any sneezing being produced until the patient was roused, many minutes afterwards: we have noticed an immunity from all shock when percussion caps have been discharged suddenly and loudly close to the ear; and we have observed a patient's little finger in the flame of a candle, and yet no indication of pain. In this latter case all idea of there having been courageous dissimulation was removed from our mind, in seeing the same patient evince both surprise and indignation at the treatment received; as, from particular circumstances, a substantial inconvenience was to result from the injury to the finger, which was by no means slight." [1]

This 'mesmeric sleep' corresponds precisely in character with what is known in medicine as 'hysteric coma;' the insensibility being as profound, while it lasts, as in the coma of narcotic poisoning or pressure on the brain; but coming on and passing off with such suddenness as to show that it is dependent upon some transient condition of the sensorium, which, with our present knowledge, we can pretty certainly assign to a reduction in the supply of blood caused by a sort of spasmodic contraction of the blood-vessels. That there is no adequate ground for regarding it as otherwise than *real*, appears further from the discovery made not long afterwards by Mr. Braid, a surgeon practising at Manchester, that he could induce it by a

[1] *British and Foreign Medical Review*, April 1845.

very simple method, which is not only even more effective than the 'passes' of the mesmeriser, but is moreover quite independent of any other will than that of the person who subjects himself to it. He found that this state (which he designated as Hypnotism) could be induced in a large proportion of individuals of either sex, and of all ranks, ages, and temperaments, who determinately fix their gaze for several minutes consecutively on an object brought so near to their eyes, as to require a degree of convergence of their axes that is maintainable only by a strong effort.[1]

The first state thus induced is usually one of profound comatose sleep; the 'subject' not being capable of being roused by sensory impressions of any ordinary kind, and bearing without the least indication of consciousness what would ordinarily produce intolerable uneasiness or even severe pain. But after some little time, this state very commonly passes into one of somnambulism, which again corresponds

---

[1] Mr. Braid's peculiar success in inducing this state seemed to depend partly upon his mode of working his method, and partly upon the 'expectancy' of his subjects. Finding a bright object preferable, he usually employed his silver lancet-case, which he held in the first place at ordinary reading distance, rather above the plane of the eyes; he then slowly approximated it towards the middle point, a little above the bridge of the nose, keeping his own eyes steadily fixed upon those of his 'subject,' and watching carefully the direction of their axes. If he perceived their convergence to be at all relaxed, he withdrew the object until the axes were both again directed to it; and then again approximated it as closely as was compatible with their continued convergence. When this could be maintained for a sufficient length of time upon an object at no more than about three inches distance, the comatose state generally supervened.

closely on the one hand with *natural,* and on the other with *mesmeric* somnambulism. In fact, it has been by the study of the Somnambulism artificially induced by Mr. Braid's process, that the essential nature of this condition has been elucidated, and that a scientific *rationale* can now be given of a large proportion of the phenomena reported by Mesmerisers as having been presented by their somnambules.

It has been claimed for certain Mesmeric somnambules, however, that they occasionally possess an intelligence altogether superhuman as to things present, past, and future, which has received the designation ' lucidity ; ' and it is contended that the testimony on which we accept the reality of phenomena which are conformable to our scientific experience, ought to satisfy us equally as to the genuineness of those designated as ' the higher,' which not only transcend, but absolutely contradict, what the mass of enlightened men would regard as universal experience. This contention, however, seems to me to rest upon an entirely incorrect appreciation of the probative force of evidence ; for, as I shall endeavour to prove to you in my succeeding lecture, the only secure basis for our belief on *any* subject, is the confirmation afforded to external testimony by our sense of the inherent probability of the fact testified to ; so that, as has been well remarked, " evidence tendered in support of what " is new must correspond in strength with the degree " of its incompatibility with doctrines generally admitted " as true ; and, where statements obviously contravene " all past experience and the universal consent of man-

C

" kind, any evidence is inadequate to the proof, which
" is not complete, beyond suspicion, and absolutely in-
" capable of being explained away."

Putting aside for the present the discussion of
these asserted marvels, I shall try to set before you
briefly the essential characters which distinguish the
state of Somnambulism (whether natural or induced),
on the one hand from dreaming, and on the other
from the ordinary waking condition. As in both
these, the mind is in a state of activity; but, as in
dreaming, its activity is free from that controlling
power of the will, by which it is directed in the waking
state ; and is also removed from this last by the complete ignorance of all that has passed in it, which is
manifested by the 'subject' when called back to his
waking self,—although the events of one access of this
'second consciousness' may vividly present themselves in the next, as if they had happened only just
before. Again, instead of all the senses being shut
up, as in ordinary dreaming sleep, some of them are
not only awake, but preternaturally impressible ; so
that the course of the somnambulist's thought may
be completely directed by suggestions of any kind
that can be conveyed from without through the sense-
channels which still remain open. But further, while
the mind of the ordinary dreamer can no more produce movements in his body than impressions on his
sense-organs can affect his mind, that of the Somnambulist retains full direction of his body (in so far, at
least, as his senses serve to guide its movements) ; so
that he *acts* his dreams as if they were his waking

thoughts. The mesmerised or hypnotised Somnambule may, in fact, be characterised as a *conscious automaton*, which, by appropriate suggestions, may be made to think, feel, say, or do almost anything that its director wills it to think, feel, say, or do ; with this remarkable peculiarity, that its whole power seems concentrated upon the state of activity in which it is at each moment, so that every faculty it is capable of exerting may become extraordinarily intensified. Thus, while vision is usually suspended, the senses of hearing, smell, and touch, with the muscular sense, are often preternaturally acute ; in consequence, it would seem, of the undistracted concentration of the attention on their indications. I could give you many curious instances of this, which I have myself witnessed ; as also of the great exertion of muscular power by subjects of extremely feeble *physique* : [1] but as they are all obviously referrible to this one simple principle, I need not dwell on their details, preferring to narrate one which I did not myself witness, but which was reported to me on most trustworthy authority, of a remarkable manifestation of a power of imitative vocalisation that is ordinarily attainable only after long practice. When Jenny Lind was singing at Manchester, she was invited by Mr. Braid to hear the performances of one of his hypnotised subjects, an illiterate factory girl, who had an excellent voice and ear, but whose musical powers had received scarcely any cultivation. This girl in the hypnotic state followed the Swedish nightingale's songs in different

[1] *Appendix F.*
C 2

languages both instantaneously and correctly ; and when, in order to test her powers, Mdlle. Lind extemporised a long and elaborate chromatic exercise, she imitated this with no less precision, though unable in her waking state even to attempt anything of the sort. " She caught the sounds so promptly," says Mr. Braid, " and gave both words and music so simultaneously " and correctly, that several persons present could not " discriminate whether there were two voices or only " one."

Now I wish you to compare this case with another, which was reported about the same time upon what seemed equally unexceptionable testimony. When Miss Martineau first avowed her conversion to Mesmerism, the extraordinary performances of her servant J—— were much talked of ; and among other marvels it was asserted that she could converse, when in her mesmeric state, in languages she had never learned, and of which she knew nothing when awake ; the particular fact being explicitly stated, that Lord Morpeth had tested this power and had found it real. You will readily perceive that supposing the testimony in this case to have been exactly the same as in the preceding, its probative force would have been very different. For the first of them, though unprecedented, presented no scientific improbability to those who were prepared by their careful study of the phenomena of Hypnotism, to believe that the power of imitative vocalisation, like any other, might be intensified by the concentration of the somnabule's whole attention upon the performance. But it seemed inconceivable that an uneducated servant girl could understand what was said to her in a language she had never learned ; still more, that she should be able to reply in the same language. And the only rational explanation of the fact, *if fact it was*, short of a miracle, must have lain, either in her having learned the language long before and subsequently forgotten it, or in her being able by ' thought-reading ' (which is maintained by some, even at the present time, to be one of the attributes of the mesmeric state) to divine and express the answer expected by Lord Morpeth. But the marvel was entirely dissipated by the enquiries of Dr. Noble ; who, being very desirous of getting at the exact truth, first applied for information to a near relative of Miss Martineau, and was told by him that the report was not quite accurate, for that on Lord Morpeth putting a question to J—— in a foreign language, J—— had replied appropriately in her own vernacular. Her comprehension of Lord Morpeth's question, however, appeared in itself sufficiently strange to be suggestive of some fallacy ; and having an opportunity, not long afterwards, of asking Lord Morpeth himself what was the real state of the case, Dr. Noble learned from him that when he put a question to J—— in a foreign language, she imitated his speech after a fashion by an unmeaning articulation of sound.

On the lesson which this case affords as to the credibility of testimony in regard to what are called the ' higher phenomena ' of Mesmerism, I shall enlarge in my succeeding lecture ; and at present I shall only remark that it was shown by careful comparison

between the phenomena displayed by the same individuals, when 'mesmerised' in the ordinary way, and
'hypnotised' by Mr. Braid's process, that there was
no other difference between the two states, than that
arising from the special *rapport* between the mesmeriser and his 'subject'; and that this was clearly expli-
cable by the 'expectancy' under which the 'subject'
passed into the state of second consciousness. For
Mr. Braid found himself able, by assuring his 'subjects' during the induction of the coma that they
would hear the voice of one particular person and no
other, to establish this *rapport* with any person he
might choose: the case being strictly analogous to
the awaking of the telegraph-clerk by the clicking of
his needles, of the doctor by his night-bell, or of the
mother by her infant's ᴄᵣᵧ, though all would sleep
soundly through far louder noises to which they felt
no call to attend. And thus, as was pointed out long
since by Dr. Noble and myself, not only may the
general reality of the Mesmeric Somnambulism be
fully admitted, but a scientific *rationale* may be found
for its supposed distinctive peculiarities, without the
assumption of any special 'magnetic' or 'mesmeric'
agency.

It is affirmed, however, that proof of this agency
is furnished by the power of the 'silent will' of the
Mesmeriser to induce the sleep in subjects who are
not in the least aware that it is being exerted, and
further, to direct from a distance the actions of the
Somnambule. Doubtless, if satisfactory proof of this
assertion could be furnished, it would go far to estab-

lish the claim. But nothing is more difficult than to
eliminate all sources of fallacy in this matter. For
while it is admitted by Mesmerisers that the belief
that the influence is being exerted is quite sufficient,
in habitual somnambules, to induce the result, it is
equally certain that such 'sensitives' are marvellously
quick at guessing from slight intimations what is expected to happen. And it has been repeatedly found
that mesmerisers who had no hesitation in asserting
that they could send particular 'subjects' to sleep, or
could affect them in other ways, by an effort of silent
will, have utterly failed to do so when these 'subjects'
were carefully kept from any suspicion that such will
was being exerted. Thus Dr. Noble has recorded the
case of a friend of his own, who, believing himself
able thus to influence a female servant whom he had
repeatedly mesmerised, accepted with the full assurance of confident faith a proposal to make this
experiment in Dr. Noble's house instead of his own.
The girl, having been sent thither with a note, was
told to sit down in Dr. Noble's consulting-room while
the answer was being written ; her chair being close
to a partially-open door, on the other side of which
her master, whom she supposed to be elsewhere, had
previously taken up his position. Although this gentleman had usually found two or three minutes
sufficient to send the girl to sleep, when he was in his
own drawing-room and she was in the kitchen, the two
being separated by intervening walls and flooring, yet
when he put forth his whole force for a quarter of an
hour within two feet of her, with only a partially closed

door between them, it was entirely without result;
and no other reason for the failure could be assigned
than *her entire freedom from expectancy.* So in
another case, in which Mr. Lewis (accounted one of
the most powerful Mesmerists of his time) undertook
to direct the actions of his somnambule in the next
room, according to a programme agreed on between
himself and one set of witnesses,—whilst the actions
actually performed were recorded and timed by
another set,—there was found to be so complete a
discordance between the programme ' willed ' and the
actions really executed, as entirely to negative the
idea of any dependence of the latter upon the directing
power of the mesmeriser.[1]   Mr. Lewis was challenged
to this test-experiment by Professors of the University
of Aberdeen, in consequence of his public assertion
that he had repeatedly induced the mesmeric sleep,
and had directed the operations of his somnambules,
by the exertion of his ' silent will ' from a distance.
His utter failure to produce either result, however,
under the scrutiny of sceptical enquirers, obviously
discredits all his previous statements ; except to such
as (like Mr. A. R. Wallace, who has recently expressed
his full faith in Mr. Lewis's self-asserted powers,) are
ready to accept without question the slenderest evidence of the greatest marvels.   Further, when challenged to give proof before the same Committee, of
the power he had publicly claimed of overcoming the
force of gravity by raising a man from the ground and
keeping him suspended in the air for a short time,

[1] *Appendix G.*

simply by holding his hand above the man's head and willing the result, Mr. Lewis admitted "that he had " no such power, and that he could only influence " a person lying on the ground so as to make him start " up, though others were endeavouring to hold him " down." Now I would ask you to compare this disclaimer, made to a body of sceptical Professors of Aberdeen, whose published report of it was never impugned by Mr. Lewis, with the assertion made to and accepted by Professor Gregory of Edinburgh:—
"When Mr. Lewis stood on a chair, and tried to draw " Mr. H., without contact, from the ground, he gradu-" ally rose on tiptoe, making the most violent efforts to " rise, till he was fixed by cataleptic rigidity. Mr. Lewis " said, that had he been still more elevated above Mr. " H., he could have raised him from the floor without " contact, and *held him thus suspended for a short time,* " *while some spectator should pass his hand under his feet.* " Although this was not done in my presence, yet the " attraction upwards was so strong, that *I see no reason* " *to doubt the statement made to me by Mr. Lewis and* " *others who saw it, that this experiment has been success-* "*fully performed.*'[1] One is inclined to say of such pretenders, and of the believers in them, "These be thy gods, O Israel."

A converse experiment performed by Dr. Elliotson himself, satisfied him that 'expectancy' would take the place of what he maintained to be the real Mesmeric influence. Having told one of his *habituées* that he would go into the next room and mesmerise her

[1] *Letters to a Candid Enquirer on Animal Magnetism,* p. 352.

through the door, he retired, shut the door, performed
no mesmeric passes, but tried to forget her, walked
away from the door, busied himself with something else, and even walked into a third room ; and
on returning in less than ten minutes found the
girl in her usual sleep-waking condition. The extreme susceptibility of many of these ' sensitive ' subjects further accounts for their being affected (without
any intentional deceit) by physical impressions which
are quite imperceptible to others :—such as slight
differences in temperature, when two coins are presented to them, of which one has been held in the
hand of the mesmeriser ; or two wine-glasses of water,
into one of which he has dipped his finger for a short
time. But the *belief* that he has transmitted his
influence in any mode is quite sufficient to produce the
result ; as was shown in an amusing case recorded by
M. Bertrand, whose treatise on *Animal Magnetism*
(Paris, 1826) is, by far, the most philosophical work
extant on the subject. Having occasion to go a journey of a hundred leagues, leaving a female somnambule under the treatment of one of his friends,
M. Bertrand sent him a magnetised letter, which he
requested him to place on the stomach of the patient,
who had been led to anticipate the expected results ;
Mesmeric sleep, with the customary phenomena, supervened. He then wrote another letter which he did
not magnetise, and sent it to her in the same manner,
and with the same intimation. She again fell into the
Mesmeric sleep, which was attributed to the letter
having been unintentionally impregnated by M. Ber-

trand with the mesmeric fluid while he was writing it. Desiring to test the matter still further, he caused one of his friends to write a similar letter, imitating his handwriting so closely that those who received it should believe it to be his ;—the same effect was once more produced.

And so it was with the large number of experiments that were made within my own knowledge during the twenty years' attention that I gave to this subject, with a view to test the Mesmeriser's power of inducing any of the phenomena of this state without the patient's consciousness.   Successes, it is true, were not unfrequent ; but these almost invariably occurred when the experiments were made under conditions to which the parties had become habituated, as in the case of Dr. Noble's friend.   For his performances were so continually being repeated to satisfy the curiosity of visitors, that Dr. Noble's call at his house would have been sufficient to excite, on the part of the 'subject,' the expectancy that would have thrown her into the sleep.   But when such expectancy was carefully guarded against, the result was so constantly negative, as—I will not say to *disprove* the existence of any special Mesmeric force,—but to neutralise completely the affirmative value of the evidence adduced to *prove* it.   For I think you must now agree with me, that, if 'expectancy' alone is competent to produce the results, as admitted by the most intelligent Mesmerisers, nothing but the most rigid exclusion of such expectancy can afford the least ground for the assumption of any other agency.   And my own prolonged study of the subject further justifies me in taking the position, that it is only when the enquiry is directed, and its results recorded, by *sceptical experts*, that such results have the least claim to scientific value. The disposition to overlook sources of fallacy, to magnify trivialities into marvels, to construct circumstantial 'myths' (as in the case of Miss Martineau's J—— and Lord Morpeth) on the slightest foundation of fact, and to allow themselves to be imposed upon by cunning cheats, have been so constantly exhibited by even the most honest believers in the 'occult' power of Mesmerism, as—not only in my own opinion, but in that of my very able allies in this enquiry—to deprive the unconfirmed testimony of any number of such believers, in regard to matters lying beyond scientific experience, of all claim to acceptance. In fact, the positions taken in regard to Mesmerism by my friend Dr. Noble, as far back as 1845,[1] and more fully developed by myself a few years later on the basis of Mr. Braid's experiments and of my own Physiological and Psychological studies,[2] have, not only in our own judgment, but by the general verdict of the Medical and Scientific world, been fully confirmed by the subsequent course of events, the history of which I shall now proceed to sketch.

[1] *British and Foreign Medical Review,* vol. xix.
[2] *Principles of Human Physiology,* 4th edition, 1853 ; *Quarterly Review,* October, 1853.

ODYLISM.

It was asserted, about thirty years ago, by Baron von Reichenbach,—whose researches on the Chemistry of the Hydrocarbons constitute the foundation of our present knowledge of paraffin and its allied products of the distillation of coal,—that he had found certain ' sensitive ' subjects so peculiarly affected by the neighbourhood of Magnets or Crystals, as to justify the assumption of a special polar force which he termed *Odyle*, allied to, but not identical with, Magnetism ; present in all material substances, though generally in a less degree than in magnets and crystals ; but called into energetic activity by any kind of physical or chemical change, and, therefore, especially abundant in the Human body. Of the existence of this Odylic force, which he identified with the ' animal magnetism ' of Mesmer, he found what he maintained to be adequate evidence in the peculiar sensations and attractions experienced by his ' sensitives' when in the neighbourhood either of Magnets or Crystals, or of Human beings specially charged with it. After a magnet had been repeatedly drawn along the arm of one of these ' subjects,' she would feel a pricking, streaming, or shooting sensation ; she would smell odours proceeding from it ; or she would see a small volcano of flame issuing from its poles, when gazing at them, even in broad daylight. As in the Mesmeric sleep light is often seen by the somnambule to issue from the operator's fingers, so the Odylic light was

discerned in the dark by Von Reichenbach's 'sensitives,' issuing not only from the hands, but from the
head, eyes, and mouth of powerful generators of this
force. One individual in particular was so peculiarly
sensitive, that she saw (in the dark) sparks and flames
issuing from ordinary nails and hooks in a wall. It
was further affirmed that certain of these 'sensitives'
found their hands so powerfully attracted by magnets
or crystals, as to be irresistibly drawn towards them ;
and thus that if the attracting object were forcibly
drawn away, not only the hand, but the whole body
of the sensitive was dragged after it. Another set of
facts was adduced to prove the special relation of
Odyle to terrestrial Magnetism,—namely, that many
'sensitives' cannot sleep in beds which lie across the
magnetic meridian ; a position at right angles to it
being to some quite intolerable.

Von Reichenbach's doctrine came before the British
public under the authority of the late Dr. Gregory,
then Professor of Chemistry in the University of
Edinburgh ; who went so far as to affirm that " by a
" laborious and beautiful investigation, Reichenbach
" had demonstrated the existence of a force, influence,
" or imponderable fluid—whatever name be given to it—
" which is distinct from all the known forces, influences,
" or imponderable fluids, such as heat, light, electricity,
" magnetism, and from the attractions, such as gravita-
" tion, or chemical attraction." It at once became apparent, however, to experienced Physicians conversant
with the proteiform manifestations of that excitable,
nervous temperament, of which I have already had to

speak, that all these sensations were of the kind
which the Physiologist terms 'subjective;' the state
of the Sensorium on which they immediately depend,
being the resultant, not of physical impressions made
by external agencies upon the Organs of Sense, but
of Cerebral changes connected with the ideas with
which the minds of the 'sensitives' had come to be
'possessed.' The very fact that no manifestation of
the supposed force could be obtained except through
a conscious Human organism, should have been quite
sufficient to suggest to any philosophic investigator
that he had to do, not with a new Physical Force, but
with a peculiar phase of Physiological action, by no
means unfamiliar to those who had previously studied
the influence of the Mind upon the Body. As Mr.
Braid justly remarked, "It unfortunately happens
"that the only test of this alleged new Force is the
" Human Nerve ; and not only so, but it is further ad-
"mitted that its existence can only be demonstrated
" by certain impressions imparted to, or experienced
" by, *a comparatively small number of highly sensitive*
" *and nervous subjects.* But it is an undoubted fact
" that with many individuals, and especially of the
"highly nervous, and imaginative, and abstractive
"classes, a strong direction of inward consciousness to
" any part of the body, especially if attended with the
"expectation or belief of something being about to
"happen, is quite sufficient to *change the physical action*
" *of the part, and to produce such impressions from this*
"*cause alone, as Baron Reichenbach attributes to his new*
"*force.* Thus every variety of feeling may be excited

" from an *internal* or *mental* cause—such as heat or
"cold, pricking, creeping, tingling, spasmodic twitching
" of muscles, catalepsy, a feeling of attraction or repul-
" sion, sights of every form or hue, odours, tastes, and
" sounds, in endless variety, and so on, according as ac-
" cident or intention may have suggested.   Moreover,
" the oftener such impressions have been excited, the
" more readily may they be reproduced, under similar
" circumstances, through the laws of association and
"habit. Such being the fact, it must consequently be
" obvious to every intelligent and unprejudiced person,
" that no implicit reliance can be placed on the Human
"Nerve, as a test of this new power in producing
" effects from *external* impressions or influences ; since
" precisely the same phenomena may arise from an
" *internal* or *mental* influence, when no external agency
" whatever is in operation." [1]

The fact, which Von Reichenbach himself was
honest enough to admit—that when a magnet was
poised in a delicate balance, and the hand of a 'sensitive'
was placed above or beneath it, the magnet was never
drawn towards the hand — ought to have convinced
him that the force which attracted the ' sensitive's '
hand to the magnet has nothing in common with
physical attractions, whose action is invariably *reci-
procal ;* but that it was the product of her own conviction that she *must* thus approximate it.   So
' possessed ' was he, however, by his pseudo-scientific
conception, that the true significance of this fact
entirely escaped him ; and although he considered
that he had taken adequate precautions to exclude

[1] A striking illustration of this principle will be found in Appendix H.

the conveyance of any suggestion of which his 'sensitives' should be conscious, he never tried the one test which would have been the *experimentum crucis* in regard to all the supposed influences of Magnets,—that of using *electro-magnets*, which could be 'made' and 'unmade' by completing or breaking the electric circuit, without any indication being given to the 'sensitive' of this change of its conditions. And the same remark applies to the more recent statement of Lord Lindsay, as to Mr. Home's recognition of the position of a permanent magnet in a totally darkened room ; the value of this solitary fact, for which there are plenty of ways of accounting, never having been tested by the use of an Electro-magnet, whose active or passive condition should be entirely unknown, not only to Mr. Home, but to every person present.

That 'sensitives' like Von Reichenbach's, in so far as they are not intentional deceivers (which many hysterical subjects are constitutionally prone to be), can feel, see, or smell anything that they were led to believe that they *would* feel, see, or smell, was soon proved by the experimental enquiries of Mr. Braid, many of which I myself witnessed.[1] He found that not only in hysterical girls, but in many men and women "of a highly concentrative and imaginative "turn of mind," though otherwise in ordinary health, it was sufficient to fix the attention on any particular form of *expectancy*,—such as pricking, streaming, heat, cold, or other feelings, in any part of the body over

---

[1] *Appendix I.*

which a magnet was being drawn ; luminous emana-
tions from the poles of a magnet in the dark, in some
cases even in full daylight ; or the attraction of a
magnet or crystal held within reach of the hand,—for
that expectancy to be fully realised. And, conversely,
the same sensations were equally produced when the
subjects of them were led to *believe* that the same
agency was being employed, although nothing whatever was really done ; the same flames being seen
when the magnet was concealed by shutting it in a
box, or even when it was carried out of the room,
without the knowledge of the subject ; and the attraction of the magnet for the hand being entirely
governed by the idea previously suggested, positive
or negative results being thus obtained with either
pole, as Mr. Braid might direct.

I had myself the opportunity of witnessing these
'vigilant phenomena' (as Mr. Braid termed them,
from their being presented by individuals not asleep,
though in a state of abstraction) upon one of Mr.
Braid's best 'subjects,' a gentleman residing in
Manchester, well known for his high intellectual
culture, great general ability, and strict probity.
He had such a remarkable power of voluntary abstraction, as to be able at any time to induce in
himself a state akin to profound Reverie (corresponding to what has been since most inappropriately
called the 'biological'), in which he became so completely 'possessed' by any idea strongly enforced
upon him, that his whole state of feeling and action
was dominated by it. Thus it was sufficient for him
to place his hand upon the table, and fix his attention

upon it for half a minute, to be entirely unable to withdraw it, if assured in a determined tone that he *could not* do so. When his gaze had been steadily directed for a short time to the poles of a magnet, he could be brought to see flames issuing from them, of any form or colour that Mr. Braid chose to name. And when desired to place his hand upon one of the poles, and to fix his attention for a brief period upon it, the peremptory assurance that he *could not* detach it was sufficient to hold it there with such tenacity, that I saw Mr. Braid drag him round the room by the traction of the magnet which he held, in a way that reminded me of George Cruikshank's amusing illustration of the German fairy story of the Golden Goose. The attraction was dissolved by Mr. Braid's loud cheery 'All right, man,' which brought the subject back to his normal condition, as suddenly as the attraction of a powerful Electro-magnet for a heavy mass of iron ceases when the circuit is broken.

ELECTRO-BIOLOGY.

Similar experiments to the foregoing (which I first witnessed about thirty years ago) have been since repeated, over and over again, upon great numbers of persons, in whom a corresponding state can be induced by prolonged fixation of the vision on a small object held in the hand. It was in the year 1850 that a new manifestation of the supposed 'occult' power first attracted public attention, through the exhibition of it by a couple of itinerant Americans, who styled themselves 'professors' of a new art which they termed *Electro-Biology* ; asserting that by an influence of which the secret was only known to themselves, but which was partially derived from a little disk of zinc or copper held in the hand of the 'subject' and steadily gazed on by him, they could subjugate the most determined will, paralyse the strongest muscles, pervert the evidence of the senses, destroy the memory of even the most familiar things or of the most recent occurrences, induce obedience to any command, or make the individual believe himself transformed into anyone else ;—all this, and much more, being done while he was still wide awake.   They soon attracted large assemblages to witness their performances ; and seldom failed to elicit some of the most remarkable phenomena from entire strangers to them, whose honesty could not be reasonably called in question. In place of a few peculiarly susceptible 'subjects' not always to be met with, and open to suspicion on various grounds, those who took up this practice found in almost every circle some individuals in whom the 'biological' state could be self-induced by the steady direction of their eyes to one point, at the ordinary reading distance, for a period usually varying from about five to twenty minutes ; a much shorter time generally sufficing in cases in which the practice has been frequently repeated.   In this condition, the whole course of thought is directed by external suggestions, the subject's own control over it being altogether suspended.   Yet he differs from the somnambulist in being awake ; that is, he has generally the use of all his senses, and usually, though not always, preserves a distinct recollection of all that has taken place.   There is, in fact, a gradational transition from the 'biological' to the 'mesmeric' state ; just as there is a passage from the state of profound reverie or 'day-dreaming' to that of ordinary sleep.   All its strange phenomena are referrible to one simple principle—the possession of the mind by a *dominant idea*, from which, however absurd it may be, the subject cannot free himself by bringing it to the test of actual experience, because the suspension of his self-directing power prevents him from correcting his ideational state by comparing it with external realities ; this suspension being often as complete as it is in dreaming, so that, though the senses are awake, they cannot be turned to account.   But it may exist in regard to one sense only, the impressions made on others being truly represented to the mind.   Thus I have seen instances in which a 'biologised' subject could be made to believe himself to be *tasting* anything which the operator might assure him that he *would* taste— such as milk, coffee, wine, or porter—when drinking a glass of pure water, though he was instantly disabused by *looking* at the liquid ; whilst another would *see* milk or coffee, wine or porter, as he was directed, but would instantly set himself right when he *tasted* the liquid.   Nothing can be more instructive than to experiment upon a subject who has no misgivings of this kind, but whose perceptions are altogether under the direction of the ideas impressed upon him.   He may be made to exhibit all the manifestations of delight which would be called forth by the viands or liquors of which he may be most fond ; and these may be turned in a moment into expressions of the strongest disgust, by simply giving the word which shall (ideally) change it into something he detests. Or if, when he believes himself to be drinking a cup of tea or coffee, he be made to believe that it is very hot, nothing will induce him to take more than a sip at a time ; yet a moment afterwards he will be ready to swallow the whole in gulps, if assured that the liquid is quite cool. Tell him, again, that his seat is growing hot under him, and that he will not be able to remain long upon it, and he will fidget uneasily for some time, and at last start up with all the indications of having found the heat no longer bearable. Whilst he is firmly grasping a stick in his hand, let him be assured that it will burn him if he continue to hold it, or that it is becoming so heavy that he can no longer sustain it ; and he will presently drop it with gestures conformable in each case to the idea.

It may, of course, be said that what I have presented to you as real phenomena are only simulated ; and as there would be nothing difficult in such simulation, the supposition is clearly admissible. But they are so perfectly conformable to the known principles of Mental action, that there is no justification for the suspicion of deceit, when they are presented by persons in whose good faith we have reasonable grounds of confidence. For everyone must be conscious of occasional mistakes as to what he supposes himself to have seen or heard, which he can trace to a previous 'expectancy.' Of this I can give you a very striking illustration in a case narrated by Dr. Tuke. A lady, whose mind had been a good deal occupied on the subject of drinking-fountains, was walking from Penryn to Falmouth, and thought she saw in the road a newly-erected fountain, with the inscription, 'If any man thirst, let him come hither and drink.' Some time afterwards, on mentioning the fact with pleasure to the daughters of a gentleman whom she supposed to have erected it, she was greatly surprised to learn from them that no such drinking-fountain existed ; and on subsequently repairing to the spot, she found nothing but a few stones, which constituted the foundation on which her expectant imagination had built an ideal superstructure.

The same may be said with regard to the control exercised over the muscular movements of the Biologised 'subject,' by the persuasion that he *must* or that he *cannot* perform a particular action. His hands being placed in contact with one another, he is assured that he cannot separate them ; and they remain as if firmly glued together, in spite of all his apparent efforts to draw them apart. Or, a hand being held up before him, he is assured that he cannot succeed in striking it; and not only does all his power seem inadequate to the performance of this simple action, but it actually is so, as long as he remains convinced of its entire impossibility. So I have seen a strong man chained down to his chair, prevented from stepping over a stick on the floor, or obliged to remain almost doubled upon himself in a stooping position, by the assurance that he *could* not move. On the other hand, an extraordinary power may be called forth in any set of muscles—as in Hypnotised subjects—by the assurance that the action to be performed by them may be executed with the greatest facility. This, again, is quite conformable to ordinary experience ; the assurance that we *can* perform some feat of strength or dexterity, nerving us to the effort ; whilst our power is weakened by our own doubts of success, still more by the unfavourable impression produced by a confident prediction of failure. It is only needed for the mind to become completely 'possessed' by the one or the other conviction, for it to produce the bodily results of this kind which I have over and over again witnessed.

Now the phenomena of the 'Biological' condition seem to me of peculiar significance, in relation to a large class of those which are claimed as manifestations of a supposed 'Spiritual' agency. When a number of persons of that "concentrative and imaginative turn of mind" which predisposes them to this condition, sit for a couple of hours (especially if in the dark) with the expectation of some extraordinary occurrence,—such as the rising and floating in the air, either of the human body, or of chairs or tables, without any physical agency ; the crawling of live lobsters over their persons ; the contact of the hands, the sound of the voices, or the visible luminous shapes,[1] of their

---

[1] I put aside the question of fraud, to which recourse has doubtless often been had for the production of these phenomena ; being satisfied that they are often genuinely 'subjective.'

departed friends,—it is perfectly conformable to scientific probability that they should pass more or less completely (like Reichenbach's 'sensitives') into a state which is neither waking nor sleeping, but between the two, in which they see, hear, or feel by touch, anything they have been led to expect will present itself. And the accordance of their testimony, in regard to such occurrences, is only such as is produced by the community of the 'dominant idea' with which they are all 'possessed,' a community of which history furnishes any amount of strangely-varied examples. And thus it becomes obvious that the testimony of a single cool-headed sceptic, who asserts that nothing extraordinary has really occurred, should be accepted as more trustworthy than that of any number of believers, who have, as it were, *created* the sensorial result by their anticipation of it.

PENDULE EXPLORATEUR.

I have now to show you that the like 'expectancy' can also produce *movements* of various kinds through the instrumentality of the nervo-muscular apparatus, without the least consciousness on the part of its subject of his being himself the instrument of their performance ; a physiological fact which is the key to the whole mystery of Table-turning and Table-talking. I very well remember the prevalence, in my schoolboy days, of a belief that when a ring, a button, or any other small body, suspended by a string over the end of the finger, was brought near the outside or

inside of a glass tumbler, it would strike the hour of
the day against its surface ; and the experiment certainly succeeded in the hands of several of my school-
fellows, who tried it in all good faith, getting up in
the middle of the night to test it, in entire ignorance—
as they declared—of the real time. But, as was pointed
out by M. Chevreul, who investigated this subject in
a truly scientific spirit more than forty years ago,[1] it
is impossible by any voluntary effort to keep the hand
absolutely still for a length of time in the position
required ; an involuntary tremulousness is always ob-
servable in the suspended body ; and if the attention
be fixed on it with the expectation that its vibrations
will take a definite direction, they are very likely to
do so.   But their persistence in that direction is found
to last only so long as they are guided by the sight
of the operator ; the oscillations at once and entirely
losing their constancy, if he closes or turns away his
eyes.   Thus it became obvious that, in the striking
of the hour, the influence which determines the number of strokes is really the knowledge or suspicion
present to the *mind* of the operator, which involuntarily
and unconsciously directs the action of his muscles ;
and the same *rationale* was applied by M. Chevreul
to other cases in which this *pendule explorateur* (the use
of which can be traced back to a very remote date)
has been appealed to for answers to questions of very
diverse character.[2]

[1] See his letter to M. Ampère in the *Revue des Deux Mondes,*
Mai, 1833.

[2] *Appendix K.*

When, however, ' Odyle' came to the front, and
the world of curious but unscientific enquirers was
again 'possessed' by the idea of an unknown and
mysterious agency, capable of manifesting itself in an
unlimited variety of ways, the *pendule explorateur* was
brought into vogue, under the name of *Odometer*, by
Dr. Herbert Mayo,[1] who investigated its action with
a great show of scientific precision ; starting, however,
with the foregone conclusion that its oscillations were
directed by the hypothetical ' odyle,' and altogether
ignoring the mental participation of the operator,
whom he supposed to be as passive as a thermometer
or a balance. By a series of elaborate experiments,
he convinced himself that the direction and extent of
the oscillations could be altered, either by a change
in the nature of the substances placed beneath the
' odometer,' or by the contact of the hand of a person
of the opposite sex, or even of the other hand of the
experimenter himself, with that from which it was suspended. And he gradually reduced his result to a
series of definite laws, which he regarded as having
the same constancy as those of Physics or Chemistry.
Unfortunately, however, other experimenters, who
worked out the enquiry with similar perseverance and
good faith, arrived at such different results, that it
soon came to be obvious that what Astronomical ob-
servers call the ' personal equation' of the individual
has a very large share in determining them. A very
intelligent medical friend of my own, then residing
abroad, wrote me long letters full of the detailed

[1] *On the Truths contained in Popular Superstitions*, 1851.

results of his own enquiries, on which he was anxious for my opinion. My reply was simply, " Shut your " eyes, or turn them away ; let some one else watch the " oscillations under the conditions you have specified, " and record their results ; and you will find, if I do not " mistake, that they will then show an entire *want* of " the constancy you have hitherto observed." His next letter informed me that such proved to be the case ; so that he came entirely to agree with me as to the dependence of the previous uniformity of his results on his own 'expectancy.'

A curious variation of the ' Odometer' was introduced by Mr. Rutter, then manager of the gas-works at Brighton, under the name of ' Magnetometer ;' which was simply a gallows-shaped frame, mounted on a solid base, and having a metallic ball suspended from its free extremity. When the finger was kept for a short time in contact with this frame, the ball began to oscillate, usually in some definite direction ; changing that direction with any change of circumstances, after the manner of Dr. Mayo's 'odometer.' To many persons, as to Mr. Rutter himself, it appeared impossible that these oscillations could have their origin in any movement of the operator ; but everyone who knew how difficult it is to prevent vibrations in the supporting frame-work of a Microscope or a Telescope, and who recognised in the construction of the ' Magnetometer' exactly such an arrangement as enabled the smallest amount of imparted motion to produce the greatest sensible effect, was prepared to anticipate that the oscillations of the suspended ball would be

as much maintained and guided by the ' expectancy '
of the operator, as they are when it is hung directly
from his own finger. Experiment soon proved this to
be the case ; for it was found that the constancy of
the vibrations entirely depended upon the operator's
watching their direction, either by his own eyes or by
those of some one else ; and further, that when such a
change was made *without his knowledge* in the conditions of the experiment, as *ought*, theoretically, to
alter the direction of the oscillations, no such alteration
took place.

A very amusing *exposé* of the mystery of the
' Magnetometer ' resulted from its application by Dr.
Madden, a Homœopathic physician at Brighton, to
test the virtues of his ' globules,' as to which he had,
of course, some pre-formed conclusions of his own.
The results of his first experiments entirely corre-
sponded with his ideas of what they ought to be ; for
when a globule of one medicine was taken into his
disengaged hand, the suspended ball oscillated longi-
tudinally ; and when this globule was changed for
another of (supposed) opposite virtues, the direction of
the oscillations became transverse.   Another Homœopathic physician, however, was going through a similar
course of experiments ; and his results, while conformable to his own notions of the virtues of the globules,
were by no means accordant with those of Dr. Madden.
The latter was thus led to re-investigate the matter
with a precaution he had omitted in the first instance ;
—namely, that the globules should be placed in his
hand by another person, without any hint being given

him of their nature.   From the moment he began to
work upon this plan, the whole aspect of the subject
was changed ; globules that produced longitudinal
oscillations at one time, gave transverse at another ;
whilst globules of the most opposite remedial virtues
gave no sign of difference.   And thus he was soon led
to the conviction, which he avowed with a candour
very creditable to him, that the system he had built
up had no better foundation than his own 'expectancy' of what the results of each experiment should
be ; that anticipation expressing itself unconsciously
in involuntary and imperceptible movements of his
finger, which communicated a rhythmical vibration to
the framework when the oscillations of the ball suspended from it were watched.

     Thus, by the investigations of scientific experts
who were alive to the sources of fallacy which the introduction of the *human* element always brings into
play, the hypothesis of Odylic force was proved to be
completely baseless ; the phenomena which were supposed to indicate its existence being traceable to the
Physiological conditions of the Human organisms
through whose instrumentality they were manifested.
The principle that the state of 'expectant attention'
is capable of giving rise either to *sensations* or to involuntary *movements*, according to the nature of the
expectancy, had been previously recognised in Physiological science, and was not invented for the occasion ;
but the phenomena I have been describing to you are
among its most 'pregnant instances.'

DIVINING ROD.

The same principle furnishes what I believe to be
the true scientific explanation of the supposed mystery of the Divining Rod, often used where water is
scarce for the discovery of springs, and in mining districts for the detection of metallic veins. This rod is
a forked twig, shaped like the letter Y, hazel being
usually preferred ; and the diviner walks over the
ground to be explored, firmly grasping its two prongs
with his hands, in such a position that its stem points
forwards. After a time the end of the stem points
downwards, often, it is said, with a sort of writhing
or struggling motion, especially when the fork is tightly
grasped ; and sometimes it even turns backwards, so as
to point towards, instead of away from, the body of the
diviner. Now there is a very large body of apparently
reliable testimony, that when the ground has been
opened in situations thus indicated, either water-
springs or metallic veins have been found beneath ;
and it is quite certain that the existence of such a
power is a matter of unquestioning faith on the part
of large numbers of intelligent persons, who have witnessed what they believed to be its genuine manifestations.[1] This subject, however, was carefully enquired
into more than forty years ago by MM. Chevreul and
Biot ; and their experimental conclusions anticipated

[1] I have lately received a pamphlet from an Engineer in the United
States, giving most circumstantial details of successes thus obtained
within his own experience.

those to which I was myself led, in ignorance of them, by Physiological reasoning. They found that the forked twig cannot be firmly grasped for a quarter of an hour or more in the regular position, without the induction of a state of muscular tension which at last discharges itself in movement; and this acts on the prongs of the fork in such a manner, as to cause its stem to point either upwards or downwards or to one side. The occasion of this discharge, and the direction of the movement, are greatly influenced—like the oscillations of bodies suspended from the finger—by the expectancy of the operator; so that if he has any suspicion or surmise as to the 'whereabouts' of the object of his search, an involuntary and unconscious action of his muscles causes the point of the rod to dip over it. This was admitted even by Dr. H. Mayo, a believer in the existence of an 'Od-force' governing the movements of the rod; for he found that when his 'diviner' knew which way the fork was expected to move, it invariably answered his expectations; whilst, when he had the man blindfolded, the results were uncertain and contradictory. Hence he came to the conclusion that several of those in whose hands the Divining Rod moves, set it in motion, and direct its motion (however unintentionally and unconsciously) by the pressure of their fingers, and by carrying their hands near-to or apart-from one another.[1]

Again, since not one individual in forty, in the localities in which the virtues of the Divining Rod are still held as an article of faith, is found to obtain any

[1] *On the Truths contained in Popular Superstitions,* Letter I., p. 19.

results from its use, it becomes obvious that its movements must be due, not to any Physical agency directly affecting the rod, but to some influence exerted through its holder. And that this influence is his expectation of the result, may, I think, be pretty confidently affirmed. For it has been clearly shown, by careful and repeated experiments, that, while the rod dips when the ' diviner ' knows or believes he is over a water-spring or a metallic vein, the results are uncertain, contradictory, or simply negative, when he is blindfolded, so as not to be aware precisely where he is. The following is a striking case of this kind, that has been lately brought to my knowledge :—

"A friend of mine (says Dr. Beard),[1] an aged clergyman, of thorough integrity and fairness, has for many years—the larger part of his natural life, I believe—enjoyed the reputation of being especially skilled in the finding of places to dig wells, by means of a divining rod of witch hazel, or the fresh branches of apple or other trees. His fame has spread far ; and the accounts that are given by him and of him, are, to those who think human testimony worth anything, overwhelmingly convincing. He consented to allow me to experiment with him. I found that only a few moments were required to prove that his fancied gift was a delusion, and could be explained wholly by unconscious muscular motion, the result of expectancy and coincidence. In his own yard there was known to be a stream of water running through a small pipe a few feet below the surface. Marching over and near this, the rod continually pointed strongly downwards, and several times turned clear over. These places I marked, blindfolded him, marched him about until he knew not where he was, and took him over the same ground over and over again; and although the rod went down a number of times, it did not once point to or near the places previously indicated."

I very well remember having heard, some 35 years ago, from Mr. Dilke (the grandfather of the present Sir Charles) of an experiment of this kind which he had himself made upon a young Portuguese, who had come to him with a letter of introduction, describing the bearer of it as possessing a most remarkable power of finding, by means of the Divining Rod, metals concealed from view. Mr. Dilke's family being at a summer residence in the country, his plate had all been sent to his chambers in the Adelphi, where he was visited by the Portuguese youth; to whom he said "Go about the room with your rod, and try if you can find any mass of metal." The youth did so; and his rod dipped over a large standing desk, in which Mr. D.'s plate had been temporarily lodged. Seeing, however, that there were circumstances which might reasonably suggest this guess, Mr. Dilke asked the youth if he was willing to allow his divining power to be tested under conditions which should exclude all such suggestion; and having received a ready assent, he took his measures accordingly. Taking his plate-box down to his country residence, he secretly buried it just beneath the soil in a newly ploughed field; selecting a spot which he could identify by cross-bearings of conspicuous trees, and getting a plough drawn again over its surface, so that the ridges and furrows should correspond precisely with those of the rest of the field. The young diviner was then summoned from London, and challenged to find beneath the soil of this field the very same plate which he had previously detected in Mr. Dilke's desk at the Adelphi; but having nothing whatever to guide him even to a guess, he was completely at fault. Mr. Dilke's impression was that he was not an impostor, but a sincere believer in his own power, as the 'dowsers' of mining districts seem unquestionably to be.—The test of blindfolding the diviner, and then leading him about in different directions so as to put him completely at fault in regard to his locality, is one that can be very readily applied when the diviner is acting in good faith ; but, as I shall show you in the next lecture, it requires very special precautions to blindfold a person who is determined to see ; and in some of the cases which seem to have stood this test, it seems not improbable that vision was not altogether precluded.

An additional reason for attributing the action of the Divining Rod to the muscular movements called forth by a state of 'expectancy' (perhaps not always consciously entertained) on the part of the performer, seems to me to be furnished by the diversity of the powers that have been attributed to it ; such as that of identifying murderers and indicating the direction of their flight, discovering the lost boundaries of lands, detecting the birth-place and parentage of foundlings, &c. The older writers do not in the least call in

question the reality of the powers of the hazel fork;
but learnedly discuss whether they are due to natural
or to diabolic agency.   When, in the last century, the
phenomena of Electricity and Magnetism became
objects of scientific study, but had not yet been com-
prehended under the grasp of law, it was natural that
those of the Divining Rod should be referred to
agencies so convenient, which seemed ready to account
for anything otherwise unaccountable.   But since Physicists and Physiologists have come to agree that the
moving power is furnished by nothing else than the
muscles of the diviner, the only question that remains
is—what calls forth its exercise?   And the conclusive
evidence I have given you, as to the dependence of
the definite oscillations of suspended bodies on involuntary movements unconsciously determined by
states of *expectancy*, clearly points to the conclusion
that we have in the supposed mystery of the Divining
Rod only another case of the same kind.   It is well
known that persons who are conversant with the
Geological structure of a district, are often able to
indicate with considerable certainty in what spot, and
at what depth, Water will be found; and men of less
scientific knowledge, but of considerable practical experience, frequently arrive at a true conclusion on this
point, without being able to assign reasons for their
opinions.   Exactly the same may be said in regard
to the mineral structure of a mining district; the
course of a Metallic vein being often correctly indicated by the shrewd guess of an observant workman,
where the scientific reasoning of the mining engineer

altogether fails. It is an experience we are continually encountering in other walks of life, that particular persons are guided,—some apparently by an original, and others by an acquired intuition,—to conclusions for which they can give no adequate reasons, but which subsequent events prove to have been correct; and I look upon the Divining Rod in its various applications as only a peculiar method of giving expression to results worked out by an Automatic process of this kind, even before they rise to distinct mental Consciousness. Various other methods of Divination that seem to be practised in perfectly good faith— such, for example, as the Bible and key test, used for the discovery of stolen property—are probably to be attributed to the same agency; the Cerebral traces of past occurrences often supplying materials for the automatic evolution of a result (as they unquestionably do in dreams), when the occurrences themselves have been forgotten.

THOUGHT-READING.

Many of the cases of so-called 'Thought-reading' are clearly of the same kind; the communication being made by unconscious muscular action on the part of one person, and automatically interpreted by the other,—as in the following instance. Several persons being assembled, one of them leaves the room, and during his [1] absence some object is hidden. On

---

[1] The experiment succeeds equally well, or perhaps better, with ladies.

the absentee's re-entrance, two persons who know the
hiding-place stand one on either side of him, and
establish some personal contact with him ; one method
being for each to place a finger on the shoulder next
him, while another is for each to place a hand on his
body, one on the front and the other on the back.
He walks about the room between the two, and
generally succeeds before long in finding the hidden
object ; being led towards it (as careful observation
and experiment have fully proved) by the involuntary
muscular action of his unconscious guides, one or the
other of them pressing more heavily when the object
is on his side, and the finder as involuntarily turning
towards that side.

These and other curious results of recent enquiry,
while strictly conformable to Physiological principles,
greatly extend our knowledge of the modes in which
states of Brain express themselves unconsciously and
involuntarily in Muscular action ; and I dwell on them
the more, because they seem to me to afford the key
(as I shall explain in my second lecture) to some of
these phenomena of Spiritualistic divination, which
have been most perplexing to many who have come
in contact with them, without being disposed to accept
the spiritualistic interpretation of them.

There seems no inherent improbability in the supposition, that the power of *intuitively* interpreting the
indications involuntarily furnished by expression of
countenance, gesture, manner, &c., so as to divine
what is passing in the mind of another person, may
be greatly intensified in that state of concentration

which has been already shown (p. 19), to produce a temporary exaltation of other faculties. There can be no question that this divining power is naturally possessed in a very remarkable degree by certain individuals ; and that it may be greatly improved by cultivation,—going in many instances far beyond what can have been learned by experience as to the *meaning* of the indications on which it rests. But I have not met with any cases, either in my own experience, or in the recorded experiments of such as have proved their competence to conduct them, of the exercise of this power without the intermediation of those expressional signs, which, as in the case I have just cited, are *made* and *interpreted* alike unconsciously.

LECTURE II.

SEVERAL years ago, an eminent Colonial Judge with whom I was discussing the subject on which I am now to address you, said to me, "According to the ordinary "rules of evidence, by which I am accustomed to be "guided in the administration of justice, I cannot refuse "credit to persons whose honesty and competence "seem beyond doubt, in regard to facts which they de-"clare themselves to have witnessed ; and such is the "character of a great body of testimony I have received "in regard to the phenomena of Spiritualism." In arguing this matter with my friend at the time, I took my stand upon the fact, well known not only to lawyers but to all men of large experience in affairs, that thoroughly honest and competent witnesses continually differ extremely in their accounts of the very same transaction, according to their mental prepossessions in regard to it ; and I gave him instances that had occurred within my own experience, in which a prepossession in favour of 'occult' agencies had given origin and currency to statements reported by witnesses whose good faith could not be called in question, which careful enquiry afterwards proved to have no real foundation in fact.

Subsequent study, however, of the whole subject

of the validity of Testimony, has led me not only to attach yet greater importance to what Metaphysicians call its ' subjective' element—that is, the state of mind of the witness who gives it ; but, further, to see that we must utterly fail to appreciate the true value of evidence, if we do not take the general experience of intelligent men, embodied in what we term ' educated common sense,' as the basis of our estimate. In all ordinary legal procedures, the witnesses on each side depose to things which *might have* happened ; and in case of a ' conflict of testimony,' the penetration of the presiding judge, and the good sense of the jury, are exerted in trying to find out what really did happen ; their search being guided partly by the relative con-fidence they place in the several witnesses, but partly by the general probabilities of the case.

Now, it would be at once accepted as a guiding principle by any administrator of justice, that the more extraordinary any assertion—that is, the more widely it departs from ordinary experience—the stronger is the testimony needed to give it a claim on our acceptance as truth ; so that while *ordinary* evidence may very properly be admitted as adequate proof of any ordinary occurrence, an *extraordinary* weight of evidence would be rightly required to establish the credibility of any statement that is in itself inherently improbable, the strength of the proof required being proportional to the improbability. And if a statement made by any witness in a Court of Justice should be *completely in opposition to the universal experience of Mankind, as embodied in those Laws of Nature which*

are accepted by all men of ordinary intelligence, the
judge and jury would most assuredly put that particular statement ' out of court ' as a thing that could
not have happened; whatever might be the value
they would assign to the testimony of the same witness as to ordinary matters.   Thus if, in order to
account for the signature of a will in London at a
certain time, by a person who could be proved, beyond
reasonable doubt, to have been in Edinburgh only an
hour before, either a single witness, or any number of
witnesses, were to affirm that the testator had been
carried by ' the spirits ' through the air all the way
from Edinburgh to London in that hour, I ask whether
the ' common sense ' of the whole Court would not
revolt at such an assertion, as a thing not *in rerum
naturâ.*   And yet there are at the present time
numbers of educated men and women, who have so
completely surrendered their ' common sense ' to a
dominant prepossession, as to maintain that any such
monstrous fiction ought to be believed, even upon the
evidence of a single witness, if that witness be one
upon whose testimony we should rely in the ordinary
affairs of life !

   There is, indeed, no other test than that of ' common sense,' for distinguishing between the delusions
of a Monomaniac, and the conclusions drawn by sane
minds from the same data.   There are many persons
who are perfectly rational upon every subject but one ;
and who, if put on their trial, will stand a searching
cross-examination without betraying themselves, especially if they know from previous experience what

it is that they should endeavour to conceal. But a questioner who has received the right cue, and skilfully follows it up, will generally succeed at last in extracting an answer which enables him to turn to the jury and say—"You see that whilst sane enough " in other matters, the patient upon this point is clearly " mad." Yet the proof of such madness consists in nothing else than the absurd discordance between the fixed conviction entertained by the individual, and what is accepted by the world at large as indubitably true ; as, for example, when he declares himself to be one of the persons of the Trinity, or affirms (as in a case now before me) that he is a victim to the machinations of infernal powers, whom he overhears to be conspiring against him. We have no other basis than the dictates of 'common sense' for regarding such persons as the subjects of pitiable delusions, and have no other justification for treating them accordingly. Their convictions are perfectly true *to themselves* ; they maintain in all sincerity that it is only *they* who are sane, and that the rest of mankind must be mad not to see the matter in the same light ; and all this arises from their having allowed their minds to fall under subjection to some 'dominant idea,' which at last takes full possession of them. Thus, for example, a man suffering under incipient *melancholia* begins by taking gloomy views of everything that concerns him ; his affairs are all going to ruin ; his family and friends are alienated from him ; the world in general is 'going to the bad.' Under the influence of this morbid colouring, he takes more and more distorted views of the occurrences of his present life, and looks back with exaggerated reprobation at the errors of his past ; and in time, not only *ideal misrepresentations* of real occurrences, but *ideal constructions* having scarcely any or perhaps no basis in actual fact, take full possession of his mind, which credits only his own imaginings, and refuses to accept the corrections given by the assurances of those who surround him. So I have seen a woman who has had the misfortune to fix her affections upon a man who did not return them, first misinterpret ordinary civilities as expressions of devoted attachment, and then, by constantly dwelling upon her own feelings, mentally construct ideal representations of occurrences which she comes to believe in as real ; not allowing herself to be undeceived, even when the object of her attachment declares that the sayings and doings attributed to him are altogether imaginary.

It is in this way that I account for what appear to me to be the strange delusions, which have laid hold at the present time of a number of persons who are not only perfectly sane and rational upon all other subjects, but may be eminently distinguished by intellectual ability. They first surrender themselves, without due enquiry, to a disposition to believe in ' occult ' agencies ; and having so surrendered themselves, they interpret everything in accordance with that belief. The best protection against such surrender appears to me to be the *early culture* of those scientific habits of thought, which shape, when once established, the whole future intellectual course of the individual.

The case is not really altered by the participation of large numbers of persons in the same delusion ; in fact, the majority sometimes goes mad, the few who retain their 'common sense' being the exceptions. Of this we have a notable instance in the Witch-persecutions of the seventeenth century, mainly instigated by King James I. and his Theological allies; who, because ' witchcraft' and other ' curious arts' are condemned both by the Mosaic law and by Apostolic authority, 'stirred up the people' against those who were supposed to practise them, and branded every doubter as an atheist.

The Witch-persecution carried on by James in Scotland, before his accession to the English throne, is believed to have caused the sacrifice of several thousand lives ; but in England, under the too celebrated Witch Act, which was passed by Parliament under his influence, in the first year of his reign, it was far more terribly destructive. No fewer than seventy thousand persons are believed to have been executed for witchcraft between the years 1603 and 1680 ; a number far larger than that of the sufferers in all the religious persecutions of the later Tudors.

The 'History of Human Error' seems to me, in fact, to have no pages more full of instruction to such as can read them aright, than those which chronicle the trials for this offence, which were presided over by judges—like Sir Matthew Hale—of the highest repute for learning, uprightness, and humanity. Not only were the most trivial and ridiculous circumstances admitted as proofs of the charge, but the most

monstrous assertions were accepted without the slightest question. Thus in 1663 a woman was hanged at
Taunton, on the evidence of a hunter that a hare which
had taken refuge from his pursuit in a bush, was found
on the opposite side in the likeness of a witch, who,
having assumed the form of the animal, took advantage
of her hiding-place to resume her proper shape. And
the proof of these marvels did not rest on the testimony of single witnesses. In 1658 a woman was
hung at Chard Assizes for having bewitched a boy of
twelve years old, who was seen to rise in the air, and
pass some thirty yards over a garden wall; while at
another time he was found in a room with his hands
flat against a beam at the top, and his body two or
three feet above the floor—*nine people at a time seeing
him in this position.*

In 1677, however, an able work was published
under the title of *The Displaying of Supposed Witchcraft,* in which the author, Webster, who had seen a
great deal of witch-trials, maintained the opinion
that the whole system of witchcraft was founded on
natural phenomena, credulity, torture, imposture, or
delusion ; and a reaction seems then to have begun in
favour of 'common sense,' which was fostered by the
Revolution of 1688. Though accusations continued
to be made, the judicious conduct of Lord Chief
Justice Holt, who presided over trials for this offence
in various parts of the kingdom, generally caused the
acquittal of the prisoners ; and when they were found
guilty and condemned, the capital sentence was
seldom carried out. The last witch-execution in

Scotland, where the Theological prepossession longest maintained its hold over the public, was in 1722 ; and the Witch Act was repealed in 1736. The belief in witchcraft still survived, however, not only among the ignorant vulgar, but in the minds of some of the most enlightened men of the last century. We find Addison, in the earlier part of it, speaking of witchcraft as a thing that could not reasonably be called in question ; while, towards its close, Dr. Johnson maintained that as the non-existence of witches could not be proved, there was no sufficient ground for denying their diabolical powers. This is one of the cases, however, in which an enlightened 'common sense'—the intelligent embodiment of the general experience of mankind—is a much safer guide than logic. The belief in Witchcraft was not killed by discussion, but perished by neglect. The 'childish things' believed in by our ancestors have been 'put away' by the full-grown sense of the present generation ; the testimony in their favour, once unquestionably accepted as convincing, is no longer deemed worthy of being even considered ; and it is only among those of our hereditarily uneducated population, whose general intelligence is about upon a par with that of a Hottentot or an Esquimaux, that 'cunning women' are able to turn this lingering superstition to the purposes of gain.

Of the rapid spread of the Witchcraft delusion in a population whose theological 'prepossession' favoured its development, and of its equally rapid decline when 'common sense' resumed its due ascendancy, no case was more remarkable than the Epidemic that spread through Puritan New England, just two hundred years ago. This was initiated by the trial and execution of a poor Irishman, who, being obnoxious as a papist, was accused of having bewitched two children who suffered from convulsive attacks. Dr. Cotton Mather, Fellow of Harvard College, received one of these children into his house ; and asserted the girl's possession by evil spirits as an indubitable fact, on the following grounds :— She would suddenly, in the presence of a number of spectators, fall into a trance, rise up, place herself in a riding attitude as if setting out for the Sabbath, and hold conversation with invisible beings. When under the influence of 'hellish charms' she took pleasure in reading or hearing 'bad' books, which she was permitted to do with perfect freedom. These books included the Prayer Book of the English Episcopal Church, the writings of Quakers, and Popish productions. On the other hand, whenever the Bible was taken up, the devil threw her into the most fearful convulsions. It was upon such testimony that the unfortunate Irishman was convicted and executed !

The judicial persecution, once begun, soon raged with such severity that its victims were hung by half a dozen or more at a time; one of them being a minister, who had provoked his judges by calling in question the very existence of witchcraft. The accusations became more and more numerous, and at last implicated people of the highest consideration, among them the wife of a minister who had been one of the most active promoters of these proceedings ; so that the authorities felt it necessary for their own safety at once to check the further progress of the infection. Judges and juries then found out that they had been 'sadly deluded and mistaken,' only Dr. Cotton Mather's father (who was President of Harvard) and other Theologians still holding their ground ; and the release, by the Governor, of a hundred and fifty witches who were under arrest, and the stoppage of proceedings against two hundred more who were about to be arrested, came to be accepted in a short time with general approval, though vehemently protested against by Cotton Mather in these remarkable terms :—" *Fleshy* people may burlesque these things; " but when hundreds of the most solemn people, in a " country where they have as much mother-wit, cer- " tainly, as the rest of mankind, *know them to be true,* " nothing but the froward spirit of Sadduceeism can " question them. I have not yet mentioned so much as " one thing that will not be justified, if it be required, " by the oaths of more considerate persons than any " that can ridicule these odd phenomena."

Now this is precisely the position taken by the modern Spiritualists ; who revive under new forms the doctrines which were supposed to have faded away under the light of Modern Science. The 'hundreds of the most solemn people,' who are ready to justify their conviction of such wonders as Mr. Home's and Mrs. Guppy-Volckman's aerial flights, the elongation of the body of the former, or the bringing in of ice, flowers, and fruits by the minister-

ing spirits of the latter, are equally bound to accept
the testimony, given on oath and in solemn form of
law, which satisfied able judges and honest juries two
centuries ago, that tens of thousands of innocent
people had entered into the guilty league with Satan,
whose punishment was death here and everlasting
damnation hereafter. The unbelieving Sadducees of
the present time, on the other hand, can appeal to the
same sad history, in justification of their refusal to
admit the testimony of the votaries of a system which
is to their minds quite as absurd and irrational as that
of Witchcraft ; and of their disbelief in the reality of
alleged occurrences which they deem it an insult to
their common sense to be asked to credit. For the
faithful few, who two centuries ago rallied round the
standard of Rationalism, in antagonism not only to
the dead weight of ignorant prejudice, but to the
active force of learning and authority, had no other
defence of their position than the *inherent incredibility*
of the opposing testimony ; notwithstanding that this
was clearly given (in many cases if not in all) in perfect good faith, and often admitted as true even by
the unfortunate victims it incriminated, who seem to
have themselves participated in what every person of
ordinary intelligence now admits to have been a pitiable delusion.

But, it may be objected, the acceptance of this
test would equally justify a disbelief in any of those
marvels which are rightly esteemed the glories of
Modern Science. Tell a man, for instance, to whom
the fact is new, that the hand may be held without

injury in the stream of liquid iron issuing from the smelting furnace, or dipped and moved about in a bucket of the molten metal ; and he will probably reject your assertion as altogether incredible. Yet this statement, while apparently antagonistic to universal experience, can be shown to be really conformable to it. For the protection of the hand from being burned by the hot metal, when the intervention of a film of vapour has been secured by moistening its surface, is just what you may see every day in the rolling off of drops of fluid from a heated iron, in the application of the familiar test by which the laundress judges of the suitability of its temperature.

Take, again, the case of the Electric Telegraph, and especially that of the Atlantic cable. If submarine telegraphy had not been led up to by progressive steps, the mass of mankind would have undoubtedly scoffed at the idea of "putting a girdle round the earth in twenty minutes"; and even after the first Atlantic cable had actually conveyed messages of great importance, to the full satisfaction of those who sent them, there were obstinate sceptics who maintained that its asserted success *must* be a falsehood, as being opposed to 'common sense.' But every person sufficiently educated to understand the scientific principles of its construction, was perfectly prepared to accept it as a real success ; the speedy failure of the first cable, so far from justifying the original scepticism, only serving to show what the conditions were, by due observance of which permanent success might be assured.

Compare this with another curious demand upon public credence—the 'panasilinic telegraph'—which was made by an ingenious hoaxer about the time that the success of land electric telegraphy first set the world to dream of uniting the New World with the Old by the like means.   It was gravely announced that a French *savant* had discovered that if two snails were brought for a time into mutual relation, such a sympathy would be established between them, that, however widely they might be separated, the movements of each would correspond with those of the other ; so that if a couple of friends, one in New York and the other in Paris, wished to converse, they had only to provide themselves with an alphabet and figure dial, get a pair of sympathetic snails, and appoint a time for their conversation.   The one who led off was to make his snail walk over the dial, and to stop him at the letter or figure he wished to indicate ; his friend's snail would do exactly the same, and thus the message would be gradually spelled out.—Now I perfectly well remember that this ridiculous absurdity found many believers.   My old friend Dr. Robert Chambers, ever on the watch for scientific novelties, gave currency to the statement in *Chambers's Journal*, without, however, committing himself to its truth. And I am sure that its very marvellousness had an attraction for those credulous subjects, who are ready to surrender their common sense to any pretender to occult powers,—the more readily, it often seems, in proportion to the extravagance of his claims.

I might cite the Spectroscope and the Radiometer

as additional cases, not merely of the readiness, but of
the eagerness of Scientific men, to extend their knowledge of the agencies of Nature in entirely new
directions ; and to accept with implicit confidence,
upon adequate evidence, revelations in regard to matters lying so completely beyond the domain covered
by previous experience, as entirely to transcend, if
not directly to violate it.   Now this, in the first case,
is because the whole of that wonderful fabric of Spec-
trum-analysis, by which we are now enabled to study
the chemical and physical constitution of every kind
of Celestial object which the telescope can render visible to us, has been built up, course by course, on the
basis of one of our most familiar scientific experiences
—the dark lines that cross the solar spectrum.   So,
Mr. Crookes's invention of the Radiometer was the
culmination of a long series of experimental enquiries,
the results of which could be demonstrated at any
time and to any number of persons ; the fundamental
fact of the vanes being driven round by radiant force
being thus put beyond dispute.   And while, as I
stated to you in my previous lecture, what at first
seemed the obvious interpretation of this fact—
namely, that radiant force here acted in a manner
altogether new to science, by direct mechanical impulse on the vanes—was almost universally accepted
by even the most distinguished Physicists, further
investigations of the most ingenious and elaborate
nature have now conclusively proved that the action
is really an indirect one, capable of being accounted
for on previously understood principles.—I hold the

warning given by the history of this enquiry, in regard to the duty of the Scientific man to exhaust every possible mode of accounting for new and strange phenomena, before attributing it to any previously unknown agency, to be one of the most valuable lessons afforded by Mr. Crookes's discoveries.

Now I maintain that it requires exactly the same kind of specially trained ability, to elicit the truth in regard to the phenomena we are now considering, as has been exerted in the researches made by the instrumentality of the Spectroscope and the Radiometer. And I cannot but believe that if Mr. Crookes had been prepared by a special training in the bodily and mental constitution, abnormal as well as normal, of the Human instruments of the Spiritualistic enquiries, and had devoted to them the ability, skill, perseverance, and freedom from prepossession, which he has shown in his Physical investigations, he would have arrived at conclusions more akin to those of the great body of scientific men whom I believe to share my own convictions on this subject.

So far are we from regarding Science as having unveiled all the mysteries of Nature, that we hold ourselves ready to accept *any* new agency, the evidence for which will stand the test of cross-examination by skilled experts. But, in default of such evidence, we are fully justified by experience in regarding it as more probable that the most honest witnesses have either been intentionally deceived or have deceived themselves, than that assertions in direct contradiction to all the 'natural knowledge' we possess should have any real justification in fact.

In support of this position, I shall now show you that in every instance (so far as I am aware) in which a thorough investigation has been made into those 'higher phenomena' of Mesmerism which are adduced in support of Spiritualism, the supposed proof has completely failed, generally by the detection of intentional fraud ; while as the unexplained marvels of the same kind which are still appealed to as valid proofs, rest on no better evidentiary foundation than seemed originally to be possessed by those which have entirely broken down, it may be fairly presumed that they too would be discredited by the like searching enquiry.

It was in France that the pretensions of Mesmeric *clairvoyance* were first advanced ; and it was by the French Academy of Medicine, in which the mesmeric state had been previously discussed with reference to the performance of surgical operations, that this new and more extraordinary claim was first carefully sifted; in consequence of the offer made in 1837 by M. Burdin (himself a member of that Academy) of a prize of 3,000 francs to anyone who should be found capable of reading through opaque substances. The money was deposited in the hands of a notary for a period of two years, afterwards extended to three ; the announcement was extensively published ; numerous cases were offered for examination ; every imaginable concession was made to the competitors, that was compatible with a thorough testing of the reality of the asserted power ; and *not one was found to stand the trial.*

But not only was there complete and ignominious failure; the fraudulent mode in which the previous successes had been obtained was detected in two of the three cases which were brought most prominently forward, and was made scarcely less evident in the third.

The first case was presented by M. Houblier, a physician of Provence, who, after a long period of preparation, sent his *clairvoyante* Mlle. Emélie to Paris, to the care of a friend and mesmeriser, M. Frappart. This gentleman, before presenting her to the Commissioners, thought it as well to put her asserted power of reading with the back of her head to some preliminary trials; and soon finding reason to suspect her good faith, he set a trap for her, into which (supposing him to be her friend) she unsuspectingly fell. Very judiciously, however, he did not immediately expose her, but let her continue her performances; bringing up M. Houblier from Provence to meet other persons interested in the enquiry, that they might see for themselves through the key-hole of the room in which Mlle. Emélie was supposed to be lying entranced in a mesmeric sleep, that she got up and examined, here and there, the pages of the book —purposely left in the room—in which her alleged *clairvoyant* power was to be tested. Of course, Mlle. Emélie was never presented to the Commissioners of the Academy; and M. Houblier confessed with grief and shame that he had not only himself been for four years the dupe of this *maîtresse femme*, but that he had unconsciously helped her to impose upon

many most respectable persons in his own neigbour-
hood. Now, all these, with M. Houblier himself,
might be presumed to have been both competent and
trustworthy witnesses ; so that if M. Burdin's prize
had never been offered, this case would have been put
on record (like others of which I shall presently tell
you) as an unimpeachable attestation of the reality of
clairvoyance. Again, the immediate detection of the
fraud, not by a hostile sceptic, but by a friendly mesmeriser, shows how easily, under the influence of a
' prepossession,' numbers of intelligent people may be
led to surrender their ' common sense ' to the extent
of believing, not only that the seat of vision may be
transferred to the back of the head, but that a distinct picture of a page of a book can be formed without any optical apparatus. The conduct of M.
Frappart in the matter should serve as a lesson to
honest Spiritualists at the present time ; who, when there
is good ground to suspect trickery, would much better
serve their own cause by helping to expose it, than by
lending themselves to the defence of the trickster.

Among the earliest claimants of the Burdin prize
was a M. Pigeaire of Montpellier ; who affirmed that
his daughter, a girl eleven years old, was able, when
her eyes were completely blinded, to read with the
points of her fingers, which then became her visual
organs ; the sole condition he required being that she
should be blinded by himself with a bandage of black
velvet. Her power of reading in this condition was
attested by peers, deputies, physicians, distinguished
littérateurs (amongst others by George Sand) and

newspaper editors, to whom it had been exhibited in
Paris before she was presented to the Commission.
But its members were nevertheless sceptical enough
to require proof satisfactory to themselves, and desired to render the girl 'temporarily blind' (to use her
father's words) by their own method ; objecting that
his velvet bandage might be so disarranged by the
working of her facial muscles, as to allow her to see
downwards beneath its lower edge, when the book
was held in a suitable position. M. Pigeaire, however, objecting to this test, the Commissioners having
satisfied themselves of the opacity of the bandage,
stipulated only that the book should not be put into
the girl's hands, to be held by herself wherever she
wished, but should be placed *opposite* her eyes at any
distance her father should desire. As he would not
consent to this condition, the Commissioners, of
course, declined to accept his daughter's performances
as furnishing any valid evidence of *clairvoyance.*
Though the bandage was opaque, the trick now became transparent ; yet it had taken in peers, deputies,
and George Sand ; and only experts in such enquiries
succeeded in discovering it.

The third case was brought forward by M. Teste,
a well-known magnetiser of that date, who affirmed
that every experienced mesmerist had witnessed the
exercise of this faculty at least twenty times. Confident in his position, he offered to submit his *clairvoyante* (a young girl) to the *experimentum crucis*—
the reading of print or writing enclosed in opaque
boxes ; stipulating only that the direction of the lines

should be previously indicated. Such a box was prepared and placed in the girl's hands, with the required indication. Being presently asked by M. Teste whether she would be able to read what was in the interior of the box, she answered *Oui* ; and on his asking her how soon, she replied confidently *dix minutes.* She then turned the box about in her hands, and in doing so tore one of the bands that secured it. This being remarked upon, she made no further attempt of the same kind, but continued (as it appeared) to exert herself in fatiguing efforts to discern the concealed lines. Whole hours having thus passed, and M. Teste having asked his *clairvoyante* how many lines there were in the box, she answered *deux.* He then pressed her to read, and she announced that she saw the word *nous*, and later the word *sommes.* As she then declared that she could read no more, the box was taken from her hands, and the girl was dismissed ; and the box being then opened, the printed slip it contained was shown to M. Teste to have on it six lines of French poetry, in which neither of the words *nous sommes* occurred.

Of course this failure does not *disprove* any of M. Teste's assertions, either in regard to the same girl under other conditions, or in regard to other alleged *clairvoyantes* ; but it fully justifies the allegation, that as this was a picked case, presented by himself, near the expiration of the third year during which M. Burdin's prize was open, with unhesitating confidence in the girl's success, his other reported cases, of which not one rests upon better authority than his own, have not the least claim upon our acceptance. He seems to have been very easily satisfied ; and it is clear that if he was not a consenting party, he was not adequately on his guard against the possibility of a furtive peep being taken by his *clairvoyante* into the interior of the box while it was being turned about in her hands,—the method which Houdin avows himself to have practised in performing his 'second sight' trick, and by which, as I shall presently tell you, one of our own most noted advocates of the 'transcendental' was afterwards completely taken in.

It was in 1844 that the *clairvoyant* Alexis came hither from Paris, with the reputation of extraordinary powers ; and though these had not been submitted to the test of investigation by the French Academy of Medicine, it was confidently affirmed by the leading mesmerisers in this country, that there was nothing in the way of 'lucidity' that this youth had not done and could not do. Not only had he divined the contents of sealed packets and thick wooden boxes, but he could give an exact account of the contents of any room in any house never before seen or heard of ; he had described occurrences taking place at a distance, which, to the great surprise of the questioners (who expected something very different), were afterwards found to have transpired exactly as he had stated ; he had revealed to persons anxious to recover important papers the unknown places of their lodgment ; in fact, if all was true that was affirmed of him, the power for which he could claim credit would have been little less than omniscience—if only it could have been commanded at will. But, by the admission of his best friends, it was extremely variable, coming in gushes or flashes; while, as he was often unable to see clearly at first, and had an unfortunate habit of 'thinking aloud,' he continually made a great many blunders before he arrived at anything like the truth.

Having myself settled in the neighbourhood of London just as Alexis came over, and having found my friend Dr. Forbes (then editor of the *British and Foreign Medical Review*) extremely interested in the enquiry into the reality of his asserted *clairvoyant* powers, I accompanied Dr. F., time after time, to public and private *séances* at which these powers were *exhibited*, though not adequately *tested*. So far from being at that time an opponent, I was much more nearly a believer; the weight of testimony seemed too strong to be overborne; and it was only after repeated experience of the numerous sources of fallacy which the keen-sightedness of Dr. Forbes enabled him to discern, that I became, like him, a sceptic as to the reality of Alexis's reputed *clairvoyance*. My scepticism was increased by seeing how, whilst he was 'thinking aloud' (according to his friends) but 'fishing' or 'pumping' (according to unbelievers), he was helped by the information he gleaned from the unconscious promptings of his questioners. And my confidence in testimony was greatly weakened, by finding that extraordinary successes were reported to have been obtained in some cases which Dr. Forbes and I regarded as utter failures, as well as in others in which it was clear to us that no adequate precautions had been taken to prevent the use of ordinary vision. For we satisfied ourselves that when he was going to read or to play cards with his eyes bandaged, it was his habit so to manœuvre, as to prevent the bandage from being drawn tight,—*cela m'étouffe* being his constant complaint, even when his nostrils were left perfectly free ; and that when he could not see under its lower edge at first, he worked the muscles of his face until he displaced it sufficiently for his purpose.   And thus we came to the conclusion that no test of his 'lucidity' could be of any value, which did not involve the reading of print or writing enclosed in perfectly opaque boxes or other envelopes, without the assistance of any response to his guesses. A *test-séance* of this kind having been arranged by Dr. Forbes at his own house, the general result (as admitted by M. Marcillet, the mesmeriser who accompanied Alexis) was *utter failure* ; the only noteworthy exception being in a case in which, having selected the thinnest of the paper envelopes, Alexis correctly stated that the word within it consisted of three letters, without, however, being able to name them.   And the value of even this very slight success was afterwards completely neutralised by the discovery, which I shall recount in connection with the case of the brother and successor of Alexis, that nothing else than ordinary vision was required to obtain it.

As M. Marcillet could not dispute the fairness with which the investigation was conducted, he could offer no other explanation of Alexis's failure on this occasion, than the presence of an 'atmosphere of incredibility' emanating from the persons of the sceptical doctors present. It may be shrewdly suspected, however, that Alexis recognised the presence of a *maître homme* in *clear-sightedness*, and felt himself foiled at every point by the keener intelligence of Dr. Forbes. For he and M. Marcillet forthwith left London for Paris, and never publicly reappeared in this country.

His place, however, was taken after a year or two by his brother Adolphe, whose powers were highly vaunted by believers as even surpassing those of his predecessor. Again Dr. Forbes applied himself to the investigation ; and again I took every opportunity afforded me of witnessing their exercise. It was at a public *séance* at which I was myself present, though Dr. Forbes was not, that a circumstance occurred which made at the time considerable impression. Slips of writing-paper having been distributed, any person who wished to put Adolphe's power to the test was desired to write a word at the top of the slip, and then to fold it over and over several times, so that the writing should be covered both in front and behind by two or three layers of the paper. Having myself written *Paris,* I folded it up in the prescribed manner ; my friend Mr. Ottley wrote *Toulon* ; several other persons did the like ; and we satisfied ourselves, by holding up our folded slips between our eyes and the light, that the writing within was completely invisible. Yet, taking one of them after another into his

hands, and making no attempt to unfold the papers
(some of which, I think, were secured by seal or
wafer), Adolphe named, without hesitation, the word
written on each. Within a day or two, however, I
learned from Mr. Ottley that his sister had discovered
that she could read by her natural eyesight the writing on his slip, which it was supposed could only be
discovered by *clairvoyant* power ; and on trying her
method upon my own slip, I found myself able to do
the same. The secret consisted in holding the slip,
not *between* the eye and the light, but in such a position that the light of the window or lamp should be
reflected obliquely from its surface. And any of
you will find that after a little practice, words written
in a legible but not large hand can be thus read,
though covered by three folds of ordinary writing-
paper. This discovery fully accounts for various successes, as well of Alexis and Adolphe, as of other
reputed clairvoyants ; and affords a further warning
as to the scrupulous care required to exclude all
possible sources of fallacy in conducting such trials.

The conclusions drawn by Dr. Forbes from his
critical examination of Adolphe's pretensions, tallied
exactly with those to which he had been led by his
previous search. All the instances of *success* could be
fairly explained without crediting the performer with
any extraordinary powers ; where, on the other hand,
due care was taken to render the ordinary operation
of the visual sense impossible, *failure invariably resulted.* Thus the claims of Adolphe, like those of
Alexis, vanished into thin air at the wand of the ex-

pert ; and, notwithstanding the great efforts made to rehabilitate his reputation, he soon found his stay in London no longer profitable, and went the way of his predecessor. Nothing, so far as I am aware, has ever been since heard of this *par nobile fratrum* ; certainly they never challenged the French Academy of Medicine to an investigation of their pretensions.

Another case of this kind was tested a few years later by Mr. Braid. In 1852 M. Lassaigne and Mdlle. Prudence Bernard, who had gained a great reputation in London by their performances at Hungerford Hall, having come to Manchester, Mr. B. went, at the desire of a friend in Edinburgh, to test the lady's *clairvoyant* pretensions. The first part of the performance consisted of feats which might be readily explained by a system of collusion ; not being so remarkable as those which M. Robin and his female confederate accomplished by means so simple, that the performer of them could scarcely refrain from laughing at the ease with which the public could be deceived.

" But now arrived," continued Mr. Braid, " the experiment which I considered by far the most interesting of all on the programme,—viz., playing at cards, and reading, when her eyes were to be so securely blindfolded that not a ray of light could reach them, in the common acceptation of the term. To effect this, folds of cotton wadding were placed across the forehead, eyes, and nose, and over the face as far as the point of the nose ; and then a white handkerchief folded several times, so as to be about $2\frac{1}{2}$ inches wide, was bound round the head and eyes, so as to maintain the cotton in its place. This done, M. Lassaigne triumphantly asked anyone to examine his subject, and say whether it was *possible* for her to see through all this apparatus. Some one having exclaimed ' No,' the lady sat down at a table to challenge any one present to play a game at cards with her. Whilst they were making arrangements for the game, I was sufficiently clairvoyant, even without being mesmerised, to observe the lady pensively lay her face upon her hands, so as to enable her very conveniently, and *by mere accident no doubt*, to give the proper twist and finish to the apparatus for *excluding* light from her eyes. I observed this manœuvre by the lady *twice*, and called the attention of some friends to it, who can also testify to the fact. The clairvoyante now became very lively ; described the personal appearance of her opponent, played dexterously, and beat him. She also did the same by another gentleman who tried a round with her ; and with a third gentleman, a friend of my own, who, by my suggestion, had taken a *new* pack of cards with him, she proved her power of describing his personal appearance correctly, and playing well, but she lost on this occasion from having bad cards.

"As the lady was now considered to have proved her clairvoyant powers to the satisfaction of all present, I stepped forward and announced my desire to have the privilege of applying a test which would be far more satisfactory to *my* mind, because I had no confidence in the supposed efficacy of the blindfolding then in use for effectually accomplishing what it professed to do. I told the audience that I felt convinced that the patient was seeing through interstices between the cotton and the face, near the side of the nose. My proposal for guarding against such a source of fallacy as this, was simply to place a thin sheet of brown cardboard under her chin and round her neck, so as to guard against the possibility of the deception which I suspected. This I intended to have accomplished by tying the sheet of pasteboard around her neck, proceeding from the bottom of the throat upwards in a conical form, after the fashion of the Elizabethan frill, extending considerably higher than the head, so as to prevent the possibility of her raising her hands or lowering her head sufficiently for seeing over it, without exciting the attention of the audience. Indeed, whoever had had the opportunity of observing the clairvoyante, as I did, during this card scene, must have felt that he would be permitting an insult to be perpetrated upon himself and upon the whole audience, were he not to endeavour to expose what appeared to me to be such an absurd farce. I was aware that my test would be objected to, on the ground that she did not profess to read *through cardboard* (although I must confess my surprise that a person who can see and read through stone or brick walls, should not be competent to penetrate through thin cardboard), so I, therefore, offered to remove that objection, by cutting out a piece of the cardboard and covering the hole with the cotton wadding and folded handkerchief which *she actually professed to see through;* but, although the audience were almost unanimous in their opinion that my proposed test was a fair one, and such as they wished to see tried. M. Lassaigne well knew that it was too certain and obvious a mode of testing to answer his purpose, and, therefore, under various pretexts, and in a most rude manner, he absolutely refused to try it. I therefore withdrew from the platform and left the room, feeling the force of the remark,—' *Ex uno disce omnes.*' "[1]

And so it always proves *in the end* with these *sham* marvels ; which, however specious they may appear at a distance, vanish under critical investigation like the *mirage* of the desert on nearer approach. The *real* marvels of Science, on the other hand, not only stand the test of the most critical examination, but prove more marvellous the more thoroughly they are investigated. Reason, it has well been said, can guide where Imagination scarcely dares to follow. And those who desire to find a true spring at which to slack their thirst for knowledge, need only follow the guidance of the Spectroscope and the Radiometer, to be led to wonders of which neither the 'Poughkeepsie Seer,' the 'Seeress of Prevorst,' nor any other of the reputed 'prophets' of Mesmerism or Spiritualism had ever dreamed.

My anxiety to impress on you the lessons which (as it seems to me) such exposures ought to afford in regard to the object of our present enquiry, leads me to ask your further attention to two other cases ; in each of which a number of apparent successes of a most remarkable kind were obtained by what was subse-

[1] See Braid on *Magic, Witchcraft, Animal Magn tism, Hypnotism, and Electro-Biology,* 1852 ; p. 115.

quently shown to have been an ingenious fraud, practised upon the honest patron of the performer, who
was (like M. Houblier) his unsuspecting dupe.

In the course of his further search for *clairvoyance*,
Dr. Forbes was requested by a legal gentleman whom
he calls Mr. A. B., to witness the performances of a
copying clerk in his employ, by name George Goble ;
whom he stated to be capable, in a large proportion
of cases, of reading printed words enclosed in opaque
boxes, without either mistake or preliminary guessing.
Being at that time in the country, I did not accompany Dr. Forbes in his repeated visits to Mr. A. B.'s
chambers ; but I well remember his writing to me in
some excitement after the first of them, that at last
he seemed to have got hold of a genuine case of *clairvoyance.* He soon, however, recovered his equanimity
and his scepticism ; and felt that he must make a much
more thorough enquiry, before he could be justified in
accepting the case as genuine.   George's ' dodge ' consisted (as was subsequently proved) in furtively opening the box or other envelope, so as to get a peep at
its contents, whilst sitting or lying face-downwards on
a sofa ; and in managing to conceal his having done
so, by tearing open the box at the moment he pro-
claimed the word : his failures occurring when the box
was so secured that he could not succeed in opening
it, after manœuvring (it might be) for half an hour or
more.   Finding that in every one of George's *successes*
the envelope *might* have been opened, whilst all the
cases in which the boxes had certainly *not* been opened
were *complete failures* —a consideration which, though

very obvious, seemed never to have suggested itself to the legal mind of George's patron—Dr. Forbes and Professor Sharpey (whom he had taken into council) devised a simple ' counter-dodge,' by which it should be rendered impossible for George to open the box for the purpose of reading the contained word, without the detection of his trick.   This entirely succeeded ; George was brought upon his knees and confessed his roguery, but protested that it was his first offence. You would scarcely credit the fact if it had not been self-recorded, that George's patron still continued to believe in his *clairvoyant* power ; accepting his assurance that he had only had recourse to trickery when the genuine power failed him, and requesting Dr. Forbes to give him another trial.   This Dr. F. consented to make, upon the sole condition that a small sealed box, containing a single word printed in large type, should be returned to him *unopened* with the word written upon the outside of it.   Some days elapsed before George's ' lucidity ' recovered from the shock of the exposure ; but his master then informed Dr. F. that he had read the word IMPLEMENTS, or, as he spelled it, *impelments*, with great assurance of correctness.   This, however, proving altogether wrong, the box was left in Mr. A. B.'s hands for a further space of two months ; and no second guess having been then made, the real word was disclosed by Dr. F. to be OBJECTIONS.

The history of this enquiry, as detailed by Dr. Forbes,[1] brings into the strongest contrast the patient

[1] *Illustrations of Modern Mesmerism from Personal Investigation,* London (Churchill) 1845, Third Series, pp. 63–89.

and honest search for truth of the cautious sceptic, willing to be convinced if satisfactory evidence could be adduced, and the easy credulity of the enthusiastic disciple, who not only eagerly accepted a conclusion opposed to universal experience, without taking any adequate precautions against trickery, but held to that conclusion after the trick had been not only exposed but confessed. And here, again, we see how, but for the interposition of a sceptical ' expert,' a case of sham *clairvoyance* would have been published to the world with the same unhesitating affirmation of its genuineness, as that which now claims credit for the exercise of ' Psychic Force ' in causing accordions to play, and heavy tables to turn round or even to rise in the air, without muscular agency.[1]

In the other case I have now to mention—that of Mr. Hewes' 'Jack,' publicly exhibited at Manchester about the same time that Alexis was performing in London—the proof of *clairvoyance*, as shown in reading when the eyes had been effectually closed, seemed as complete as it was possible to obtain. Jack's eyelids were bound down by surgeons of that town (who were assuredly not confederates) with strips of adhesive plaster, over which were placed folds of leather, which again were kept in place by other plasters ; the only condition made by Mr. Hewes being that the ridges of the eyebrows should not be covered, as it was there that Jack saw when ' lucid.' The results were truly surprising ; there was no guessing, no need of prompting, no failure ; ' Jack ' read off, without the

[1] See Serjeant Cox's letter in the *Spectator*, Nov. 11, 1876.

least hesitation, everything that was presented to him. The local newspapers were full of this new wonder ; and no documentary testimony in favour of *clairvoyance* could possibly be more conclusive. But, as usual, the marvel would not stand the test of close examination. A young Manchester surgeon, who had been experimenting upon himself, gave a public exhibition of his power of reading when his eyes had been ' made up ' in precisely the same manner as ' Jack's,' and by the same gentlemen ; the means he adopted being simply to work the muscles of his face, until he so far loosened the plasters as to obtain a crevice through which he could read by looking upwards. Mr. Hewes, who witnessed this performance, readily agreed that ' Jack ' should be further tested ; and it was settled, *en petite comité*, that after protecting his eyelashes with narrow strips of plaster, his eyelids should be covered with a thick coating of shoemaker's wax, leaving the superciliary ridges free. When this was done (not without considerable resistance on the part of ' Jack,' only kept under by the influence of his patron) the *clairvoyant* power was completely annihilated ; but one thing ' Jack' plainly saw, even with his eyes shut— that ' his little game was up.' His patron, a gentleman of independent fortune, who had become an active propagandist of the belief he had honestly embraced, returned all the money which had been received for ' Jack's ' performances, and ' Jack ' withdrew into private life.

Now I readily concede that neither the detection of ' Jack ' and George Goble, nor the failure of Alexis

and Adolphe under test-conditions, disproves the reality
of *clairvoyance*; but my position is, that since the
choicest examples of its manifestation are found to
break down when thoroughly investigated, not one of
the reported instances in which *no* such thorough investigation has been made, has the least claim to be
accepted as genuine. It must, I think, have become
abundantly obvious to you, that until the existence of
the *clairvoyant* power shall have been established beyond question, by every test that the skill of the most
wary and inveterate sceptic can devise, the scientific
expert is fully justified in refusing to accept the
testimony of any number of witnesses, however
honest, but of no *special* intelligence in regard to the
subject of the enquiry, as to particular instances of
this power. George Goble's master would have re-
counted the performances of his *protégé* in perfect
good faith, and would have been very angry with
anyone who should express a doubt either of his
veracity or his competence. And not only Mr.
Hewes, but a large body of lookers-on, would have
stoutly contended for the impossibility of 'Jack'
having read with his eyes, when they had been carefully covered by a surgeon with plasters and leather.
But to me it seems the 'common sense' view of the
matter, that the fact of 'Jack' having read with his
eyes covered, should have been accepted as a proof—
not of his *clairvoyance*—but of his eyes *not* having
been *effectually* covered ; and that the very fact of
George Goble having found out the words in certain
boxes which he *might* have opened, while he did not

find out any in the boxes he *could not* open, should
have been accepted as valid evidence—not of his
clairvoyance—but of his having taken a furtive peep
with his natural eyes into the unsecured boxes. And
in each case, 'common sense' would have been justified by the result.

The ordinary rules of Evidence, as I have endeavoured to show you, apply only to ordinary occurrences. To establish the reality of such an extraordinary condition as *clairvoyance*, extraordinary
evidence is required ; and it is the entire absence of
this, which vitiates the whole body of testimony put
forward by Prof. Gregory (*Letters on Animal Magnetism*), doubtless in the most complete good faith,
regarding the performances of Major Buckley's *clairvoyantes* ; whom he states to have collectively read
the mottoes enclosed in 4,860 nut-shells (one of them
consisting of 98 words), and upwards of 36,000 words
on papers enclosed in boxes, one of these papers containing 371 words. Now, that Professor Gregory lent
not only himself, but the authority of his public position, with reprehensible facility, to the attestation of
Major Buckley's statements, might be fairly anticipated from his eager endorsement of Reichenbach's
doctrines, and his credulous acceptance of Mr.
Lewis's claims, of which I spoke in my previous lecture ; and the complete untrustworthiness of his
statements in regard to *clairvoyance* becomes obvious
to any sceptical reader of his 'Letters.' For not
only is there an entire absence of detail, in regard to
the precautions taken to prevent the ingenious tricks,

to which (as all previous experience had indicated) the claimants to this power are accustomed to have recourse , but the narrative of one of his cases shows such an easy credulity on the very face of it, as at once to deprive his other statements of the least claim to credence. I refer to that (*Op. cit.*, p. 364) in which folded papers or sealed envelopes were forwarded to the *clairvoyantes*, who returned them—the seals apparently unbroken—with a correct statement of the contained words. Now the unsealing of sealed letters, and the resealing them so as to conceal their having been opened, are practised on occasion in the Post-office of probably every Continental capital, if not in our own ; and, as some of you have probably seen in the public prints, the doings in this line of a ' medium ' who professed to be able to return answers under spiritual influence to questions contained in sealed letters, have lately been exposed in the Law-courts of New York ; the medium's own wife disclosing the manner in which the unsealing and resealing of these letters were effected. Common sense, it might have been thought, would dictate that if the contents of a sealed letter had been made known by a person in whose possession it had lain, that letter had been opened and resealed. Yet Prof. Gregory prefers to believe that these letters had been read by *clairvoyance* ; and numbers of persons in various parts of the Union, including many of high social consideration, were found to have placed such confidence in the ' spiritual' pretensions of the New York swindler, as to submit to him questions of the most private nature, with fees that gave him an annual income of more than a thousand pounds!

It was to put the value of Professor Gregory's evidence in support of *clairvoyance* to the test, that his colleague, Dr. (afterwards Sir James) Simpson, offered a bank-note of large value, enclosed in a sealed box and placed in the hands of a public official in Edinburgh, as a prize to anyone who could read its number; and I am informed by Sir Dominic Corrigan, M.P., that Sir Philip Crampton (Surgeon to the Queen in Ireland) did the like in Dublin. Though these rich prizes remained open to all comers for at least a year, none of Major Buckley's one hundred and forty-eight *clairvoyantes* succeeded in establishing a claim to either of them; in fact, I believe that not even a single attempt was made. And yet there are even now men of high scientific distinction, who adduce Professor Gregory's testimony on this subject as unimpeachable![1]

Still more akin to the powers claimed for Spirit-

[1] It was publicly suggested by Mr. Wallace at the Glasgow Meeting of the British Association, that the failure of the *clairvoyantes* in the case of Dr. Simpson's bank-note might be due to there having been really no note placed in the box. This suggestion I indignantly repudiated at the time, as an unworthy imputation upon the character of a public man whose honesty was above all suspicion. But I might have replied that if the fact had been so, some of Major Buckley's 148 *clairvoyantes* ought to have found it out. Dr. Simpson informed me that Dr. Gregory, on being asked the reason of their complete abstention, could give no other account of it, than that the very offer of the reward, by introducing a selfish motive for the exercise of this power, prevented its access; as if Alexis, Adolphe, and numerous other professors of the art of reading without eyes, had not been daily practising it for the purpose of pecuniary gain.

ualistic 'mediums,' is that form of alleged Mesmeric *clairvoyance* which consists in the vision of scenes or occurrences at a distance ; so that they are described exactly as they are at the time, and not according to the expectation of the questioners. Numerous cases of this kind have been very circumstantially recorded ; and I most freely admit that a body of thoroughly well-attested and well-sifted evidence in their favour would present a strong claim to acceptance. Every one knows, however, that plenty of marvels of the same class have been current as 'ghost stories ;' and that even some of what were regarded as the best attested of these, have faded out of the credit they once enjoyed, under the advancing light of a healthy rationalism. And while such as have a 'transcendental' turn of mind will accept the most wonderful story of *clairvoyance* at a distance with little or no hesitation, those of a more sceptical habit will admit none that has not been subjected to the test of a searching cross-examination ; thinking it more probable that some latent fallacy is concealed beneath the ostensible facts, than that anything so marvellous should have really happened.

My own attention was very early drawn to this subject by certain occurrences which fell under my immediate observation. A Mesmeric 'somnambule' said to be possessed of this power of 'mental travelling' being the subject of a *séance* at my own house, and being directed to describe what she saw in the rooms above, gave a correct and unhesitating reply as to the occupants of my nursery ; whilst in regard to the very unusual contents of a store-room at the top of the house, she was entirely at fault, until I purposely prompted her by leading questions. The next day I found out that she had enjoyed ample previous opportunities of information as to the points which she had described correctly ; whilst it soon came to my knowledge that a most circumstantial narrative was current in Bristol (where I then resided) of her extraordinary success in discerning in the store-room the very objects which she had entirely failed to see. Here, then, was a marked instance of two sources of fallacy in narratives of this description : first, the disposition to attribute to ' occult ' agencies what may be readily explained by natural causes ; and second, the ' myth-making ' tendency—far more general than is commonly supposed—which, as I have already shown you, builds up the most elaborate constructions of fiction upon the slenderest foundation of fact.

In my interviews with Alexis and Adolphe, also, both of whom were reputed to possess a very high degree of this power, I tested them as to the contents of my house, which they described in a vague and general way that would apply to almost any ordinary domicile. But both of them spoke of my drawing-room as having pictures on its walls, which was not then the fact ; and neither of them, though pressed as to something very conspicuous which they could not help seeing, gave the least hint of the presence of an organ with gilt pipes. Their failure with me does not, of course, invalidate any *real* successes they may

have gained with others ; but my previous experience
had led me to entertain grave doubts as to the reality
of the *reputed* successes ; and these doubts were subsequently strengthened by the complete breakdown,
under the persevering and sagacious enquiries prose-
cuted by Dr. Forbes, of a most notable case which
excited great public interest at that time.

The wonderful performances of Miss Martineau's
servant J., which she announced to the public in 1844,
through the medium of the *Athenæum*, culminated in
a detailed description—given by J. in the mesmeric
sleep—of the particulars of the wreck of a vessel of
which her cousin was one of the crew, as also of the
previous loss of a boy overboard ; with which particulars it was positively affirmed by Miss Martineau, and
believed by many on her authority, that the girl
could not possibly have been previously informed, as
her aunt had only brought the account to the house
when the *séance* was nearly terminated. On being
asked, says Miss M., two evenings afterwards, when
again in the sleep, "whether she knew what she
"related by seeing her aunt telling the people
"below," J. replied "No; I saw the place and the
"people themselves—like a vision." And Miss
Martineau believed her.

My sceptical friend, Dr. Forbes, however, would
not pin his faith to hers ; and determined to institute,
through a Medical friend on the spot, a more searching investigation than Miss Martineau had thought
necessary. The result of this enquiry was to prove,
unequivocally, that J.'s aunt had told the whole story

to her sister, in whose house Miss M. was residing, about *three hours before the séance*; and that, though J. was not then in the room, the circumstances were fully discussed in her presence before she was summoned to the mesmeric performance.[1]—Thus not only was J. completely discredited as a seer; but the value of *all* testimony to such marvels was seriously lowered, when so honest and intelligent a witness as Harriet Martineau could be so completely led astray by her ' prepossession,' as to put forth statements as facts, which were at once upset by the careful enquiry which she ought to have made before committing herself to them.

It is the wise rule of our law, that no Evidence (save that of dying declarations) is admissible in Court, that is not capable of being tested by cross-examination; and no well-trained investigator will put forth a new discovery in Science, until he has verified it by ' putting it to the question ' in every mode he can think of.

If, in the case I have just cited, the ' common sense ' view had been taken from the beginning, the correspondence of J.'s circumstantial narrative with the actual facts of the case, would have been accepted as proving—not that she had received them in Mesmeric vision—but that she had learned them through some ordinary channel; and the truth of this conclusion would have at once become apparent, when the proper means were taken to verify it. The same

---

[1] *Illustrations of Modern Mesmerism*, pp. 91–101.

ground should (I contend) be taken in regard to all the marvels of this class which rest on the testimony of believers only. For no one of them is better attested than that which I have just cited ; and until the evidence in support of any case of *clairvoyance* can be shown to have been sifted in the same thorough manner, I maintain that it has no more claim on our acceptance, than has the specious 'opening' of a case in a Court of Law, before it has been subjected to the hostile scrutiny of the counsel on the other side.

TABLE-TURNING AND TABLE-TALKING.

I need not detain you long with the scientific discussion of the phenomena of *Table-turning* and *Table-talking*; since no facts have been established in regard to them, which are not susceptible of a very simple explanation. A number of persons seat themselves round a table, and place their hands upon it, with a preconceived idea that the table will turn ; and after some time, it may be, during which the movement has been attentively waited for, the rotation begins. If the parties retain their seats, the turning only takes place as far as the length of their arms allows, but not unfrequently they all rise, feeling themselves obliged (as they assert) to *follow* the table; and, from a walk, their pace may be accelerated to a run, until the table actually spins round so fast that they can no longer keep up with it. And since this happens, not merely without consciousness on the part of the performers that they are exercising any

H

force of their own, but for the most part under the
full conviction that they do not ;—and, moreover, as
tables thus move, which the performers declare themselves unable to move to the same extent by any
voluntary effort ;—it is not unnatural that they should
conclude that *some other force* than their own Muscular action must have put it in motion.

But the man of science, whether Physicist or Physiologist, cannot rest content without adequate proof
of this conclusion ; and a test is very easily applied.
You see here a little apparatus consisting of two
pieces of board, two cedar pencils, two india-rubber
bands, two pins, and a slender index-rod, which was
devised by Faraday to ascertain whether the table
ever moves round without a lateral pressure from the
hands of the operators. For this 'indicator' is so
constructed, that when the hands are placed upon
it, instead of resting immediately on the table, any
lateral pressure exerted by them makes the upper
board roll upon the lower ; and the slightest movement of this kind is so magnified by the leverage of
the index, as to show itself by a very decided motion
of its point in the opposite direction. By this simple
test, anyone may experimentally satisfy himself that
the table never goes round unless the index of the
'indicator' shows that lateral muscular pressure is
being exerted in the direction of its movement ; and,
conversely, that when such lateral pressure, as shown
by the 'indicator,' is being adequately exerted, the
table moves round. The Physicist, therefore, has a
right to assert, that, until a table shall be found to
turn *without* lateral pressure of the hands laid upon

the 'indicator,' as shown by the fixity of its index, *there is no evidence whatever of the exertion of any other force than the Muscular action of the operators.* And the Physiologist, who is familiar with the fact that every human being is continually putting forth a vast amount of muscular energy, of the exercise of which he is entirely unconscious, and who has also studied that unconscious influence of mental preconception of which I have already given you illustrations in the *pendule explorateur*, at once perceives that the absence of any consciousness of exertion on the part of the operators, affords no proof whatever that it is not being put forth ; while he is further well aware that *involuntary* muscular contractions are often far more powerful than any which the *will* can excite.

The same explanation applies to the tilting of the table, which is made in response to questions asked of 'the spirits' by which it is supposed to be influenced. Nothing but a strange prepossession in favour of some 'occult' agency, can attribute such tilting to anything but the *downward* pressure of the hands laid upon it ; the hypothetic exertion of *any other* force being scientifically inadmissible, until it shall have been experimentally shown that the table tilts without being manually pressed down. An 'indicator' might be easily constructed, which should test *downward* pressure, on the same principle that Faraday's indicator tests *lateral* pressure ; but no one, so far as I am aware, has ever ventured to affirm that he has thus demonstrated the *absence* of muscular pressure, although I long since pointed out that only in

this manner could the matter be scientifically tested.
Until such demonstrations shall have been given, the
tilting—like the turning—of tables, may be unhesita-
tingly attributed to the unconscious muscular action
of the operators ; while the answers which are brought
out by its instrumentality may be shown to be the expressions, either (like the movements of the *pendule
explorateur*) of ideas actually present to the mind of
one or other of the performers ; or (as often occurs in
Somnambulism and other allied states) of past ideas
which have left their traces in the brain, although they
have dropped out of the conscious memory.

That such is the nature of the responses ordinarily
obtained by those who (in entire good faith) have
practised this ' curious art ' in any of its varied forms
— including planchette-writing — is shown by the
analysis of a number of cases observed by myself
and recorded by others.[1] And there is this very
curious indication of it : that when the ' table-talking '
epidemic first spread in this country, a number of
Low-church Clergymen, strongly imbued with the
belief that it was a manifestation of Satanic agency, put
to the tables a series of what they regarded as ' test '
questions, and got just the answers they expected.[2]

SPIRITUALISM.

I now come to the existing phase of the Epidemic
belief in the ' occult,' which, as I have already pointed
out, differs from the preceding rather in its outward
manifestations than in its essential nature. You have

[1] *Appendix L.*   [2] *Appendix M.*

all heard of the ghostly visitations, which, in the days of our ancestors, were reputed to have disclosed by means of raps the places in which treasure had been hidden, or a murdered corpse had been buried. Ghosts, however, like witchcraft, seem to have lost credit with the present generation, until brought into vogue again as 'spirits' by the Rochester rappings. A family of the name of Fox, including two girls aged respectively about *nine* and *eleven* years, went to inhabit a house at Hydesville (Rochester County, New York State), in which a murder was said to have been committed many years before. They had not resided in it long, when raps were heard in the girls' chamber ; sometimes obviously issuing from their persons, but sometimes apparently proceeding from other parts of the room. Curiosity was excited ; the neighbourhood flocked to witness the marvel ; no one could detect any movement on the part of either of the girls while the raps were sounding ; and no concealed instrumentality could be discovered by careful search. The rappings soon began to show a certain coherence ; a code of signals was arranged, according to which one rap was to mean *no*, three raps *yes*, and two raps *doubtful* or *wait* ; and communications having been thus opened with the rappers, visitors were enabled, through the medium of these two girls, to summon and interrogate the 'spirits' of their departed friends. Multitudes now flocked from all parts to witness the phenomena ; and the girls having gone to live with an elder married sister at Rochester-town, the alphabetical system was established at her suggestion ; which enabled the 'spirits' to spell out their messages by rapping at the required letters, when either the alphabet was repeated by the enquirer, or the letters on an alphabet-card were successively pointed to. The excitement continuing to increase, a Committee of Investigation was appointed by a town-meeting. Every opportunity was given for the enquiry ; but the committee was completely baffled. The enquiry was taken up, however, by an eminent anatomist, Dr. Austin Flint, of New York ; who, having first convinced himself that the sounds issued from the legs or feet of the girls themselves, notwithstanding their apparent stillness, sought for a physiological explanation of them ; and soon found one in the power which certain persons can acquire, of giving a jerking or snapping action to particular tendons of either the knees, ankles, or toes,— a patient of his own being able thus to produce an exact imitation of the Rochester rappings. Dr. Austin Flint's explanation subsequently received full confirmation from Professor Schiff, since of Florence, who not only himself acquired the power of producing the raps, by the repeated displacement of a tendon which slides through a sheath behind the external protuberance of the ankle, but exhibited this acquirement to the French Academy of Medicine in April, 1859, baring his legs, and producing the raps without any apparent movement. And not more than six years ago, Mrs. Culver, a female relative of the Fox family, made a deposition before the magistrates of the town in which she resided ; [1] stating that while visiting the

----
[1] *Appendix N.*

girls at Rochester many years before, she had become acquainted with the entire secret, which she
fully disclosed; and herself reproducing the raps in
verification of her narrative.

But the very rationality of this explanation caused
it to be disbelieved by such as were anxious to be
placed in communication with 'the spirit world.' The
fame of the Fox girls spread through the United States;
they established themselves as 'mediums' in New
York; and before long they were drawing a large
income from the pockets of their credulous visitors.

Under the fostering influence of pecuniary temptation, imitators of the Fox girls soon sprang up in
various parts of the United States; 'mediums'
became numerous; and one of them, Mrs. Hayden,
brought the contagion to this country, where the
'spirit-rapping' Epidemic rapidly spread. The manner
in which, according to the experience of those who
witnessed Mrs. Hayden's performances (subsequently
confirmed by Mrs. Culver), the 'medium' divined at
what letters to make the raps, was very simple; consisting merely in carefully watching the countenance
or gestures of the questioner, who almost invariably
gives, in some way or other, involuntary expression to
his or her expectancy. Of this I could cite many
proofs. An eminent scientific friend told me that
having been at a party by one member of which after
another Mrs. Hayden's powers were tested, he was
at first greatly surprised at the accuracy of the replies
he obtained regarding the name, date of death, and

place of death, of a deceased friend of whom he was thinking ; but that he soon obtained a clue, by observing that her success varied with the demonstrativeness of the individual, and that she utterly failed with one of peculiarly imperturbable habit. He then made a fresh trial, with the fixed predetermination to withhold any manifestation of his expectancy ; and Mrs. Hayden was completely baffled. The secret was divined also by Professor Edward Forbes, who, by pausing on particular letters, made Mrs. Hayden spell ' Lord Tomnoddy ' and other waggeries. And the most complete exposure of the trick was given by Mr. G. H. K. Lewes ; who caused Mrs. Hayden to rap out the most absurd replies to questions which he had previously written down and communicated to another member of the party ; finally obtaining, in answer to the question ' Is Mrs. Hayden an impostor ? ' three unhesitating raps at the letters Y, E, S.[1]

In the ' Report on Spiritualism of the Committee of the London Dialectical Society,' you will find that Dr. Edmunds, the chairman of that Committee, not only detected a well-known professional ' medium ' in making the raps with her foot, but observed that she regulated her raps by intently watching the questioner, and that when she was prevented from doing this by the interposition of a screen, her raps were altogether

---

[1] Mr. Wallace explains this result by assuming that the raps were caused by ' invisible beings,' who, reading what was in the questioner's mind, answered a fool according to his folly. Where the folly lies, the readers of Mr. Wallace's letter (*Appendix O*) will judge for themselves.

meaningless. My own experience with other 'mediums' has been to exactly the same effect.[1]

Of the 'higher phenomena' of Spiritualism—the 'levitation' of chairs and tables, and even of men and women; the 'elongation' of Mr. Home's body, his handling of heated bodies, and his heaping hot coals on the head of a bald gentleman without any discomfort to him; the untying of knots and change of coats; the production of 'spiritual photographs;' the bringing-in of fruits, flowers, or live lobsters, in dark *séances*; and the like—I have left myself no time to speak. The very catalogue speaks, to any sober and unprepossessed mind, of the extreme improbability that any 'spiritual' agents should so manifest their presence. And in regard to the spirit-writing by pens or pencils, I can only say that of the revelations given by its means, I have seen none that could claim any higher character than that of unmitigated 'twaddle.' It is because the present generation knows little of the history of former Epidemics of this kind, and is therefore not in a position to profit by the experience they have afforded, that I have rather dwelt in these lec-

---

[1] *Appendix P.*—Much stress is laid by the Editor of the *Spectator*, and by Mr. Wallace, upon a statement made by the late Professor De Morgan, that Mrs. Hayden's success was *not* interfered with by the interposition of a screen. But I have it on the authority of an eminent Scientific colleague of Professor De Morgan's, who was repeatedly present at the spiritualistic *séances* held at his house, that the experiments were habitually conducted there in so loose a manner as to be altogether unsatisfactory; frauds of the most transparent kind (which my friend himself more than once exposed) being accepted as valid proofs; and nonnatural interpretations being always preferred, when natural explanations were obvious.

tures on the lessons of the past in regard to the *credibility of testimony* on these subjects, than discussed
the truth or falsehood of statements now in currency
in regard to the recent doings of 'the spirits.' It is
not because I have not investigated Spiritualism for
myself, that I refrain from bringing before you in
detail the results of my own enquiries. At the out-
break of the Epidemic I devoted to the examination
of its pretensions an amount of time and attention
which might have been far more profitably employed ;
and I did not give up the enquiry until I had satisfied myself, by long and careful study, that its character was fundamentally the same with that of the
epidemics I had previously witnessed, differing only
in the particular form of its manifestations. I could not
afford to sacrifice the time that might be much more
profitably spent in adding to our stock of real knowledge, in the (so-called) scientific investigation of such
performances as those of the 'Davenport Brothers ; '
when I found that the investigation was to be so
carried on, that I should be precluded from using
either my eyes or my hands, the most important instruments of scientific enquiry. I felt assured that
these performances would turn out to be mere conjuring tricks : and that they really are so has been
shown, not merely by Mr. Maskelyne's discovery of
the secret, and his repetition of the performances *as*
conjuring tricks, but by the recent public *exposé* of the
whole method, in Boston (N.E.), by one who formerly
practised it for gain. So, again, in other cases in which
I strongly suspected the supposed 'spiritualistic'

manifestations to be intentional deceptions, and proposed their repetition under test-conditions admitted to be fair, I waited hour after hour for the manifestations, the non-production of which was attributed to my 'atmosphere of incredulity.'

Thus, having accompanied a scientific friend to a Spiritualistic *séance*, at which we saw a small light table dance up and down under the hands of a professional 'medium' (Mrs. M.) as she moved across the room, I pointed out to my friend, who regarded this as an example of 'spiritual' agency, that since the 'medium' wore a large crinoline which completely concealed her feet, it was quite possible for her to have lifted the table upon one foot, while moving across the room on the other—as any opera-dancer could do. My friend, candidly admitting the possibility of this explanation, subsequently invited me to a *séance* at his own house, with a non-professional 'medium;' and asked me if I was satisfied with the 'crinoline-guard' of wire and paper which he had so placed round the legs of a small table, that the 'medium' could not lift the table on her foot without breaking through the 'guard.' I replied that I was perfectly satisfied ; and that if I should see the table dance up and down under his 'medium's' hands, in the same manner as under Mrs. M.'s, I should admit that it was a case for further investigation. During a *séance* of two hours, however, no other manifestation took place than 'raps,' indicating the presence of 'spirits;' the interposition of the 'crinoline-guard' apparently keeping them away from the table.[1]

[1] Since the delivery of this Lecture, Mr. A. R. Wallace has pub-

In regard to professional 'mediums' who make their living by the exercise of their supposed gifts, I came to the conclusion that we have as much right to assume fraud until the contrary shall have been proved, as we have in the case of a gipsy fortune-teller, who has managed to learn a good deal about the chief people of the country neighbourhood into which she comes, before she allows herself to be consulted, and then astonishes her credulous clients by the knowledge of their affairs which she displays. I need not tell you how one after another of such pretenders has been detected in England. In Paris the frauds of a 'spiritual' Photographic establishment were brought into the law courts, and the persons concerned in them sentenced to severe punishment, a year or two ago. And in America, the 'Katie King' imposture, which had deluded some of the leading spiritualists in this country, as well as in the United States, was publicly exposed at about the same time.

But, it is affirmed, such exposures *prove* nothing against the genuineness of any new manifestation. I quite admit this. But I affirm that to anyone accustomed to weigh the value of evidence, the fact that the testimony in favour of a whole series of antecedent claims has been completely upset, seriously invalidates (as I have shown in regard to Mesmeric *clairvoyance*) the trustworthiness of the testimony in favour of any new claimant to 'occult' powers. Why should

licly avowed himself to be the 'scientific friend' to whom I referred ; and has stated that on subsequent occasions the table *did* rise within the 'crinoline guard.' Has it ever done so, I ask, in the presence of a sceptical expert ?

I believe the testimony of any believer in the genuineness of D's performances, when he has been obliged to admit that he has been egregiously deceived in the cases of A, B, and C?

The case is not essentially different in regard to 'mediums' who do *not* practise for gain. For it is perfectly well known to those who have had adequate opportunities of observation, that there is a class of persons (especially, I am sorry to have to say, of the female sex) who have an extraordinary proclivity to deceit, even from a very early period of life ; and who enjoy nothing better than ' taking-in ' older and wiser people, even when doing so brings no special advantage to themselves.[1] Every Medical practitioner of large experience has met with cases in which young ladies have imposed in this way, by feigning disease, not only upon their families, but upon their previous doctors ; the supposed patients sometimes undergoing very severe treatment for its cure. And when the new attendant has sagaciously found out the cheat, and has honestly exposed it to the parents, he is in general ' morally ' kicked out of the house for his unfounded aspersion ;—not every one having the good

---

[1] Thus Mr. Braid gives (*Magic, Witchcraft, &c.*, p. 117) the case of a boy who got credit in his own town for *clairvoyant* power ; being able to read, play cards, &c., when the upper part of his face was covered with a mask of nine folds of silk stuffed with cotton-wool. Hundreds of respectable people were ready to attest the fact ; but when the precaution suggested by Mr. Braid—of guarding against interspaces near the nose—was put in practice, the trick was made apparent, as in the case of Madlle. Pigeaire (p. 74). Mr. Braid was requested not to make any public exposure of the cheat ; " because the boy's father was " such a respectable man, being one of the Town-Council." '

fortune of my old friend Dr. A. T. Thompson, who was sent for some years afterwards by a young married lady to attend her family, on account of the high opinion she had formed of his ability, as the only one of the many doctors formerly consulted about her, who had found out the real nature of her case. I could tell you the particulars, in my possession, of the detection of the imposture practised by one of the most noteworthy of these Lady-mediums, in the distribution of flowers which she averred to be brought-in by the 'spirits' in a dark *séance*, fresh from the garden, and wet with the dew of heaven ; these flowers having really been previously collected in a basin upstairs, and watered out of a decanter standing by,—as was proved by the fact, that an inquisitive sceptic having furtively introduced into the water of the decanter a small quantity of a nearly colourless salt (ferrocyanide of potassium), its presence in the 'dew' of the flowers was afterwards recognised by the appropriate chemical test (a per-salt of iron) which brought out 'prussian blue.'

In other instances, again, I have witnessed the most extraordinary *self*-deception : which, as in the Mesmeric performances, invested occurrences which could be readily accounted for on 'natural' principles, with a 'supernatural' character ; often through the omission of some essential fact, which is entirely ignored by the narrator. Thus I was seriously informed, during the Table-turning epidemic, that a table had been moved round by the will of a gentleman sitting at a distance from it ; but it came out upon cross-examination, that a number of hands were laid upon it in the usual way, and that after the performers had sat for some time in silent expectation, the operator called upon 'the spirit of Samson' to move the table, which then obediently went round.—Sometimes the essential fact, under the influence of this proclivity, completely passes out of the mind of the narrator ; as in the instance of a lady, cited by Miss Cobbe in her paper on the 'Fallacies of Memory,' who assured Miss C. that a table in her drawing-room had some years before correctly rapped out her age in the presence of several persons, *none of whom were near the table* ; the fact being impressed on her mind by her annoyance at the disclosure, which was so great that she sold the table ! Having assured Miss Cobbe that she could verify her statement by reference to notes made at the time, she subsequently corrected it, very honestly, by telling Miss C. that she found that there *were* hands on the table.—So, I have been recently requested by a gentleman to go and see a light table made heavy at the will of a person standing apart from it ; a table which could be ordinarily lifted on a single finger, requiring the strength of the hands to raise it when so commanded. Thinking that this might be a trick of the kind that Houdin played upon the Arabs by means of an electro-magnet, I made some preliminary enquiries with a view to satisfy myself whether the phenomenon was to be thus accounted for ; and finding that it was not, I was about to go to witness it, when I received a letter from the brother of my correspondent, who told me that he thought I ought to know the real conditions of the performance ; which were that, the hands of two of the operator's family being first laid upon the table, the table was upset and lay on the floor on its side ; and that then, their hands still pressing sideways upon the top of the table, it could be made light or heavy by the will of the operator at a distance, a single finger being able to raise it up in the once case, while the whole hand was required in the other. And thus, as in the case of ' the spirit of Samson,' it became evident that the will of the operator was exercised in regulating the pressure of the hands in contact with the table, there being no evidence whatever of any alteration in its actual weight.

One potent source of this self-deception, I find in the state of *expectancy* that results from prolonged and repeated *séances* ; in which, by mere continued monotony of impression, the mind tends towards a state in which the will and discrimination are suspended, and the expected phenomenon (such as the rising of a table in the air) takes place *subjectively,*— that is, in the belief of the person or persons who report it—without any *objective* reality. Of this mental condition an admirable description was given by Mr. Braid,[1] on the basis of his own investigations, before ' Spiritualism ' became epidemic in this country; its existence is not, therefore, a hypothesis invented *ad hoc.* Sceptical enquirers, like myself, are continually told :— " You must not form your negative conclusions from " one or two failures ; but you must persevere in your " enquiries until you get positive results." This is just

[1] *Appendix Q.*

like John Wesley's advice to a young preacher, who was lamenting his want of 'faith,' and asking his advice as to continuing in the ministry :—" Preach " faith *till* you have it, and then you will preach it *be-* " *cause* you have it." Spiritualistic disciples are bidden to sit hour after hour, and day after day, until they pass into the state of mind in which they can be brought to believe anything they have been led to expect ; and thenceforth they rail at scientific sceptics for not abnegating their intellectual discrimination, by submitting themselves to a process which dethrones their higher powers from their normal supremacy, and leaves their imaginations free scope.

I have thus endeavoured to set before you what a long sequence of experiences seems to me to teach in regard to this subject ; namely, that we should rather trust to the evidence of our *sense*, than to that of our *senses*. That the latter is liable to many fallacies, we are almost daily finding out. If we go to see the performances of a Conjuror, we *see* things which we *know* to be impossibilities ; and that knowledge makes us aware that they *cannot really* happen as they *seem* to happen. Thus every conjuror can pour out scores of glasses of different kinds of wine from a single bottle ; or can tumble a great pile of bouquets out of a single hat ; but we know that he *must* do this from some larger store, which he dexterously conceals from our view. So, the celebrated conjuror Bosco seemed even to those who were closely watching him within a very short distance, to convert a living

I

hare into two living rabbits ; the movements by which he made the exchange from a bag behind him, being so extraordinarily rapid as to elude the observation of the bystanders, whose attention he fixed (the great secret alike of conjurors and professional 'mediums') upon something else. And I conclude, therefore, as I began, with the affirmation that we have a right to reject the testimony of the most truthful and honest witnesses, as to asserted phenomena which are as much opposed to the 'Laws of Nature' as the transport of a human being through the air, the conversion of an old woman into a hare (or *vice versâ*), or the change of a hare into two rabbits ; until the facts of the case shall have been so thoroughly sifted by the investigation of 'sceptical experts' as to present an irresistible claim on our belief. In every case within my knowledge, in which such investigation *has* been made, its fallacies have become apparent ; and when, therefore, I receive narratives from persons quite credible in regard to *ordinary* matters, as to *extraordinary* occurrences which have taken place within their knowledge, I think myself justified in telling them plainly that their conviction cannot govern my belief, because both theory and experience have led me to the conclusion that no amount of testimony is good for anything, which is given by persons 'possessed' with a 'dominant idea' in regard to the subject of it, and which has not been tested by severe cross-examination.

As I wrote twenty-three years ago :—" In all ages " the possession of men's minds by dominant ideas has

" been most complete, when these ideas have been *reli-*
" *gious* aberrations. The origin of such aberrations has
" uniformly lain in the preference given to the feelings
" over the judgment, in the inordinate indulgence of
" emotional excitement without adequate control on
" the part of the rational will. Those who are thus
" affected place themselves beyond the pale of any ap-
" peals to their reasoning faculty, and lead others into
" the same position. They are no more to be argued
" with, than are insane patients. They cannot accept
" any proposition which they fancy to be in the least
" inconsistent with their prepossessions ; and the evi-
" dence of their own feelings is to them the highest
" attainable truth." [1]

Many of the victims of these delusions have become the subjects of actual Insanity ; which has been
attributed by believers to ' a spirit having entered in
and taken possession.' What kind of spirits they are
which thus take possession of credulous and excitable
minds, I hope that I have now made sufficiently
plain : they are *Dominant Ideas.*

[1] *Quarterly Review*, October 1853.—A sensible Clergyman has lately
written in almost the same words, in regard to the 'dominant ideas'
by which his ultra-ritualistic brethren are at present possessed. "I
"know well (says ' Clericus,' *Times*, Dec. 29, 1876) that when men have
" once committed themselves to a false principle or theory, it becomes a
" monomania with them for a time ; and those who on all other points
" are reasonable and capable of forming just conclusions, become utterly
" blind and illogical, so that argument with them is hopeless."

APPENDICES.

―◦◦―

APPENDIX A.

MAGIC AND DEMONIACAL AGENCY AT THE CHRISTIAN ERA.

"For many years before this time, and for many years
after, impostors from the East, pretending to magical powers,
had great influence over the Roman mind. All the Greek
and Roman literature of the empire, from Horace to Lucian,
abounds in proof of the prevalent credulity of this sceptical
period. Unbelief, when it has become conscious of its
weakness, is often glad to give its hand to superstition. The
faith of educated Romans was utterly gone. We can hardly
wonder, when the East was thrown open—the land of mystery—the fountain of the earliest migrations—the cradle of
the earliest religions—that the imagination both of the
populace and the aristocracy of Rome became fanatically
excited, and that they greedily welcomed the most absurd
and degrading superstitions. Not only was the metropolis
of the empire crowded with hungry Greeks, but Syrian for-
tune-tellers flocked into all the haunts of public amusement.
Every part of the East contributed its share to the general
superstition. The gods of Egypt and Phrygia found unfailing votaries. Before the close of the republic, the temples
of Isis and Serapis had been more than once erected, des-

troyed and renewed. Josephus tells us that certain disgrace-
ful priests of Isis were crucified at Rome by the second
emperor ; but this punishment was only a momentary check
to their sway over the Roman mind. The more remote districts of Asia Minor sent their itinerant soothsayers ; Syria
sent her music and her medicines ; Chaldæa her Babylonian
numbers and mathematical calculations. To these corrupters
of the people of Romulus we must add one more Asiatic
nation—the nation of the Israelites ;—and it is an instructive
employment to observe that, while some members of the
Jewish people were rising, by the Divine power, to the
highest position ever occupied by men on earth, others were
sinking themselves, and others along with them, to the lowest
and most contemptible degradation."—Conybeare and How-
son's *Life of St. Paul*, vol. i. p. 158.

The reputation of Simon Magus of Samaria stood so
high in Rome, alike with the Senate and the people, that he
was even adored as a god ; a statue being raised to him in
the island of the Tiber, with the inscription, *Simoni Deo
Sancto.* Several of the early Christian Fathers who speak
of this inscription, fully admit the reality of Simon's miraculous powers, as shown in his making statues which walked
at his command in the midst of a crowd thunderstruck with
wonder and fright ; his remaining unhurt in the midst of the
flames of a burning pile ; his changing stones into bread ;
his making a scythe mow without hands, and the like:—some
of them merely protesting against his being credited with
the attribute of Divinity, whilst others affirm that it was only
after having failed to obtain these powers from the Apostles
by the offer of money, that he gained them by allying himself with Demons. Apollonius of Thyana was another celebrated magician of the first century, who figures much in the
writings of the early fathers as an opponent of the Christ-
ians, to whom he did all the mischief he could by his
diabolical arts ; in which these Fathers believed as firmly as

they did in those of Simon Magus. There is a singular passage in Tertullian (Apologies, chap. xxiii.), which refers to magicians who could bring up phantoms, evoke the spirits of the dead, force the mouths of infants to utter oracles, and make chairs and tables prophesy by means of 'circles' or chains formed by the joined hands of several individuals — exactly after the manner of modern Spiritualists. If 'the spirits' are powerful enough, argues Tertullian, to do these things at the orders of others, what must they be able to effect when working with redoubled zeal on their own account? Against these he sets two Christian miracles which occurred within his own knowledge ; the first, of a corpse, at its own funeral, raising and clasping its hands in the usual attitude of supplication at the first word of the priest in prayer, and then replacing them at its sides when the prayer was over ; and the second, of a Christian corpse long dead and buried, which, on its grave being re-opened for the admission of a recently defunct, courteously moved to one side to make room for the new-comer! These statements, doubtless made in all honesty and good faith, curiously illustrate that influence of 'dominant ideas' over an intellect powerful, subtle, and profound in many respects, but totally destitute of scientific discrimination, which it is the object of these Lectures to elucidate.

APPENDIX B.

FLAGELLANT MANIA.

The private practice of individual flagellation, as an act of self-mortification, was common among religious communities from an early period of Christianity ; but it was not until the thirteenth century, when a general belief prevailed that the end of the world was at hand, that regular associations and fraternities were formed for its public performance, and that the mania spread epidemically over a large part of Europe. Of the *Devoti* of Italy in the year 1260, we are told by a contemporary historian that " noble and ignoble, old and young, and even children of five years of age, marched through the streets with no covering but a scarf round the waist. They each carried a scourge of leathern thongs, which they applied to their limbs, amid sighs and tears, with such violence that the blood flowed from the wounds. Not only during the day, but even by night, and in the severest winter, they traversed the cities with burning torches and banners in thousands and tens of thousands, headed by their priests, and prostrated themselves before the altars. They proceeded in the same manner in the villages ; and the woods and mountains resounded with the voices of those whose cries were raised to God. The melancholy chaunt of the penitent alone was heard. Enemies were reconciled ; men and women vied with each other in splendid works of charity, as if they dreaded that Divine Omnipotence would pronounce on them the doom of annihilation." (Monachus Paduanus, in Hecker's *Epidemics of the Middle Ages*, translated by Dr. Babington for the Sydenham Society, p. 36.)

It was in the middle of the fourteenth century (1347–1350) that Europe was devastated by the Black Death, a most malignant form of the Oriental Plague, which is believed to have carried off *one fourth* of its entire population ; and under the terror inspired by this visitation the flagellant Mania, which had previously almost entirely abated, broke out with new fury, apparently in many places at once ; and the excesses of this fanaticism became even more violent than before. But though it prevailed over nearly the whole of Continental Europe, this Mania does not seem to have become epidemic in Britain. We are told by Stow that a band of Flagellants reached London in the reign of Edward III., their number consisting of 120 men and women. Each day, at an appointed hour, they assembled, ranged themselves in two lines, and paraded the streets scourging their naked shoulders and chanting a hymn. At a given signal, all with the exception of the last, threw themselves flat on the ground; and he who was last, as he passed by his companions, gave each a lash, and then also lay down. The others followed in succession, till every individual in his or her turn had received a stroke from the whole brotherhood. The citizens of London gazed and marvelled, pitied and commended; but they went no farther. Their faith was too weak, or their skins too delicate ; and they allowed the strangers to monopolise all the merits of such a religious exercise. The missionaries did not make a single convert, and were obliged to return without any other success than the conviction of having done their duty to an unbelieving generation.

Though the practice was at first encouraged by the Church, the Flagellants subsequently fell under its ban as heretical ; for they taught that many of its doctrines were false, and that faith and flagellation, with a belief in the Apostles' Creed, were alone necessary to salvation. The priests complained of their loss of influence ; the hierarchy took the alarm ; and the Pope prohibited throughout Christendom the continuance of the flagellant pilgrimages, under pain of excommunication. The flagellants were then everywhere persecuted, and some of them were burned as heretics ; but it was long before the Mania was completely repressed. It broke out several times in the later part of the fourteenth century ; in the fifteenth it was deemed necessary in several parts of Germany to exterminate the flagellants with fire and sword ; yet as late as 1710 their processions were still seen in Italy. Of the strength of this 'possession,' it is scarcely possible to conceive a stronger instance than is presented by the depo-

sition of a citizen of Nordhäusen, in 1446, that his wife, in
the belief of performing a Christian act, wanted to scourge
her children as soon as they were baptised !

APPENDIX C.

DANCING MANIA.

" In the year 1374, assemblages of men and women were
seen at Aix-la-Chapelle, who had come out of Germany, and
who, united by one common delusion, exhibited to the public,
both in the streets and in the churches, the following strange
spectacle :—They formed circles hand in hand, and appear-
ing to have lost all control over their senses, continued
dancing, regardless of the bystanders, for hours together, in
wild delirium, until at length they fell to the ground in a state
of exhaustion. They then complained of extreme oppres-
sion, and groaned as if in the agonies of death, until they
were swathed in clothes bound tightly round their waists ;
upon which they again recovered, and remained free from
complaint until the next attack. This practice of swathing
was resorted to, on account of the tympany which followed
these spasmodic ravings ; but the bystanders frequently relieved patients in a less artificial manner, by thumping and
trampling upon the parts affected. While dancing they
neither saw nor heard, being insensible to external impressions through the senses ; but were haunted by visions, their
fancies conjuring up spirits, whose names they shrieked out;
and some of them afterwards asserted that they felt as if
they had been immersed in a stream of blood, which obliged
them to leap so high. Others, during the paroxysm, saw
the heavens open, and the Saviour enthroned with the Virgin Mary ; according as the religious notions of the age
were strangely and variously reflected in their imaginations.

Where the disease was completely developed, the attack commenced with epileptic convulsions. Those affected fell to the ground senseless, panting and labouring for breath. They foamed at the mouth, and suddenly springing up began their dance amidst strange contortions.

" A few months after this dancing malady had made its appearance at Aix-la-Chapelle, it broke out at Cologne, where the number of those possessed amounted to more than five hundred ; and about the same time at Metz, the streets of which place are said to have been filled with eleven hundred dancers. Peasants left their ploughs, mechanics their workshops, housewives their domestic duties, to join the wild revels ; and this rich commercial city became the scene of the most ruinous disorder.

" The St. Vitus's dance attacked people of all stations, especially those who led a sedentary life, such as shoemakers and tailors ; but even the most robust peasants abandoned their labours in their fields, as if they were possessed by evil spirits ; and those affected were seen assembling indiscriminately, from time to time, at certain appointed places, and, unless prevented by the lookers-on, continued to dance without intermission, until their very last breath was expended. Their fury and extravagance of demeanour so completely deprived them of their senses, that many of them dashed their brains out against the walls and corners of buildings, or rushed headlong into rapid rivers, where they found a watery grave. Roaring and foaming as they were, the bystanders could only succeed in restraining them by placing benches and chairs in their way, so that, by the high leaps they were thus tempted to take, their strength might be exhausted. As soon as this was the case, they fell, as it were, lifeless to the ground, and, by very slow degrees, recovered their strength. Many there were, who, even with all this exertion, had not expended the violence of the tempest which raged within them ; but awoke with newly revived powers, and again and again mixed with the crowd of dancers ; until at length the violent excitement of their disordered nerves was allayed by the great involuntary exertion of their limbs ; and the mental disorder was calmed by the exhaustion of the body. The cure effected by these stormy attacks was in many cases so perfect, that some patients returned to the factory or the plough, as if nothing had happened. Others, on the contrary, paid the penalty of their folly by so total a loss of power, that they could not regain their former health, even by the employment of the most strengthening remedies."—(Hecker's *Epidemics of the Middle Ages*, pp. 87–104.)

APPENDIX D.

THE 'ANIMAL MAGNETISM' OF MESMER.

"Animal Magnetism is a fluid universally diffused ; it is the medium of a mutual influence between the heavenly bodies, the earth, and animated bodies ; it is everywhere continuous, so as to leave no void ; its subtlety admits of no comparison ; it is capable of receiving, propagating, communicating all the impressions of motion ; it is susceptible of flux and of reflux. The animal body experiences the effects of this agent ; by insinuating itself into the substance of the nerves it affects them immediately. There are observed, particularly in the human body, properties analogous to those of the magnet ; and in it are discerned properties equally different and opposite. The action and the virtues of animal magnetism may be communicated from one body to other bodies, animate and inanimate. This action takes place at a remote distance, without the aid of any intermediate body ; it is increased, reflected by mirrors; communicated, propagated, augmented by sound ; its virtues

may be accumulated, concentrated, transported. Although
this fluid is universal, all animal bodies are not equally susceptible of it; there are even some, though a very small
number, which have properties so opposite, that their very
presence destroys all the effects of this fluid on other bodies.
Animal Magnetism is capable of healing diseases of the
nerves immediately, and others mediately. It perfects the
action of medicines ; it excites and directs salutary *crises* in
such a manner that the physician may render himself master
of them ; by its means he knows the state of health of each
individual, and judges with certainty of the origin, the nature,
and the progress of the most complicated diseases ; he prevents their increase, and succeeds in healing them without
at any time exposing his patient to dangerous effects or
troublesome consequences; whatever be the age, the temperament, and the sex. In animal magnetism, nature presents a universal method of healing and preserving mankind."—(*Mémoire sur la Découverte du Magnétisme Animal,*
par M. Mesmer.   Paris, 1779, p. 74, *et seq.*—*Ibid, Avis du
Lecteur,* p. 6.)

APPENDIX E.

REPORT ON MESMER'S PRETENSIONS, BY THE COMMISSION
APPOINTED BY THE ACADEMY OF SCIENCES, PARIS.

"The sick persons, arranged in great numbers and in
several rows around the *baquet,* receive the magnetism by
all these means ; by the iron rods which convey to them that
of the baquet ; by the cords wound round their bodies ; by
the connection of the thumbs which communicate to them
that of their neighbours ; by the sound of the pianoforte, or
of an agreeable voice diffusing the magnetism in the air ; by

the finger and rod of the magnetiser moved before their faces, above or behind their heads, and on the diseased parts, always observing the direction of the poles; by the eye of the magnetiser; but above all by the application of his hands and the pressure of his fingers on the hypochondria and on the regions of the abdomen; an application often continued for a long time, sometimes for several hours. Meanwhile the patients, in their different conditions, present a varied picture. Some are calm, tranquil, and experience no effect; others cough, spit, feel slight pains, local or general heat, and have sweatings; others again are agitated or tormented with convulsions. These convulsions are remarkable in regard to the number affected with them, and to their duration and force; and are characterised by the precipitous involuntary motions of all the limbs and of the whole body, by the constriction of the throat, by the violent heavings of the hypochondria and the epigastrium; by the dimness and wandering of the eyes; by piercing shrieks, tears, sobbing, and immoderate laughter. They are preceded or followed by a state of languor and reverie, a kind of depression, and even drowsiness. The smallest unforeseen noise occasions shudderings; even a change of tone and measure in the airs played on the pianoforte influences the patients, a quicker motion agitating them more and renewing the vivacity of their convulsions. Nothing is more astonishing than the spectacle of these convulsions; one who has not seen them can form no idea of them. The spectator is equally astonished at the profound repose of one part of the patients, and at the agitation of the rest; at the various accidents which are repeated, and the sympathies which are established. Some patients devote their exclusive attention to each other, rushing towards one another, smiling, speaking with affection, and mutually soothing their *crises*. All are under the power of the magnetiser; it matters not in what state of drowsiness they may be; his voice, a look, a gesture brings them out of it."—*(Report of the Commission of the French Academy of Sciences.)*

The Commissioners further reported—"That this pretended agent certainly is not common Magnetism; for on examining the *baquet*, the grand reservoir of this wonderful fluid, by means of a needle and electrometer, not the slightest indication of the presence either of common magnetism or of electricity was afforded; that it is wholly inappreciable by any of the senses, or by any mechanical or chemical process; that they tried it upon themselves and upon many others, without being able to perceive anything; that on blindfolding those who seemed to be most susceptible to its influence, all its ordinary effects were produced when nothing was done to them, but when they imagined they were being magnetised, while none of its effects were produced when they were really magnetised, but imagined that nothing was being done; that, in like manner, when brought under a magnetised tree, nothing happened if the subjects of the experiment thought they were at a distance from the tree, while they were immediately thrown into convulsions if they believed they were near the tree, although really at a distance from it; that, consequently the effects actually produced were produced purely by the imagination; that these effects, though some cures might be wrought, were not without danger, since the convulsions excited were often violent and exceedingly apt to spread, especially among men feeble in body and weak in mind, and almost universally among women; and finally, that there were parts of the operation of magnetising which might readily be turned to vicious purposes, and that immoral practices had already actually grown out of them.'—*(Ibid.)*

APPENDIX F.

EXTRAORDINARY MUSCULAR ENERGY PRODUCIBLE BY
MENTAL CONCENTRATION.

It is a well-known fact that when the whole energy is concentrated upon some Muscular effort, especially under the influence of an overpowering emotion, the body seems endowed with superhuman strength and agility, so as to be able to accomplish some extraordinary feat, at which the performer himself stands aghast when he contemplates it after his return to his sober senses. Thus an old cook-maid who heard an alarm of fire, seized an enormous box containing the whole of her property, and ran down stairs with it as easily as she would have carried a dish of meat ; yet after the fire had been extinguished, she could not lift it a hair's breadth from the ground, and two men were required to carry it upstairs again.—It was by the artificial induction of a like state of concentrated effort, coupled with the assurance of easy success, ('it will go up like a feather.') with which he had completely possessed his 'subject's' mind, that Mr. Braid (in my presence) enabled a man so remarkable for the poverty of his *physique*, that he had not for many years ventured to lift a weight of twenty pounds, to take up a weight of 28 lbs. upon his little finger, and swing it round his head, with the greatest apparent ease.   Neither Mr. Braid nor his son, both of them powerful men, could do anything like this ; and I could not myself lift the same weight on my little finger to more than half my own height. Trickery in this case was obviously impossible ; since, if the 'subject' had been trained to such feats, the effect of such training would have become visible in his muscular development.

APPENDIX G.

EXAMINATION OF MR. LEWIS'S EXPERIMENTS ON MES-
MERISM, AT THE MEDICAL SCHOOL OF THE UNIVERSITY
AND KING'S COLLEGE, ABERDEEN.

The Committee consisted of three professors, two medical
men, and a clergyman, who undertook the investigation at
the earnest solicitation of the pupils in the Medical School.
The experiments were conducted in a perfectly fair spirit,
with every desire to do ample justice to the operator, and
at the same time in such a manner as to guard against all
obvious sources of fallacy. The 'subjects' were chosen by
Mr. Lewis from among the students; their susceptibility
having been previously tested by him. Three of the Committee remained in the Class-room where the 'subject' was
seated, and recorded the time and description of the movements he performed; whilst the other three went into an
adjoining room with Mr. Lewis, to direct at successive intervals the various movements they wished him to excite by
his silent will and bodily gestures, recording each direction
with the time at which it was given. When the round of
the experiments was finished, these three gentlemen returned
into the Class-room, and both reports were then read aloud
and compared.

The following is the first act in the performance :—

Exactly at three P.M. Mr. Lewis was desired by his committee to 'make Mr. M.—— lie on the floor with his face
on the floor.' No other direction was given for *five
minutes;* during which Mr. M. made *fourteen* movements,
not one of which had been willed by Mr. Lewis, or bore the
least resemblance to that which he did will.

K

H. M.   *Mr. M's. Movements.*

3.1½ P.M.—Raised himself up in the chair and shook himself.

3.2 P.M.—Slipped down a little. Got up and sat down.
Changed his seat.

3.2½ P.M.—Rubbed his hand on his thigh, and his left arm
with his right hand.

3.3¼ P.M.—Stamped on the floor and moved his feet sideways ; then got up and changed his seat
again.

3.3⅔ P.M.—Folded arms. Put left hand behind.

3.4½ P.M.—Rocked his body from side to side.

The divergence was equally great in all the other experiments ; so that the Committee unanimously agreed in the
Report (to which Mr. Lewis could make no objection) that
"these experiments afford no ground whatever for the
" opinion that either Mr. L—— or any other person can in-
" fluence another at a distance from him." Mr. Lewis being
further challenged to prove his control over the influence of
gravitation, by making Mr. M. stand on one leg, with the
same side of his body and his foot pressed close to the
wall, he utterly failed to do so.

In accordance with an arrangement previously made, Mr.
Lewis left the Class-room when this series of experiments
had been brought to an end ; and the spectators were requested to remain quiet for a while, as another experiment
was about to be tried—this being as to Mr. Lewis's asserted
power of mesmerising from a distance. This power he was
to exercise from his lodgings upon Mr. M., the subject of
his previous experiments, at 4 hours 5 min. P.M. Instead,
however, of passing into the mesmeric sleep, Mr. M. got up
from his seat at 4 hours 5 min., came suddenly forward to a
chair, sat upon it in a state of apparent excitement for half a
minute, then rushed back, snatched his hat from the
ground, and ran off to Mr. L.'s lodgings, where, however,

he did *not* find Mr. L. Another gentleman, Mr. H., who had been previously acted on, seemed to suppose that he was again affected by Mr. L.'s manœuvres; for, after Mr. M. first got up, he bent down his head, and appeared to be in a state of great nervous excitement; refusing to leave on being pressed to do so. He remained in this state for half an hour, and was at last induced to go away, in company of two students who took charge of him. Before he could be prevailed upon to go home, he also went to Mr. L.'s lodgings, feeling himself irresistibly drawn thither by Mr. L.'s silent will; but it was ascertained that all this occurred without Mr. Lewis having directed his mind to him at all! The supposed 'attraction' thus obviously existed only in the imaginations of the 'subjects,' who had heard of Mr. Lewis's asserted power, and supposed that it was being exerted upon them.—*Edinburgh Monthly Journal of Medical Science*, February, 1852.

APPENDIX H.

SUPPOSED INFLUENCE OF MAGNETS ON MESMERISED SUBJECTS SHOWN TO BE DUE TO MENTAL SUGGESTION.

"When in London lately," says Mr. Braid, "I had the pleasure of calling upon an eminent and excellent physician who is in the habit of using mesmerism in his practice, in suitable cases, just as he uses any other remedy. He spoke of the extraordinary effects which he had experienced from the use of magnets applied *during the mesmeric state*, and kindly offered to illustrate the fact on a patient who had been asleep all the time I was in the room, and in that stage, during which I felt assured she could overhear every word of our conversation. He told me, that when he put the magnet into her hands, it would produce catalepsy of the hands and arms, and such was the result. He wafted the hands, and the catelepsy ceased. He said that a mere touch of a magnet on a limb would stiffen it, and such he proved to be the fact.

"I now told him, that I had got a little instrument in my pocket, which, although far less than his, I felt assured would prove quite as powerful ; and I offered to prove this by operating on the same patient, whom I had never seen before, and who was in the mesmeric state when I entered the room. My instrument was about three inches long, the thickness of a quill, with a ring attached to the end of it. I told him that when put into her hands, he would find it catalepsize both hands and arms as his had done ; and such was the result. Having reduced this by wafting, I took my instrument from her, and again returned it, *in another position*, and told him it would *now* have the very reverse effect —that she would not be able to hold it, and that although I closed her hands on it, they would open, and that it would drop out of them ; and such was the case, to the great surprise of my worthy friend, who now desired to be informed *what I had done to the instrument to invest it with this new and opposite power.* This I declined doing for the present ; but I promised to do so, when he had seen some further proofs of its remarkable powers. I now told him that a touch with it on either extremity would cause the extremity to rise and become cataleptic, and such was the result ; that a second touch on the same point would reduce the rigidity, and cause it to fall, and such again was proved to be the fact. After a variety of other experiments, every one of which proved precisely as I had predicted, she was aroused. I now applied the ring of my instrument on the third finger of the right hand, from which it was suspended, and told the doctor, that when it was so suspended, it would send her to sleep. To this he replied "*it never will*," but I again told him that I felt confident that it would send her to sleep. We then were silent, and very speedily she was once more asleep. Having aroused her, I put the instrument on the second finger of her right hand, and told the doctor that it would be found she could NOT go to sleep, when it was placed there. He said he thought she would, and he sat steadily gazing at her, but I said firmly and confidently that she would not. After a considerable time the doctor asked her if she did not feel sleepy, to which she replied 'not at all'; could you rise and walk? when she told him she could. I then requested her to look at the point of the fore-finger of her right hand, which I told the doctor would send her to sleep, and such was the result; and, after being aroused, I desired her to keep a steady gaze at the nail of the thumb of the left hand, which would send her to sleep in like manner, and such proved to be the fact.

"Having repaired to another room, I explained to the doctor the real nature and powers of my little and apparently magical instrument,—that it was nothing more than my *portmanteau-key and ring*; and that what had imparted to it such apparently varied powers, was merely the predictions which the patient had overheard me make to him, acting upon her in the peculiar state of the nervous sleep, as irresistible impulses to be affected, according to the results she had heard me predict. Had I predicted that she would see any flame, or colour, or form, or substance, animate or inanimate, I know from experience that such would have been realised, and responded to by her; and that, not from any desire on her part to impose upon others, but because she was self-deceived, the vividness of her imagination in that state, inducing her to believe as real, what were only the figments of fancy, suggested to her mind by the remarks of others. The power of suggestions of this sort also, in paralysing or energising muscular power, is truly astounding; and may all arise in perfect good faith with almost all patients who have passed into the second conscious state, and with some, during the first conscious stage; and with some weak-minded, or highly imaginative or credulous and concentrative people, *even in the waking condition."* (Braid on *The Power of the Mind over the Body,* 1846; p. 31.)

APPENDIX I.

MR. BRAID'S EXPERIMENTS ON SUBJECTIVE SENSATIONS.

" A lady, upwards of fifty-six years of age, in perfect health, and wide awake, having been taken into a dark closet, and desired to look at the poles of the powerful horse-shoe magnet of nine elements, and describe what she saw, declared, after looking a considerable time, that she saw nothing. However, after I told her to look attentively, and she would see fire cóme out of it, she speedily saw sparks, and presently it seemed to her to burst forth, as she had witnessed an artificial representation of the volcano of Mount Vesuvius at some public gardens. Without her knowledge, I closed down the lid of the trunk which contained the magnet, *but still the same appearances were described as visible.* By putting leading questions, and asking her to describe what she saw from *another* part of the closet (where there was nothing but bare walls) she went on describing various shades of most brilliant coruscations and flame, according to the leading questions I had put for the purpose of changing the fundamental ideas. On repeating the experiments, similar results were repeatedly realised by this patient. On taking this lady into the said closet after the magnet had been removed to another part of the house, she still perceived the same visible appearances of light and flame when there was nothing but the bare walls to produce them ; and, two weeks after the magnet was removed, when she went into the closet by herself, the mere association of ideas was sufficient to cause her to realise a visible representation of the same light and flames. Indeed such had been the case with her on entering the closet ever since the few first times she saw the light and flames. In like manner when she was made to touch the poles of the magnet when wide awake, no manifestations of attraction took place between her hand and the magnet, but the moment the idea was suggested that she would be held fast by its powerful attraction, so that she would be utterly unable to separate her hands from it, such result was realised; and, on separating it, by the suggestion of a new idea, and causing her to touch the *other* pole in like manner, predicating that *it* would *exert no attractive power* for the fingers or hands, such negative effects were at once manifested. I know this lady was incapable of trying to deceive myself, or others present; but she was self-deceived and spell-bound by the predominance of a pre-conceived idea, and was not less surprised at the varying powers of the instrument than others who witnessed the results." (*Op. cit.*, p. 19.)

Other 'subjects' taken by Mr. Braid into his dark closet, and unable to see anything in the first instance, when told to look steadily at a certain point (though there was no magnet there) and assured that they would see flame and light of various colours issuing from it, very soon declared that they saw them; and in some of them the same sensations could be called up in open daylight.—The following was an experiment made, *with* and *without* the magnet, upon the sensations of the general surface; the 'subject' being a young gentleman twenty-one years of age :—

" I first operated on his right hand, by drawing a powerful horse-shoe magnet over the hand, without contact, whilst the armature was attached. He immediately observed a sensation of cold follow the course of the magnet. I reversed the passes, and he felt it *less cold*, but he felt no attraction between his hand and the magnet. I then removed the cross-bar, and tried the effect with both poles alternately, but still there was no change in the effect, and decidedly no proof of attraction between his hand and the magnet. In the afternoon of the same day I desired him to look aside, and hold his hat between his eyes and his hand, and observe the effects when I operated on him, whilst he could not see my proceedings. He very soon described a recurrence of the same sort of sensations as those he felt in the morning, but they speedily became more intense, and extended up the arm, producing rigidity of the member. In the course of two minutes this feeling attacked the other arm, and to some extent the whole body; and he was, moreover, seized with a fit of involuntary laughter, like that of hysteria, which continued for several minutes—in fact, until I put an end to the experiment. His first remark was, 'Now this· experiment clearly proves that there must be some intimate connection between mineral magnetism and mesmerism; for I was most strangely affected, and could not possibly resist laughing during the extraordinary sensations with which my whole body was seized, as you drew the magnet over my hand and arm.' I replied that I drew a very different conclusion from the experiments, as *I had never used the magnet at all,* nor held it, nor anything else, near to him; and that the whole proved the truth of my position as to the extraordinary power of the mind over the body." (*Op. cit.,* p. 14.)

Phenomena of the same kind were found to be producible without the use of a magnet at all:—

"Another interesting case of a married lady, I experimented with, in the presence of her husband, as follows. I requested her to place her hand on the table, with the palm upwards, so situated as to enable her to observe the process I was about to resort to. I had previously remarked, that by my drawing something slowly over the hand, without contact, whilst the patient concentrated her attention on the process, she would experience some peculiar sensations in consequence. I took a pair of her scissors, and drew the bowl of the handle slowly from the wrist downwards. I had only done so a few times, when she felt a creeping, chilly sensation, which was immediately followed by a spasmodic twitching of the muscles, so as to toss the hand from the table, as the members of a prepared frog are agitated when galvanised. I next desired her to place her *other* hand on the table, in like manner, but placed so that by turning her head in the opposite direction she might not see what was being done, and to watch her sensations in that hand, and tell us the result. In about the same length of time similar phenomena were manifested as with the other hand, although in this instance *I had done nothing whatever*, and was not near her hand. I now desired her to watch what happened to her hand, when I predicated that she would feel it become *cold*, and the result was as predicted ; and *vice versâ*, predicating that she would feel it become intensely hot, such was realised. When I desired her to think of the tip of her nose, the predicated result, either of heat or cold, was speedily realised in that part.

" Another lady, twenty-eight years of age, being operated on in the same manner, whilst looking at my proceedings, in the course of half-a-minute, described the sensation as that of the blood rushing into the fingers ; and when the motion of my pencil-case was from below, upwards, the sensation was that of the current of blood being reversed, but less rapid in its motion. On resuming the downward direction, the original feeling occurred, still more powerfully than at first. This lady being requested now to look aside, whilst I operated, *realised similar sensations*, and that whilst *I was doing nothing*.

" The husband of this lady, twenty-eight and a half years of age, came into the room shortly after the above experiment was finished. She was very desirous of my trying the effect upon him, as he was in perfect health. I requested him to extend his right arm laterally, and let it rest on a chair with the palm upwards, to turn his head in the opposite direction so that he might not see what I was doing, and to concentrate his attention on the feelings which might arise during my process. In about half-a-minute he felt an *aura* like a breath of air passing along the hand; in a little after a slight pricking, and presently a feeling passed along the arm, as far as the elbow, which he described as similar to that of being slightly electrified. *All this while I had been doing nothing*, beyond watching what might be realised. I then desired him to tell me what he felt NOW—speaking in such a tone of voice as was calculated to lead him to believe I was operating in some different manner. The result was that the former sensations ceased; but, when I requested him once more to tell me what he felt *now*, the former sensations recurred. I then whispered to his wife, but in a tone sufficiently loud to be heard by him, observe now, and you will find his fingers begin to draw, and his hand will become clenched—see how the little finger begins to move, and such was the case; see the next one also going in like manner, and such effects followed; and finally, the entire hand closed firmly, with a very unpleasant drawing motion of the whole flexor-muscles of the fore-arm. I did nothing whatever to this patient until the fingers were nearly closed, when I touched the palm of his hand with the point of my finger, which caused it to close more rapidly and firmly. After it had remained so for a short time, I blew upon the hand, which dissipated the previously existing mental impression, and instantly the hand became relaxed. The high respectability and intelligence of this gentleman rendered his testimony very valuable; and especially so, when he was not only wide awake, but had never been either mesmerised, hypnotised, or so tested before." (*Op. cit.*, pp. 15–17.)

APPENDIX K.

PENDULE EXPLORATEUR.

We are told by Ammianus Marcellinus (the last of the Roman Historians) that, in the reign of the Emperor Flavius Valens (4th century) a conspiracy was formed, including many persons of high rank, who devoted themselves to 'curious arts,' among them the celebrated Iamblicus, a mystic philosopher of the Alexandrian School ; their objects being to learn who would be the successor of the reigning Emperor, which piece of curiosity was held to be a capital crime. Of the magical procedure they employed, of which a full description was given by one of them named Hilarius when put on his trial, the oscillations of a suspended ring, that pointed to one letter after another of an alphabet circularly disposed, constituted the essential part. The three letters ΘΕΟ having been thus spelled-out, the conspirators made up their minds that Theodosius was indicated ; and although the principal members of the conspiracy were afterwards put to death by the Emperor, the destiny of Theodosius was accomplished, for he ultimately became the successor of Valens.

APPENDIX L.

TABLE-TALKING AND PLANCHETTE-WRITING.

" Several years ago we were invited, with two medical friends, to a very select *séance*, to witness the performance of a lady, the Hon. Miss N——, who was described to us as a peculiarly gifted 'medium;' not merely being the vehicle of 'spiritual' revelations of the most elevating character, but being able to convince incredulous philosophers

like ourselves of the reality of her 'spiritual' gifts, by
'physical' manifestations of the most unmistakable kind.
Unfortunately, however, the Hon. Miss N—— was not in
great force on the occasion of our visit ; and nothing would
go right. It was suggested that she might be exhausted by
a most successful performance which had taken place on
the previous evening ; and that 'the spirits' should be asked
whether she stood in need of refreshment. The question
was put by our host (a wine-merchant, be it observed), who
repeated the alphabet *rapidly* until he came to N, and then
went on *slowly*; the table tilted at P. The same process
was repeated, until the letters successively indicated were
P, O, R, T. But this was not enough. The spirits might
prescribe either *port* or *porter* ; and the alphabet was then
repeated *slowly from the beginning,* a prolonged pause being
made at E ; as the table did *not* tilt, a bumper of port was
administered 'as directed.' It did not, however, produce
the expected effect.

"On another occasion, we happened to be on a visit at a
house at which two ladies were staying, who worked the
planchette on the original method (that of attaching to it a
pointer, which indicated letters and figures on a card), and
our long previous knowledge of whom placed them beyond
all suspicion of anything but *self*-deception. One of them
was a firm believer in the reality of her intercourse with the
spirit-world ; and her 'planchette' was continually at work
beneath her hands, its index pointing to successive letters
and figures on the card before it, just as if it had been that
of a telegraph-dial acted on by galvanic communication.
After having watched the operation for some time, and
assured ourselves that the answers she obtained to the
questions she put to her 'spiritual' visitants were just what
her own simple and devout nature would suggest, we addressed her thus :—' *You* believe that your replies are dic-
' tated to you by your " spiritual " friends, and that your hands

' are the passive vehicles of the " spiritual " agency by which
' the planchette is directed in spelling them out. *We* believe,
' on the other hand, that the answers are the products of your
' own Brain, and that the planchette is moved by your own
' Muscles. Now we can test, by a very simple experiment,
' whether *your* view or *ours* is the correct one. Will you be
' kind enough to *shut your eyes* when you ask your question,
' and to let *us* watch what the planchette spells out? If " the
' spirits " guide it, there is no reason why they should not do
' so as well when your eyes are shut, as when they are open.
' If the table is moved by your own hands, it will not give
' definite replies except under the guidance of your own
' vision.' To this appeal our friend replied that she could
not think of making such an experiment, as ' it would show
a want of faith ; ' and all our arguments and persuasions
could only bring her to the point of *asking the spirits* whether
she *might* comply with our request. The reply was, ' No.'
She then, at our continued urgency, asked ' Why not ? '
The reply was, ' Want of faith.' Putting a still stronger
pressure upon her, we induced her to ask, ' Faith in what ? '
The reply was, ' In God.'

" Of course, any further appeal in that quarter would have
been useless; and we consequently addressed ourselves to
our other fair friend, whose high culture and great general
intelligence had prepared her for our own rationalistic
explanation of marvels which had seriously perplexed her.
For having been engaged a short time before in promoting
a public movement, which had brought her into contact
with a number of persons who had previously been strangers
to her, she had asked questions respecting them, which
elicited replies that were in many instances such as she
declared to be quite unexpected by herself,—specially tending to inculpate some of her coadjutors as influenced by
unworthy motives. After a little questioning, however, she
admitted to us that she had previously entertained *lurking*

suspicions on this point, which she had scarcely even *acknowledged to herself,* far less made known to others ; and was much relieved when we pointed out that the planchette merely revealed what was going on in *the under-stratum of her own mind.* Her conversion to our view was complete, when, on her trying the working of the planchette with her eyes shut, its pointer *went astray altogether."* (*Quarterly Review,* Oct. 1871, p. 315.)

It is often cited as a proof that the performers are *not* expressing by involuntary muscular actions what is passing in their own minds, that the answers given by the tables are *not known to any of themselves, though known to some other person in the room.* Of this the following instance was recorded by Mr. Godfrey:—

" I procured an alphabet on a board, such as is used in a National School ; this board I laid down on the floor at some little distance from the table, and I lay down on the ground beside it. I then requested one of the three persons at the table to command it to spell the Christian names of Mr. L——, of B——, by lifting up the leg next him as I pointed to the letters of the alphabet in succession. He did so, and I began to point, keeping the pointer about three seconds on each letter in succession (I must say, that neither of the three persons at the table had ever heard of Mr. L—— ; and B—— is 150 miles from this place). When I arrived at G, they said, that's it ; the table is lifting its leg. When I came to E, it rose again; and in this way it spelt George Peter, whicn was perfectly correct." (*Table-turning, the Devil's Modern Master-piece,* p. 22.) Of course the person who influenced the movements of the table was guided by the indications afforded by Mr. Godfrey's own unconscious expression of his expectancy.

So, again, the late Dr. Hare, an American Chemist and Physicist of some reputation, thought that he had obtained *a precise experimental proof of the immortality of the soul* (!) by means of an apparatus by which the answers communicated through the 'medium' were spelled out by a hand pointing to an alphabet-dial which was hidden from her eyes. But it is clear from his narrative of the experiment, that her eyes were fixed upon the person to whom the expected answer was known, and that her movements were guided by the indications she received from *his* involuntary movements.

REPRODUCTION OF UNREMEMBERED IDEAS.

A 'planchette,' made in Bath, which had been on a visit in various families for several months, having been asked where it was made, replied 'Bath;' although the questioners all thought it came from *London*, and disbelieved its statement, which was afterwards verified. The rational explanation of this obviously is, that the writing was guided by the *cerebral* memory (so to speak), instead of by the *conscious* memory; just as in the case of the movements in acted dreams, by which articles long lost have been found again.

The Rev. Mr. Dibdin, M.A. (in his *Lecture on Table-Turning*, published in 1853), states that he and a friend having directed the table to say, 'How many years is it since her Majesty came to the throne?' the table struck *sixteen*, though no one present knew the date of her accession; and having directed it to 'give the age of the Prince of Wales,' which was not known either to Mr. Dibdin or his friend, the table struck *eleven*, and then raised the foot a little way. On referring to an Almanack, both these numbers were found to be correct. Further, the question being put (in the house of a tailor), 'How many men are at work in the shop below?' the table replied by striking *three*, and giving *two* gentle rises; on which the employer, who was one of the party, said, 'There are *four* men and *two* boys, so *three* is a mistake;' but *he afterwards remembered* that one of the young men was out of town.

" An eminent literary man, in whose veracity we have had

the fullest confidence, informed us that 'the spirit of a
friend, whose decease had taken place some months previously, having announced itself in the usual way, and the
question having been put, 'When did I last see you in life?'
the answer given was inconsistent with the recollection of
the interrogator.   But, on his subsequently talking over the
matter with his family, it was brought to his remembrance
that he *had* seen his deceased friend on the occasion mentioned, and had spoken of it to them at the time, although
he had afterwards quite forgotten the circumstance."—
(*Quarterly Review,* October 1871, p. 319.)

    Another instance, supplied by Mr. Dibdin (*op. cit.*),
affords yet more remarkable evidence to the same effect;
especially as being related by a firm believer in the 'diabolical' origin of Table-talking :—A gentleman, who was at
the time a believer in the 'spiritual' agency of his table,
assured Mr. Dibdin that he had raised a *good* spirit instead
of *evil* ones—that, namely, of Edward Young, the poet.
The 'spirit' having been desired to prove this identity by
citing a line of his poetry, the table spelled out, 'Man was
not made to question, but adore.'   'Is that in your "Night
Thoughts"?' was then asked.   'No.'   'Where is it, then?'
The reply was, 'J O B.'   Not being familiar with Young's
Poems, the questioner did not know what this meant; but
the next day he bought a copy of them; and at the end of
'Night Thoughts' he found a paraphrase of the Book of
Job, the last line of which is, 'Man was not made to question, but adore.'   Of course he was very much astonished;
but not long afterwards he came to Mr. Dibdin, and assured
him that he had satisfied himself that the whole thing was a
delusion,—numerous answers he had obtained being obviously the results of an influence unconsciously exerted on
the table by those who had their hands upon it ; and when
asked by Mr. Dibdin how he accounted for the dictation of
the line by the spirit of Young, he very honestly confessed,

' Well, the fact is, I must tell you, that I had the book in my house all the time, although I bought another copy ; and *I found that I had read it before.* My opinion is that it was *a latent idea*, and that the table brought it out.' (p. 7.)

APPENDIX M.

DIABOLICAL ORIGIN OF TABLE-TURNING.

In his *Table-moving Tested*, the Rev. N. S. Godfrey began by " tracing the existence of Satanic influence from the time of Moses to the time of Jesus ; connecting the ' witch,' the ' familiar spirit,' the spirit of Python, &c. with the Evil Spirit in its actual and separate existence : " and asserting without the least hesitation, that although ' so long as the supernatural gifts of the Spirit remained among men, so long the evil spirits were cast out and their presence detected,' yet that when those miraculous powers were withdrawn, they could no longer be discerned, but have continued to exist to the present time, and make themselves known in these ' latter times ' as the ' wandering (seducing) spirits,' whose appearance was predicted by St. Paul (1 Tim. iv. 10). That the answers to the ' test questions ' were exactly contrary to Mr. Godfrey's ideas of truth, was in his judgment peculiarly convincing ; " for if indeed these tables do become possessed " by some of the ' wandering spirits ' at the command of the " Devil, it would be most impolitic, and quite at variance with " the subtlety of his character, to scare people at the very " outset." The following answers, therefore, are obviously what Mr. G. expected :—

" I spoke to the table, and said, ' If you move by electricity, stop.' It stopped instantly ! I commanded it to go on again, and said, while it was moving, ' If an evil spirit

L

cause you to move, stop.' It moved round without stopping!
I again said, ' If there be any evil agency in this, stop.' It
went on as before. I was now prepared with an experiment
of a far more solemn character. I whispered to the school-
master to bring a small Bible, and to lay it on the table when
I should tell him. I then caused the table to revolve rapidly,
and gave the signal. *The Bible was gently laid on the table,
and it instantly stopped.* We were horror-struck. However,
I determined to persevere. I had other books in succession
laid on the table, to see whether the fact of a book lying
upon it altered any of the conditions under which it revolved.
It went round with them without making any difference. I
then tried with the Bible four different times, and each time
with the same result : *it would not move so long as that precious volume lay upon it.* . . . I now said, ' If there be a
hell, I command you to knock on the floor with this leg (the
one next me) twice.' It was motionless. ' If there be *not*
a hell, knock twice ; ' no answer. ' If there be a devil, knock
twice ; ' no motion. ' If there be *not* a devil, knock twice ; '
to our horror, the leg slowly rose and knocked twice ! I then
said, ' In the name of the Lord Jesus Christ, if there be *no*
devil, knock twice ; ' it was motionless. This I tried four
several times, and each time with the same result." (p. 24.)

It is clear that Mr. Godfrey and his associates, if they
had not distinctly *anticipated* these results, were fully *prepared*
for them. Thus, although he assures his readers that, when
the Bible was placed on the table, the emotion in the minds
of all the parties was *curiosity*, and that, if they *had* a bias,
it was *against* the table stopping, the very fact of the experiment being tried by a man imbued with his prepossessions
on the subject of Evil Spirits, Witchcraft, &c., sufficiently
indicates what his *real* state of mind was, although he may
not have been himself aware of it. His *involuntary* muscular actions responded to this, although no *voluntary* movement would have done so, because he had not *consciously*

accepted the Idea whose 'physical basis' had been shaping itself in the under-stratum. The experience of everyone must have convinced him that there is often a contrariety between our *beliefs as to our own states of mind*, and the *facts* of that state as they afterwards come to be *self-revealed* to us; and it is a very marked peculiarity of these movements, that they often express more truly what is buried (as it were) in the vaults of our storehouse, than what is displayed in the ware-rooms above.

The Rev. E. Gillson, M.A., a Clergyman of Bath, fully partaking of his predecessor's convictions on the subject of Satanic Agency, and also in the excitement prevailing in many circles at that time on the subject of 'Papal Aggression,' gave the following *inter alia* as his experiences (*Table-Talking: Satanic Wonders and Prophetic Signs*, 1853) :—

" I placed my hand upon the table, and put a variety of questions, all of which were instantly and correctly answered. Various ages were asked, and all correctly told. In reply to trifling questions, possessing no particular interest, the table answered by quietly lifting up the leg and rapping. But in answer to questions of a more exciting character, it would become violently agitated, and sometimes to such a degree that I can only describe the motion by the word *frantic*. I inquired, 'Are you a departed spirit?' The answer was ' Yes,' indicated by a rap. ' Are you unhappy?' The table answered by a sort of writhing motion (!), which no natural power over it could imitate. It was then asked, ' Shall you be for ever unhappy?' The same kind of writhing motion was returned. ' Do you know Satan?' ' Yes.' ' Is he the Prince of Devils?' ' Yes.' 'Will he be bound?' ' Yes.' ' Will he be cast into the abyss?' ' Yes.' ' Will you be cast in with him?' ' Yes.' 'How long will it be before he is cast out?' He rapped *ten*. ' Will wars and commotions intervene?' The table rocked and reeled backwards and forwards for a length of time, as if it intended a pantomimic

acting of the prophet's predictions (Isaiah xxiv. 20). I
then asked 'Where are Satan's head-quarters? Are they in
England?' There was a slight movement. 'Are they in
France?' A violent movement. 'Are they in Spain?'
Similar agitation. 'Are they at Rome?' *The table literally
seemed frantic.* At the close of these experiments, which
occupied about two hours, the invisible agent, in answer to
some questions about himself, did not agree with what had
been said before. I therefore asked, 'Are you the same
spirit that was in the table when we began?' 'No.' 'How
many spirits have been in the table this evening?' 'Four.'
This spirit informed us that he had been an infidel, and had
embraced Popery about five years before his death. Amongst
other questions, he was asked, 'Do you know the Pope?'
The table was violently agitated. I asked, 'How long will
Popery continue?' He rapped ten ; exactly coinciding with
the other spirits' account of the binding of Satan. Many
questions were asked, and experiments tried, in order to ascertain whether the results would agree with Mr. Godfrey's ;
and on every occasion they did, *especially that of stopping
the movement of the table with the Bible.* As we proceeded
with our questions, we found an indescribable facility in the
conversation, from the *extraordinary intelligence and ingenuity
displayed in the table* (!) *E. g.*—I inquired if many devils
were posted in Bath. He replied by the most extraordinary
and rapid knocking of the three feet in succession, round
and round, for some time, as if to intimate that they were
innumerable !" (*Op. cit.*, pp. 4–8.)

A third Clergyman, the Rev. R. W. Dibdin, M.A., while
agreeing with his predecessors in the belief that the movements of the tables are the result of Satanic (or diabolic)
agency, differed from them in maintaining 'that devils alone
(not departed spirits) are the agents in these cases ; and
being *lying* spirits, it is quite credible that, for purposes of
their own, they might *assume* the names of departed men

and women.' Of course he got the answers he expected on
this hypothesis. The following is his set of 'test questions,'
the answers to which — being entirely *opposed* to his own
notions of truth—satisfied *him*, and were expected to satisfy
his partners in the experiment, of the *diabolical* character of
the respondent :—

" 'Are we justified by works?' 'Yes.' — 'By faith
alone?' 'No.'—'Is the whole Bible true?' 'No.'—
'Were the miracles of the New Testament wrought by supernatural power?' 'No.'—'By some hidden law of Nature?'
'Yes.' — 'Was Oliver Cromwell good?' 'No.' — 'Was
Charles I. a good man?' 'Yes.'—'Is it right to pray to
the Virgin?' 'Yes.'—'Is Christ God?' 'No.'—'Is he
a man?' 'No.'—'Is he something between God and
man, a sort of angel?' 'Yes.'—'Is he in heaven?' 'No.'
—'Where is he?' It spelt slowly H E L L.—As the last
letter was indicated, the girl drew her hands quickly off the
table, much as a person would do who was drawing them off
a hot iron. Her brother-in-law turned very pale, and took
his hands off the table also." (*Lecture on Table-turning*,
1853 ; p. 8.)

The character, position, and obvious sincerity of the
actors in these performances place them beyond suspicion
of intentional deception ; and the phenomena they narrate
afford a singularly apposite illustration of the principle which
I desire to enforce. But that such obvious products
of the questioners' own mental states should have been
accepted by men of education, occupying the position of religious teachers in the National Church, as the lying responses of *evil* spirits, sent expressly to delude them, can
only be deemed—by such, at least, as are prepared to accept
a scientific *rationale* of the phenomena—a pitiable instance
of the readiness with which minds of a certain type may
allow themselves to become ' possessed ' by dominant ideas.

APPENDIX N.

MRS. CULVER'S STATEMENT.

"I am by marriage a connection of the Fox girls. Their brother married my husband's sister. The girls have been a great deal at my house ; and for about two years I was a very sincere believer in the rappings ; but something which I saw when I was visiting the girls at Rochester made me suspect that they were deceiving. I resolved to satisfy myself in some way, and sometime afterwards I made a proposition to Catherine to assist her in producing the manifestations. I had a cousin visiting me from Michigan, who was going to consult the spirits ; and I told Catherine that if they intended going to Detroit, it would be a great thing for them to convince him. I also told her that if I could do anything to help her, I would do it cheerfully ; that I should probably be able to answer all the questions he would ask, and I would do it if she would show me how to make the raps. She said that as Margaretta was absent, she wanted somebody to help her ; and that if I would become a medium, she would explain it all to me. She said that when my cousin consulted the spirits, I must sit next to her, and touch her arm when the right letter was called. I did so, and was able to answer all the questions correctly. After I had helped her in this way a few times, she revealed to me the secret. The raps are produced by the toes. All the toes are used. After nearly a week's practice with Catherine showing me how, I could produce them perfectly myself.

" At first it was very hard work to do it. Catherine told me to warm my feet, or put them in warm water, and it would then be easier to rap. She said that she had some-times to warm her feet three or four times during the evening. I found that heating my feet did enable me to rap a great deal easier. I have sometimes produced 150 raps in succession. I can rap with all the toes on both feet; it is most difficult to rap with the great toe. Catherine told me how to manage to answer the questions. She said it was generally easy enough to answer right, if the one who asked the question called the alphabet. She said the reason why she asked people to write down several names on paper, and then point to them till the spirits rapped at the right one, was to give them a chance to watch the countenance and motions of the person, and that in that way they could nearly always guess right. She also explained how they held down and moved tables. (Mrs. Culver here gave some illustration of the tricks.) She told me that all I should have to do to make raps heard on the table, would be to put my foot on the bottom of the table when I rapped; and that when I wished to make the raps sound distant on the wall I must make them louder, and direct my own eyes earnestly to the spot where I wished them to be heard. She said if I could put my foot to the bottom of the door, the raps would be heard on the top of the door.

" Catherine told me that when her feet were held down by the Rochester Committee, the Dutch servant-girl rapped with her knuckles under the floor from the cellar. The girl was instructed to rap whenever she heard their voices calling the spirits. Catherine also showed me how they made the sounds of sawing and planing boards. When I was at Rochester last January, Margaretta told me that when people insisted on seeing her feet and toes, she could produce a few raps with her knees and ankles.

" Elizabeth Fish (Mr. Fish's daughter), who now lives with her father, was the first one who produced these raps. She accidentally discovered the way of making them by playing with her toes against the foot-board while in bed. Catherine told me that the reason why Elizabeth went west to live with her father, was because she was too conscientious to become a medium. The whole secret was revealed to me, with the understanding that I should practise as a medium when the girls were away. Catherine said that whenever I practised, I had better have my little girl with me, and make folks believe that she was the medium; 'for,' she said, 'they would never suspect so young a child of any tricks.' After I had obtained the entire secret, I plainly told Catherine that my only object was to find out how these tricks were done, and that I should never go any further in this imposition. She was very much frightened, and said she believed I meant to tell of it and expose them, and if I did, she would swear it was a lie. She was so nervous and excited that I had to sleep with her that night. When she was instructing me how to be a medium, she told me how frightened they used to get in New York, for fear somebody would detect them; and gave me the history of all the tricks they played upon the people there. She said that once Margaretta spoke aloud, and that the whole party believed it was a spirit."

(Signed) MRS. NORMAN CULVER.

Certificate.

"We hereby certify that Mrs. Culver is one of the most respectable and intelligent ladies in the town of Arcadia. We were present when she made the disclosures. We had heard the same from her before, and we cheerfully bear testimony that there cannot be the slightest doubt of the truth of the whole statement."

(Signed) C. J. POMEROY, M.D.
REV. D. S. CHASE.

APPENDIX O.

Sir,—In your comment on Mr. Lewes's letter you seem to imply that the experiment described may prove imposture, but that Professor De Morgan's experiment was equally decisive against imposture. Will you allow me very briefly to point out that the alleged exposure proves nothing without assuming the very fact at issue—that Mrs. Hayden herself caused the raps following the indications given by the person who pointed to the letters of the alphabet? For let us assume, on the other hand, that the raps were, as alleged, caused by invisible beings, perhaps not superior in intelligence to Mrs. Hayden, and equally liable to be affected by insult or impulse, and that these beings could read, *more or less imperfectly*, the questioner's mind. Nonsense questions were asked these intelligences, and absurd or contradictory answers were *sought to be obtained* by dwelling on certain letters. These absurd answers were obtained. This is consistent with the supposition on two theories. Either the intelligence could read only the questioner's active desire for a certain answer while pointing to the letters, and accordingly gave that answer; or, if it were able also to perceive the question (though less vivid in the questioner's mind at the moment), it might well adopt the human principles of answering what would be impertinent questions in the only way they deserved an answer. It is a fact within my own knowledge, and it is well-known to all spiritualists, that both kinds of answers are obtained in private circles where any imposture is out of the question. Professor De Morgan's experiment on the other hand absolutely precluded imposture on Mrs. Hayden's part, since not only were the letters and pointer carefully concealed from her, but the

answer, though correct, was in words which the Professor
was not expecting. The one experiment was purely negative and inconclusive, the other positive ; and I cannot
understand how so logical a mind as that of Mr. G. H.
Lewes can put the two results even in the category, much
less allow the negative evidence to prevail.—I am, Sir, &c.,

ALFRED R. WALLACE.

APPENDIX P.

" We were requested by a lady who had known Mr. Foster
in America, to accompany her and her son-in-law (an
eminent London Physician) on a visit to Mr. Foster, who
had arrived in London only a few days previously. We
were not introduced to him by name, and we do not think
that he could have had any opportunity of knowing our
person. Nevertheless, he not only answered, in a variety of
modes, the questions we put to him respecting the time and
cause of the death of several of our departed friends and
relatives, whose names we had written down on slips of
paper which had been folded-up and crumpled into pellets
before being placed in his hands ; but he brought out names
and dates correctly, in large red letters, on his bare arm, the
redness being produced by the turgescence of the minute
vessels of the skin, and passing away after a few minutes,
like a blush. We must own to have been strongly impressed
at the time by this performance ; but on subsequently thinking it over, we could see that Mr. Foster's divining power
was probably derived from his having acquired the faculty
of interpreting the movements of the *top* of a pen or pencil,
though the *point* and what was written by it was hid from
his sight, with the aid of an observing power sharpened by
practice, which enabled him to guide his own movements

by the indications unconsciously given by ourselves of the answers we expected. For though we were fully armed with the knowledge which had been acquired of the source from which Mrs. Hayden drew her inspiration, and did our utmost to repress every sign of anticipation, we came, on reflection, to an assured conviction that Mr. Foster *had* been keen-sighted enough to detect such signs, notwithstanding our attempt to baffle him. For, having asked him the *month* of the death of a friend, whose name had previously appeared in red letters on his arm, and the *year* of whose death had also been correctly indicated in another way, he desired us to take up the alphabet-card and to point to the successive letters. This we did, *as we believe*, with pendulum-like regularity; nevertheless, distinct raps were heard at the letters J, U. When, however, on the next repetition, we came to L, M, N, Mr. Foster was obviously baffled. He directed us to try-back two or three times, and at last confessed that he could not certainly tell whether the month was *June* or *July*. The secret of this was, that *we did not ourselves recollect*.

" Wishing to clear up the matter further, we called on Mr. Foster, revealed ourselves to him *in propria personâ*, and asked him if he would object to meet a few scientific investigators, who should be allowed to subject his powers to fair tests. As he professed his readiness to do so, we brought together such a meeting at our own house ; and previously to Mr. Foster's arrival, we explained to our friends the arrangements we proposed. One of these was, that one of the party should sit outside the ' circle,' and should devote himself to observing and recording all that passed, without taking any part whatever in the performance. Another was, that instead of writing down names on slips of paper, whilst sitting at the table within Mr. Foster's view, we should write them at a side-table, with our backs turned to him. On explaining these arrangements to Mr. Foster, he immediately said that the first could not be permitted, for that every person present *must* form part of the circle. To the second he made no objection. After handing him our slips of paper carefully folded-up, we took our seats at the table, and waited for the announcement of spiritual visitors. The only one, however, who presented himself during an hour's *séance*, was the spirit of our own old master, whose name Mr. Foster might very readily have learned previously, but about whom he could give no particulars whatever. *Not one of the names written on the papers was revealed.*

" The patience of our friends being exhausted, they took their leave ; but as Mr. Foster's carriage had been ordered for a later hour, we requested him to sit down again with the members of our own family. ' Now,' we said, ' that these incredulous philosophers are gone, perhaps the spirits will favour us with a visit.' We purposely followed *his* lead, as on our first interview, and everything went on as successfully as on that occasion ; until, whilst the name of a relative we had recently lost was being spelled out on our alphabet-card, *the raps suddenly ceased* on the interposition of a large music-book, which was set-up at a preconcerted signal so as to hide the *top* as well as the bottom of our pointer from Mr. Foster's eyes. Nothing could more conclusively prove that Mr. Foster's knowledge was derived from observation of the movements of the pointer, although he could only see the portion of it not hidden by the card, which was so held as to conceal the lower part of it ; and nothing could be a better illustration of the principle of ' unconscious ideo-motor action,' then the fact, that *whilst we were most care-fully abstaining from any pause or look from which he might derive guidance, we had enabled him to divine the answer we expected.* The trick by which the red letters were produced was discovered by the inquiries of our medical friends."— (*Quarterly Review*, October 1871, p. 332.)

APPENDIX Q.

MR. BRAID ON THE INFLUENCE OF SUGGESTION AND EXPECTANCY.

" The most curious and important fact of all, however, is this,—that by engendering a state of mental concentration, by a simple act of sustained attention, fixed upon some unexciting and empty thing,—'for poverty of object engenders abstraction,'—the faculties of the minds of *some* patients are thereby thrown out of gear, (*i.e.*, their ordinary relations are changed,) so that the higher faculties—reason, comparison, and will, become dethroned from their supremacy, and give place and power to imagination, (which now careers in unbridled liberty,) easy credulity, and docility or passive obedience ; so that, even whilst apparently wide awake, and conscious of all around, they become susceptible of being influenced and controlled entirely by the suggestions of others, upon whom their attention is fixed.   In fact, such subjects, are in a sub-hypnotic condition,—in that intermediate state between sleeping and waking, when the mind becomes wavering, the attention off duty, or engrossed with a predominant idea, so that, in reality, the subjects are only half conscious of what is passing around ; and their minds, therefore, become easily imposed upon by any suggestion, audibly expressed or visibly exhibited before them.   Thus they may be made to perceive, and mistake for realities, whatever mental illusions or ideas are suggested to them.   In common parlance they *see* and *feel* AS REAL, and they consider themselves *irresistibly* or *involuntarily fixed, or spell-bound*, or *impelled to perform whatever may be said or signified by the other party upon whom their attention has become involuntarily and vividly riveted,* until a new idea has been suggested, by which the spell is broken, and the subject is left in a condition again to be subjugated and controlled by other suggestions of his temporary fascinator. This is just similar to what we see occurring to anyone spontaneously engaged in deep abstraction, who is instantaneously aroused to consciousness of all around by a tap on the shoulder, or by a word sharply addressed to him.

" It requires considerable tact to manage this, adroitly and successfully, with *some* patients ; for the will and belief of certain subjects can only be successfully subjugated and controlled by an earnest and energetic, and confident and authoritative manner, on the part of the operator ; such as by his *insisting* that *such* and *such* MUST be the case, according to his audible suggestions, or visible manœuvres for influencing the subjects through the power of sympathy and imitation. I have had ample evidence to convince me of the fact, that, in cases where these waking illusions and delusions could not be excited by giving the suggestions in an apparently doubting tone of voice, or with a hesitating manner, they became quite efficient for the purpose, the instant I assumed a commanding and confident tone of voice and deportment. By these means the *Reason* and *Will* become temporarily paralysed ; they lose their freedom of action, through the mind being so much engrossed by the suggested thought, as to allow every idea which has been vividly and energetically addressed to such individual, to assume all the force of present reality,—just as we know to occur spontaneously, in case of *monomania* and *delirium tremens.*" (See Braid *On Magic, Witchcraft, Animal Magnetism, Hypnotism, and Electro-Biology*, 1852, pp. 65–67.)

LONDON : PRINTED BY
SPOTTISWOODE AND CO., NEW-STREET SQUARE
AND PARLIAMENT STREET

For EU product safety concerns, contact us at Calle de José Abascal, 56–1°,
28003 Madrid, Spain or eugpsr@cambridge.org.

 www.ingramcontent.com/pod-product-compliance
Ingram Content Group UK Ltd.
Pitfield, Milton Keynes, MK11 3LW, UK
UKHW012342130625
459647UK00009B/461